Recruiting, Interviewing, Selecting & Orienting New Employees

Second Edition

RECRUITING, INTERVIEWING, SELECTING & ORIENTING NEW EMPLOYEES

Second Edition

Diane Arthur

American Management Association

*This publication is designed to provide accurate and authoritative
information in regard to the subject matter covered. It is sold with
the understanding that the publisher is not engaged in rendering
legal, accounting, or other professional service. If legal advice or
other expert assistance is required, the services of a competent
professional person should be sought.*

Library of Congress Cataloging-in-Publication Data

Arthur, Diane.
    Recruiting, interviewing, selecting & orienting new employees /
Diane Arthur.—2nd ed.
      p. cm.
   Rev. ed. of: Recruiting, interviewing, selecting, and orienting
new employees. c1986.
   Includes index.
   ISBN 0-8144-5007-5 (hardcover)
   1. Employees—Recruiting. 2. Employment interviewing.
3. Employee selection. I. Arthur, Diane. Recruiting,
interviewing, selecting, and orienting new employees. II. Title.
III. Title: Recruiting, interviewing, selecting, and orienting new
employees.
  HF5549.5.R44A75 1991
  658.3'11—dc20   90-56198
                                              CIP

Printing number

10 9 8

To
Warren, who challenged me with
his probing questions and invaluable suggestions,
and
Valerie, who brought me immeasurable joy
with her hugs, kisses, and games of catch

Contents

Preface to the Second Edition   **xi**

1   Recruitment Challenges and Opportunities   **1**

- *Changing Work Force*   • *Workplace Literacy*
- *Target Populations*   • *Work and Family Issues*
- *Alternative Work Arrangements*   • *Other Responses to*
Employee Needs   • *Summary*

2   Familiarization With the Details of a Job   **28**

- *Duties and Responsibilities*   • *Education and Prior*
Experience   • *Intangible Requirements*   • *Reporting*
Relationships and Decision Making   • *Work*
Environment   • *Exemption Status*   • *Salary Ranges*
- *Benefits*   • *Union Status*   • *Growth Opportunities*
- *Special Requirements*   • *Job Descriptions*
- *Summary*

3   Recruitment Sources   **48**

- *Job Posting*   • *Employee Referral Programs*
- *Newspaper and Magazine Advertising*   • *Employment*
Agencies and Search Firms   • *Personnel Files*
- *Walk-Ins, Call-Ins, and Write-Ins*   • *School Recruiting*
- *Job Fairs*   • *Open House*   • *Government Agencies*
- *Direct Mail Recruitment*   • *Radio and Television*
- *Computerized Systems*   • *Research Firms*
- *Preemployment Training*   • *Outplacement Firms*
- *Billboard Advertising*   • *Response Cards*   • *Military*
- *Newspaper Inserts*   • *Professional Associations*

• *Consulting Firms*   • *Temporary Help Agencies*
• *Employee Leasing*   • *Voice Ads*   • *On-Site
Recruitment*   • *Summary*

4   Preparing for the Interview   83

• *Telephone Screening*   • *Reviewing the Application and
Résumé*   • *Keeping Applicant Data Records*
• *Allowing Sufficient Time for the Interview*   • *Planning
an Appropriate Environment*   • *Being Clear About Your
Objectives*   • *Planning Your Basic Questions*
• *Considering the Applicant's Feelings*   • *Reviewing Your
Own Perceptions*   • *Summary*

5   Employment and the Law   105

• *EEO Legislation and Affirmative Action: Categories of
Discrimination*   • *The Impact of EEO and Affirmative
Action on the Employment Process*   • *Bona Fide
Occupational Qualifications*   • *Preemployment Inquiries*
• *Education and Experience*   • *Employment and
Termination-at-Will*   • *Negligent Hiring and Retention*
• *Summary*

6   Conducting the Interview   146

• *Establishing the Format*   • *Establishing Rapport*
• *Asking the First Question*   • *Active Listening*
• *Taking Notes*   • *Interpreting Nonverbal Communication*
• *Encouraging the Applicant to Talk*   • *Providing
Information*   • *Asking Different Types of Interview
Questions*   • *Asking Specific Employment Interview
Questions*   • *Interviewing Problem Applicants*
• *One-on-One Versus Team Interviewing*   • *Avoiding
Stress Interviews*   • *Interviewing Guidelines and Pitfalls*
• *Closing the Interview*   • *Summary*

7   Writing Up the Interview   181

• *Avoiding Subjective Language*   • *Avoiding Recording
Opinions*   • *Referring to Job-Related Facts*   • *Being
Descriptive*   • *Tape-Recording Interviews*   • *Assigning
Numerical Values*   • *Interviewing for Jobs With No
Requirements*   • *Taking Effective Notes*   • *Summary*

8   Preemployment and Employment Testing   201

    • *Testing Characteristics*   • *Uniform Guidelines on Employee Selection*   • *Testing and Discrimination*   • *Testing Policies*   • *Types of Tests*   • *Alternative Selection Procedures*   • *Summary*

9   Making the Selection   230

    • *Conducting Reference Checks*   • *Considering Other Factors*   • *Determining Who Should Choose*   • *Notifying the Chosen Candidate*   • *Writing Rejection Letters*   • *Summary*

10   Orientation   246

    • *The First Day of Work*   • *Organizational Orientation*   • *Sample Organizational Orientation Program*   • *Organizational Orientation Evaluation*   • *Departmental Orientation*   • *Summary*

Appendixes   275

A.   Work Environment Checklist   275
B.   Job Description Form   276
C.   Job Posting Notice Form   278
D.   Job Posting Application Form   279
E.   Sampling of Job Ads   280
F.   Application for Employment Form   286
G.   Completed Application for Employment Form   294
H.   Interview Evaluation Form   302
I.   Employment Reference Form for Exempt Positions   304
J.   Employment Reference Form for Nonexempt Positions   308
K.   Selection Checklist   312
L.   Checklist for New Employees   314
M.   Organizational Orientation Evaluation   317

Index   319

Preface to
the Second Edition

The second edition of *Recruiting, Interviewing, Selecting & Orienting New Employees,* like its predecessor, is designed to serve as a comprehensive guide throughout the employment process. For those who are not human resources specialists, it will provide the skills, tools, and techniques needed to operate effectively in this field. For those recently hired as human resources professionals, or who lack formal training in this area, this book will provide step-by-step guidance, beginning with preparation prior to recruitment, through an employee's first few weeks at work. It will also be a useful refresher for those who have worked in the field for some time and wish to update or upgrade their skills. The methods and techniques described in this book are applicable to all work environments: corporate and nonprofit, union and nonunion, technical and nontechnical, large and small. They may also be applied to both professional and nonprofessional positions. Readers are urged to consider the particulars of their own environment and apply the concepts discussed accordingly.

The book may also be used as a reference for training workshops in various aspects of the employment process, and as a basic text for college, university, and other courses dealing with employment.

A unique feature of this book, as with the original edition, is the recognition that selection is not the end of the employment process. With all the time, energy, and resources expended toward hiring the best possible candidate, it is crucial that the process not begin over again soon after hire for the same position. And yet, this is precisely what can, and frequently does, occur when the new hire grows disenchanted with his or her new surroundings, often within the first few weeks of employment. One way to avoid this is to make certain that all new hires receive a full and complete indoctrination into their new work culture. This is best accomplished through various aspects of the orientation process. This book addresses the role orientation plays in the employee's introduction to a new job and organization by discussing the all-important first day of work, companywide orientation, and the less formal, but no less important, departmental orientation.

While the basics of recruiting, interviewing, selecting, and orienting new employees have not changed since the first edition of this book was published (1986), other factors in our society have, thereby warranting the revisions made in this edition. These begin with a new chapter (Chapter 1) that looks to the future by exploring the various recruitment challenges confronting employers in the 1990s and into the next century. Issues such as tomorrow's changing work force, emerging work and family issues, and the host of alternative work arrangements arising over the past few years are addressed. In addition, the impact of illiteracy on business is reviewed.

Each subsequent chapter has been expanded and revised to encompass recent employment-related developments. For example, Chapter 3 now covers twenty-six methods employers can use to fill job openings, twice as many as were described in the original edition; and Chapter 5 has been updated to reflect recent legislation, termination-at-will, and negligent hiring.

Because of the increased focus on various types of testing, i.e., drug tests and polygraphs, a chapter on preemployment and employment testing has been added (Chapter 8). In addition to analyzing many different types of tests, this chapter explores such issues as test validation and the benefits and disadvantages of testing.

Many of these revisions have affected the appendixes appearing in the original edition. Consequently, in this edition several employment forms have been added and significant changes have been made to others, such as the application form.

Readers are cautioned on two points: First, any reference made to specific publications, services, or institutions is for informational purposes only and is not to be considered an endorsement; second, this book is not intended to provide legal advice. If such advice is required, the services of an attorney specializing in employment law should be sought.

Recruiting, interviewing, selecting, and orienting new employees are specific skills. How well you practice these skills can directly affect many common organizational problem areas, such as turnover, employee morale, and absenteeism. By carefully practicing and implementing the methods described in this book, an organization can greatly improve its employer/employee relations and its level of productivity.

D.A.

Recruiting, Interviewing, Selecting & Orienting New Employees

Second Edition

1

Recruitment Challenges and Opportunities

Human resources specialists and managers involved in the hiring process are viewing future job openings with a combination of excitement and apprehension. As we approach the year 2000, it is becoming increasingly apparent that the labor pool from which employers select new hires is changing at every level, from minimum wage and hourly paid workers right up the ranks to professionals and executives. In addition, it is projected that tomorrow's work force will have a different set of requirements and expectations that companies will need to understand and, ultimately, embrace, if they are to continue to produce and prosper. Unless employers have a clear picture of the new work ethic, they may find somewhat unnerving the transition from traditional nine-to-five, Monday through Friday jobs performed by known employee populations to more innovative work arrangements utilizing the talents of different target groups.

Changing Work Force

Tomorrow's work force will reflect some of the economic changes that began about ten years ago. For example, according to the Bureau of Labor Statistics (BLS), a branch of the Labor Department, between 1981 and 1986 approximately 10.8 million workers lost their jobs because of closings, mergers, and takeovers. One-third of those out of work during that five-year period are not considered part of the work force today due to their age and low retraining potential. It is believed that training for replacement work would have been more feasible if those workers had had a better command of basic reading, writing, and math skills. A 1988 National Academy of Science study revealed that from 20 to 30 percent of all dislocated or displaced workers in the past decade lacked basic skills. This contributed to their inability to compete with younger (under 50), educated workers who, according to the BLS, found new jobs in a shorter period of time. A greater tolerance for older workers might also have helped the more than 50 percent of workers, aged 50 plus, who could not find comparable work.

The shortage of labor created during the 1980s continues into the 1990s. The flood of baby-boomers who have entered the labor market since the mid-1960s has not been matched in recent years because of lower birthrates. The Census Bureau projects that the number of eighteen-year-olds will drop by 8 percent in 1991 and will not reach 1989 levels again until the year 2003. The greatest population increase will be in middle-aged Americans. The nation's elderly population will grow, as well. In addition, the number of women and minorities in the labor force will increase substantially in the next decade.

This means that companies will have to become more innovative in their recruitment efforts by entering inner-city minority and immigrant neighborhoods, and by reaching out to older workers and women with young children. Unfortunately, many of these new employees will be unskilled and require training, even for many entry-level jobs. In the 1990s, the most basic jobs are demanding new, more complex skills; even simple clerical work necessitates computer knowledge. The greatest demand in the 1990s will be in jobs that require independent thinking, reasoning, logic, and the ability to diagnose and take action. Many commentators are concerned that these skills are not being adequately taught in our schools.

A shortage of adequately trained employees is only one trend that will shape the employment picture of the 1990s. Another has to do with where job opportunities will lie. According to BLS projections, four of the fastest-growing industries between 1991 and 2000 will be computer and data processing services, health services and outpatient facilities, personnel services such as temporary agencies, and miscellaneous business services such as credit reporting. Other fast-growing jobs will include paralegals, medical assistants, physical therapists, data processing equipment repairers, home health aides, podiatrists, and computer systems analysts. Significantly, these openings are in service industries, as opposed to manufacturing, the traditional source of most jobs in the United States.

Profiles of workers for the start of the next century are already starting to emerge. According to the U.S. Department of Labor, by the year 2000 the labor force will grow by more than 21 million. More specifically, the data project that nearly 90 percent of all new workers will be women and minorities, with women accounting for more than 45 percent of the entire labor force. Immigrants are expected to represent some 23 percent. The black labor force will grow 74 percent. Only 15 percent of all new workers will be white males, as compared with 47 percent before 1986. Other ethnic groups, including Native Americans, Asians, and Pacific Islanders, will account for more than 11 percent of the total labor force growth.

The Department of Labor also projects which jobs will be the most prevalent in the beginning of the next century. The fastest-growing positions will be in the professional, technical, service, and sales fields, requiring the highest levels of education and skill. Engineering jobs will increase by more than 165,000, and there will be more than 85,000 additional managerial positions available.

The Department of Labor statistics also indicate that all groups are not likely to be equally represented in these fields. For example, blacks and Hispanics are not expected to do well in the service industries, technical positions, sales, or management. The average worker will be aged 39 in the year 2000; the number of workers aged 16–34 is expected to decline; the number of workers aged 35–54 is expected to increase; and the percentage of fifty-five to sixty-four year olds is likely to increase rapidly after 1995.

Scrutinizing these numbers too closely can leave one feeling dizzy and somewhat confused. By looking at the overall picture, however, employers can begin to better understand what lies ahead in the field of recruitment. Essentially, employers may anticipate the following changes based on the above data:

- Due to the overall shortage of labor, employers can no longer be as selective as in years past when they could afford to seek out the ideal candidate. Indeed, for some positions, finding any qualified applicants at all may be a challenge.
- Employers can no longer rely on traditional forms of recruitment, i.e., word of mouth, to find suitable workers.
- As the percentage of women, minorities, immigrants, and senior citizens in the work force continues to increase, employers must extend fair thinking and behavior well beyond

the minimal standards required by equal employment opportunity laws and affirmative action programs.

- Since the fastest-growing industries will require a higher level of skill and knowledge than in years past, greater emphasis must be placed on education and training.

Preparing now for the changes predicted for the next century will better enable employers to look forward to recruitment challenges and opportunities instead of problems.

Workplace Literacy

The heading for this section might better read "Workplace Illiteracy," for that more accurately describes the situation American businesses are facing today and will face tomorrow if we do not start taking some critical steps soon. Illiteracy in adults, however, implies a certain irreversible hopelessness and seems somehow unreal—How can it be that so many adults in our country cannot read or write? And exactly what impact has illiteracy, or literacy, had on business to date? More significantly how is it expected to affect business in the future?

We can begin to address these questions by looking at more Department of Labor statistics. They tell us that 2.5 million illiterate Americans enter the work force each year. In the immediate future, 80 percent of all available jobs will require at least a high school education, but only 74 percent of Americans finish high school. In addition, only an approximate 66 percent will graduate with adequate skills.

The U.S. Department of Education offers some additional disturbing statistics. One in every seven American adults is a functional illiterate, unable to read, write, calculate, or solve even simple problems. Functionally illiterate people presently comprise 30 percent of unskilled workers; 29 percent of semiskilled workers; and 11 percent of all managers, professionals, and technicians. Another 47 million adults are borderline illiterates. In addition, one-half of our nation's industrial workers read at or below the eighth-grade level.

The impact of illiteracy on business is far-reaching. According to Jonathan Kozol in *Illiterate America* (NAL Books, 1986), illiteracy accounts for a loss of at least $20 billion in profits each year. In addition, there are the problems of lowered productivity, declining international competitiveness, and reduced promotability. The pool of available workers that industries can hire from is affected; workers who cannot read instructions may endanger the lives of co-workers; illiterate customers cannot read advertisements; and illiterate consumers cannot read instructions. The problem has become so severe that a toll-free hot line at 1-800-228-8813 has been set up enabling companies to find groups within their community that can help fight illiteracy.

As part of the effort to reduce the growing gap between the reading, writing, and math skills of the work force and the current and future needs of industry, many businesses have begun offering in-house programs and encouraging outside education and training. In 1987 the Center for Public Resources reported that 75 percent of the country's largest corporations provided some kind of basic skills training in an effort to help eradicate illiteracy. Among them, American Telephone & Telegraph offered remedial courses to its employees; General Motors and International Business Machines financed adult education for many of their employees; Ford Motor Co. offered basic reading courses at many of its plants; Texas Instruments reimbursed the tuition of thousands of employees each semester; New York Telephone provided a program designed to elevate the educational level of barely literate employees to ninth- and tenth-grade levels; Aetna Life and Casualty and United Technologies implemented a tutorial program whereby employees tutored co-workers one-on-one; B. Dalton Bookseller launched a four-year national literacy campaign; Standard Oil Co. in Indiana employed a former schoolteacher to conduct classes in grammar and spelling for newly hired secretaries; Nabisco Brands' Virginia factory offered several hours of elementary school courses weekly; Polaroid identified hundreds of employees each year for remedial programs; and Liberty Mutual Insurance Group offered remedial and advanced literacy training. The program included a career center at corporate headquarters where basic office-skills courses were conducted.

These organizations are being joined today by other companies trying to help reduce the number of illiterate employees in American businesses. For example, Olsten Corp., a provider of temporary services, sponsors spelling bees and provides how-to guides for its employees in grammar, spelling, and punctuation. In April of 1989, the company launched a major advertising campaign, focusing on the difficulty that the alphabet presents to functionally illiterate people and how this affects productivity. Spring Industries, a textile manufacturer, provides on-site facilities for classes in basic literacy and basic technical skills. Travelers Insurance Co., in cooperation with the Urban League, established MOST (Modern Office Skills

Training) to prepare disadvantaged individuals for jobs at Travelers. BEST (Business English for Spanish-Speaking Trainees) is another program offering to teach the same skills to those for whom English is a second language. MOST/BEST graduates are offered jobs at Travelers. The UAW-Ford Eastern Michigan University Academy teaches basic skill enhancement to three hundred Ford employees each year. Classes include reading, writing, speaking, and listening. Philadelphia Newspapers, Inc. has a two-part "PNI Read Program"—"Help Others Read," in which employees are trained as tutors, and "Learn to Read Better," a referral system for those who need help. And Rocco, Inc., a poultry company, has launched a companywide campaign against illiteracy by implementing a "career enhancement program" (Rocco felt this title was more positive than "reading" program or "literacy" program).

Preemployment screening offers an opportunity for employers to identify job applicants with skill deficiencies who may require remedial training. Unfortunately, at this stage, recruiters and interviewers often assume that a business school or college graduate can automatically master basic reading, writing, and math skills. This, sadly, is not so. It has been found that many college graduates cannot write a coherent business letter and many are deficient in critical reasoning skills.

Some human resources departments actually help illiterate applicants conceal their deficiencies by allowing them to take employment applications home to complete. Such illiteracy may remain further concealed when employers shy away from preemployment tests out of fear of discrimination charges. In addition, employment and educational reference checks are increasingly difficult to conduct, and many employers do not even attempt them. Consequently, employees are placed on the payroll even though their literacy levels are unknown.

Many employers who are concerned with screening potential employees for basic literacy have found the following techniques to be helpful:

- Applicants should be required to complete the employment application form by themselves, at the time of the interview.
- Job descriptions, defining both the requirements for the job and primary duties and responsibilities, should be shown to applicants during the course of the interview. Sufficient time should then be allotted for the applicant to read the contents and ask questions.

- Job-related, validated tests may be used as one of the selection criteria. Chapter 8 addresses this area in detail.
- Thorough employment and educational reference checks should be conducted whenever possible. See Chapter 9 for additional information regarding references.
- In-depth, face-to-face interviews should be conducted by trained interviewers. The emphasis should be on open-ended questions so that the interviewers can evaluate such factors as word use, clarity of thought, organization of information, and analytical ability relevant to a given job opening. Details regarding employment interviews appear in Chapter 6.

Target Populations

Since the composition of the work force is changing, employers must begin to reconsider who will make the best workers. Traditional views that certain jobs are appropriate for men or women only, or unsuitable for older people, or undesirable for minorities, may be not only discriminatory and in violation of certain equal employment opportunity laws, but impractical and self-defeating from the standpoint of productivity and profitability. The populations from which employers will hire tomorrow's workers are expanding and changing to include older workers, the disabled, women, the homeless, minorities, and immigrants, all in greater numbers than ever before.

Older Workers

One of the groups most certain to be recruited in greater numbers at the turn of the century is older workers. As the first group of baby-boomers approaches the age of 50, Ken Dychtwald, the "guru of aging," and founder/chairman of Age Wave Inc., tells us that we are on the brink of a "senior boom"; that is, we are rapidly refocusing from youth orientation to a mature population of healthier Americans who are living longer than ever before. In the February 1990 issue of *Training & Development Journal,* Dychtwald reports that one hundred years ago only 3 million Americans were over 65—a mere 4 percent of our population. Now, as we approach the next century, there are more than 30 million over-65 Americans, or 12 percent of our population. Changes in diet and exercise habits are also producing a generation of more vigorous Americans. And yet, in spite of the statistics regarding their longevity and ability to make valuable contributions to business, there is resistance to hiring older workers.

The list of reasons offered for not hiring this increasingly visible group of would-be employees is topped by the belief that older people have more accidents on the job, poorer attendance, and lower productivity. In addition, many managers assume that the older one gets the less able or willing one is to learn new ideas or skills. Paradoxically, more mature workers are also considered to be less stable than younger workers.

Each one of these statements is easily refuted, says Dychtwald: Older workers, who make up more than 13 percent of the labor force, are responsible for less than 10 percent of on-the-job accidents, as opposed to twenty-to-twenty-four-year-old workers who account for 50 percent of accidents at work. Older workers also have fewer avoidable absences than do younger workers and good attendance records overall. Additionally, there are no data available to indicate that one age group is superior to another when it comes to productivity. In fact, with the exception of a slight decline in productivity in jobs requiring a great deal of physical exertion, many studies indicate that older workers perform at least as well as, and in many instances better than, younger workers do. As for an unwillingness or inability to change, historically older workers have experienced a great deal of social and technological change and are, therefore, more familiar with the necessity of change. Finally, with regard to the suggestion that they are not as stable as younger workers, consider this: Older workers exhibit less stress on the job, have a lower rate of illegal drug use, and have a lower rate of admission to psychiatric facilities.

Another reason for unwillingness to employ older workers is the concern that they will start a job, perhaps receive training, and then retire. In reality, older people are products of a time when the job one held was all-important and loyalty to one's company was the norm. Hence, older workers tend to stay on a job for ten to fifteen years, while many young professionals stay with one company for a maximum of four to five years.

Not everyone views older job applicants negatively. Many are enthusiastic over the findings of a 1985 Gallup survey in which the overwhelming majority of the over-63 workers polled said they worked because they wanted to and that working made them feel useful. Those recognizing that older workers represent a valuable labor pool are implementing active recruitment campaigns that include job fairs; contact with the American Association of Retired Persons (AARP) Worker Equity Initiative, a program established in

1985 to encourage employers to hire and retain senior workers; and such creative advertising phrases as "life experience a plus" to encourage elderly people to apply.

Several companies are beginning to stand out for their aggressive attempts to recruit and hire older workers. Among them are Days Inn of America, Inc., the hotel chain; McDonald's, the fast-food chain; and The Travelers Companies, with headquarters in Hartford, Connecticut. Days Inn sees senior citizens as a prime solution to the labor shortage problem. Not only are they found to be available and willing to work, but according to Richard Smith, Days Inn's vice-president of human resources, they seem to enjoy their jobs much more than the average employee does. As of fall 1989, senior workers comprised 25 percent of the staff at Days Inn's company headquarters; older workers are also employed at other Days Inn locations.

The management of McDonald's also believes in the worth of older workers. It actively recruits them through aggressive advertising and visits to senior citizens' clubs, offers them a special Mc-Master's training program, and allows them to choose their own work schedules. And at Travelers, senior workers may join the Older Americans Program, a job bank designed to help fill the company's temporary needs. As of January 1989, the retirees in Travelers' job bank filled approximately 60 percent of its temporary positions. Managers report that, in general, these retirees rate higher in work performance than do outside temporary hires.

One of the greatest benefits of hiring older workers, it seems, is the impact on turnover. At Days Inn, senior workers have a one percent turnover rate as compared with 40 percent among younger employees. The Great American Savings Bank in San Diego recently began hiring older people as tellers and found its turnover rate was dramatically reduced. Naugles, a major West Coast restaurant chain, found that once it began to hire older workers the turnover rate dropped dramatically from 400 percent per year to 80 percent.

As Dychtwald says, people don't grow old at 65 anymore. In addition, not all older people want or need the same benefits or rewards from employment. Many "younger" older workers, between the ages of 50 and 62, are looking for advancement opportunities and more money. Translated, that means full-time employment and full benefits. Retirees over the age of 62 are often on Social Security; therefore, they may be seeking part-time work that will provide a supplemental income. But this is not always the case. Other reasons given by older people for returning to work include the desire to feel useful and needed, an interest in staying in touch with current developments, a need to provide structure to their days, and a need to retain a sense of productivity and worth.

It would, therefore, appear to be in the best interests of American businesses to sweep aside traditional generalizations about an entire population of people who could prove to be among our most valuable assets.

The process of recruiting older workers may require some deviation from customary hiring practices. To begin with, it is a good idea to actively seek out older candidates, as opposed to expecting them to come to you via traditional recruitment avenues, such as job ads or employment agencies. Many retirement-age job hunters have been rejected a number of times and some may have been victims of age jokes and age discrimination. Consequently, they may believe that potential employers have written them off.

One way of recruiting older workers is to contact the Senior Employment Service, which maintains a job clearinghouse and may help put you in touch with qualified older candidates. Visiting senior citizen community centers with information about available job openings is another recruitment technique that has proved to be successful. Approaching social service agencies and organizations with large senior memberships should also be helpful. Contacting Forty Plus, a national organization that helps those over age 40 to find employment, is yet another way of recruiting older workers. The American Association of Retired Persons offers a free booklet entitled "How to Recruit Older Workers," which can help employers with their recruitment efforts. Also, do not overlook the obvious resource of your company's own retirees. In addition, if you do run advertisements, use language that encourages older workers to apply, for example, "This job is suitable for retired persons." Also, describe the kind of employees your company wants to hire, in terms of qualities and not just qualifications. You might also want to have pictures of older workers in your ads.

When hiring older workers, recruiters should be prepared to answer questions regarding how the return to work will affect a retiree's income. The limitations on what Social Security recipients can earn without penalty have been reduced in recent years, but regular employment could still produce too high a level of income for some. Also, be familiar with what benefits full- and part-time workers may be entitled to, including medical and life insurance, sick leave, paid vacations, and holidays.

Once hired, older employees should be reassured that their work is valued. They should be offered the same opportunities for advancement and challenging work that their younger peers have.

Disabled Workers

According to a report in *HR News*, February 1990, 68 percent of all disabled persons (the term now favored over *handicapped*) are employable and want to work. Yet, this has been a relatively untapped labor source. In fact, *Personnel Administrator* reported in October 1989 that only 34 percent of the disabled population in this nation are employed. While recent legislation, such as the Americans with Disabilities Act, has drawn greater attention to this group than ever before, there is still resistance to hiring them.

One of the primary reasons for this resistance has to do with how disabled people are perceived. Many of us are locked into an image of someone in a wheelchair. In reality, the term *disabled* encompasses a broad spectrum of impairments, including mental illness, heart disease, visual or hearing impairments, acquired immune deficiency syndrome (AIDS) or human immunodeficiency virus (HIV)-positive status, and limitations resulting from accidents. We also have a tendency to feel uncomfortable around people who are disabled.

As of the end of 1989, there were 36 million disabled Americans. Over 16 million were over the age of 65, indicating that the majority of disabilities are acquired through the aging process. Since the percentage of older workers is steadily rising, employers must pay greater attention to the disabled.

Another reason commonly cited for not hiring the disabled is that it will cost more money than hiring nondisabled workers. There are laws requiring many employers to make reasonable accommodations when considering disabled applicants, without creating an undue hardship (Chapter 5). In determining whether a particular accommodation would result in an undue hardship, the law assesses employers on the basis of the overall size of their business, the nature of their business, and the nature and cost of the required accommodation.

If a job should require the modification of certain equipment or procedures to accommodate a disabled worker, employers are advised to contact organizations such as the Job Accommodations Network, established by the President's Committee on Employment of People with Disabilities, at 1-800-JAN-PCEH, or the National Support Center for Persons with Disabilities, established by IBM, at 1-800-IBM-2133, for advice and assistance.

Many believe that any additional costs incurred through the process of accommodation are well worth the effort. Days Inn, known for extending employment opportunities to older workers, has also extended its "special sector" program to encompass disabled workers. The hotel chain reports that it gladly accommodates any special access needs, such as wider doors and lower lavatory fixtures, and only purchases workstations, desks, and other furnishings that can easily accommodate wheelchair-bound individuals. Pizza Hut, Inc. also has an aggressive hiring policy regarding the disabled and is determined to hire over sixteen hundred severely disabled individuals throughout its more than eight hundred locations by 1991. Eventually, Pizza Hut hopes to have 5 percent of its total labor force represented by severely disabled employees.

There are also tax incentives for hiring the disabled. For example, Section 190 of the Tax Reform Act of 1986 provides for up to a $35,000 tax credit annually for site improvements that make businesses more accessible to the disabled; state agencies will provide funds to compensate employers, in part, for the time devoted to training disabled employees; and qualified employers are entitled to a tax credit of 50 percent of a disabled employee's first $6,000 in wages for one year.

As with older workers, traditional recruitment methods are not usually successful when applied to the disabled. Some techniques that have proved successful, however, include distributing circulars at shopping centers, grocery stores, and drugstores and networking with civic centers and associations for the disabled. These associations, such as the National Association of Rehabilitation Facilities (703-648-9300), exist at the national, state, and local levels and are, reportedly, very helpful.

Interviewing disabled job applicants can initially be an unsettling experience if bias and stereotypical thinking get in the way. Aware of the problems interviewing disabled applicants can present, AT&T has a training program that helps receptionists and interviewers develop a keener sense of understanding toward, and a greater tolerance for, disabled applicants. Among other things, it permits blind applicants to submit employment applications through the mail or has an interviewer help with the completion process; questions are written out and shown to hearing-impaired applicants; and physically disabled applicants are provided with a detailed description of entrances and elevators.

Beyond such preparatory steps, the format of the actual employment interview should be essentially the same as with any candidate. The questions should all be job-related and tied in to the skills, education, and experience required to perform the job. If it is believed that a person's impairment might interfere with his or her ability to perform the essential functions of the job, then the interviewer should ask a series of pertinent questions, such as "This job requires typing; if you are visually impaired, how are you able to type?" "What accommodations would you require in order to perform this job?" "Is there anything to prevent you from successfully performing the essential functions of this job?"

Interviewers should carefully evaluate the responses to questions such as these to determine whether or not a reasonable accommodation may be made without creating an undue hardship for the company.

Women

According to "Workforce 2000: Work and Workers for the 21st Century," prepared in 1986 by the Hudson Institute, 61 percent of all women will be working by the turn of the century. Also, nearly one out of every two workers in the nation will be a woman. These statistics should send a clear message to every company in this nation to examine its structure and environment for compatibility with hiring women at all levels. This is advisable because many of the women in the work force will be mothers requiring alternative work arrangements from the traditional eight-hour day, five-day week. Such alternatives might include flexible work schedules, job sharing, at-home work arrangements, and on-site child care facilities or support.

While gains have been made toward eliminating discrimination against women in nontraditional female jobs, bias still prevails. Equal employment opportunities are still not available for qualified women at all types and levels of work. Relatively few women are found at the upper levels of management, on corporate boards, or in chief executive officer positions. This is something that needs to change, beginning now, if employers are to fully avail themselves of a most valuable pool of human resources.

The Homeless

Hiring the homeless is one of the newest areas of recruitment. In fact, until recently this was virtually unheard of. Today a handful of companies are cautiously venturing into this as-yet-unexplored labor pool. With little data available to help structure a recruitment plan, these adventuresome organizations are essentially making up guidelines as they go along and hoping for the best.

One such organization is Days Inn. Already known for its commitment to hiring older and disabled workers, this hotel chain began taking steps toward recruiting homeless people in February of 1988. With the help of a shelter for the homeless in the Atlanta suburb of Jonesboro, President and Chief Operating Officer Michael Leven developed a creative hiring program. The arrangement included housing in addition to a salary. Those homeless individuals who were hired to work at Days Inn were required to sign a statement that outlined certain rules and conditions, including no drugs or alcohol on the premises and no more than one visitor at a time.

Leven admits that the program got off to a rough start, with some new hires cashing their first paycheck and taking off. However, by more carefully screening applicants, Days Inn can now boast of ten successful hires. Leven hopes to increase that number to at least twenty and recommends that other employers also hire the homeless.

To succeed at hiring the homeless one must avoid the trap of assuming that every homeless person will be grateful and make a good employee. Leven learned that there are two primary groups of homeless people: those who have lost their homes through unfortunate circumstances and want to work, and those who are unwilling to work. Carefully screening applicants and practicing sound interviewing techniques can help lead to successful hires. Once they are hired, both general training to help reacclimate them into the work force and specific training relative to the position they have been hired for are necessary.

Youth

A shortage of younger workers at the turn of the century is imminent. As cited earlier, the number of workers aged 16 to 34 is expected to decline considerably.

One technique for attracting some of the limited number of youthful workers is to provide funding for scholarships. Some businesses are beginning to award scholarships to employees who attend college or technical school while they work. Others provide local school scholarship funding in the hope that graduates will work for them. One such company is Burger King. In 1985 Burger King established its Crew Education Assistance Program, which offers up to $2,000 to hourly employees who want to go to any licensed, accredited college or vocational/technical school. Eligibility requirements include working an average of fifteen hours per week for three months. While enrolled, employees must maintain a C average or better. Students who maintain a B average or better are eligible for an additional $1,000.

Eastman Kodak Co. has a similar program, entitled Kodak Scholars. The top students at thirty-five colleges are granted 100 percent tuition aid from the second year of school through graduation. The one stipulation is that students must work one summer at Kodak. Tied in with the scholarship program is a mentor program, which helps familiarize students with Kodak operations.

Information regarding the management of scholarship programs is available to employers from the Council for Aid to Education (212-689-2400).

Some companies are starting to stretch far to attract the dwindling number of youthful workers. For example, one fast-food company experimented with uniforms until it found one that particularly appealed to teenage applicants.

The recruitment of young workers is even more challenging because the youths who will comprise tomorrow's work force are already making it very clear that they plan to balance a fulfilling career with family and personal responsibilities. That will mean alternative work arrangements, such as job sharing, flextime, and at-home work. In addition, they will expect their employers to provide financial incentives, career opportunities, and comprehensive benefits.

Minorities

It is projected that the term *minority*, here intended to encompass a broad spectrum of ethnic groups including, but not limited to, blacks, Hispanics, Asians, and American Indians, will soon disappear from our vocabulary as we discuss employment in the next century. How can we call "minority" a collective group of people who, according to the Department of Labor, will account for nearly one-third of the labor force by the year 2000?

Unfortunately, while these groups may represent a large percentage of tomorrow's work force, few will be targeted for professional positions. Those who are qualified will be drawn to employers offering not only the usual growth opportunities and benefits, but also a multicultural environment.

The idea of a multicultural environment is one that may be difficult for some to grasp. Traditionally, employers have tended to hire candidates who most resemble themselves in terms of skills, interests, background, and even appearance. That simply will not work anymore. Recruiters are better advised to concentrate on ability, not ethnicity.

One way of establishing and promoting a multicultural environment is to develop and maintain an ongoing relationship with minority professional associations. There are numerous national associations with local chapters. Groups such as the National Black MBA Association, the American Association of Hispanic CPAs, and the American Indian Science and Engineering Society are possible sources of job candidates.

One minority recruitment source that is often overlooked is a company's own employees. Training existing staff for higher-level jobs can not only resolve recruitment woes, but also help to establish management as committed to minority development and placement.

Immigrants

As stated earlier in this chapter, immigrants will account for some 23 percent of the change in the labor force by the turn of the century. Like minorities, this group of applicants will be concerned with selecting companies offering multicultural environments. Hence, recruiters need to begin both focusing on sources that will put them in touch with qualified immigrants (networking with professional organizations is likely to yield the greatest results) and remodeling their corporate setting to be more accepting of different cultures.

Actually, finding immigrants who want to work for you is not likely to be as problematic as being able to hire them legally. The Immigration Reform and Control Act of 1986 (IRCA) has developed a set of restrictions and requirements relating to the employment of immigrants. This includes examination and verification of certain documents that confirm the identity of the person presenting the document and certification that an individual is legally authorized to work in the United States. Details of this Act are provided in Chapter 5. For now, it is important to note that all human resources professionals and managers who are involved in the hiring process must acquire a basic knowledge of IRCA and understand its implications.

Work and Family Issues

For a long time it was assumed that one would enter the labor market, work a forty-hour week five days a week for approximately forty years, and then retire to a life of fun and relaxation. Today's workers are starting to say, in an increasingly louder voice, that an arrangement committing much of the first half of their lives (we are now living to age 80, 90, and beyond) to an inflexible schedule with little time for familial activities and other interests is no longer acceptable. The focus on better balancing work and family is due, largely, to the increase of women and aging baby-boomers in the labor market. They bring with them a desire to reevaluate how careers, relationships, and life in general should be approached. Since the labor pool is shrinking and companies must become more creative and competitive in their recruitment and retention efforts, employers have little choice but to try to accommodate their workers' desire to integrate work and family.

Child Care Programs

Some forty-two hundred employers nationwide are responding to the need for a greater balance between work and family by heeding the increasing need for child care programs. The specific level and extent of care offered depends on several factors, including an organization's financial resources and the age of its employees. Services may include help in locating local care, financial aid for child care, support for near-site child care centers, and on-site care facilities. Johnson & Johnson's program provides its working parents with the names of local child care providers who have been screened by counselors and with other related services, such as workshops and educational materials. In addition, some of their locations are establishing on-site child care facilities. AT&T's Work and Family program helps employees locate day care centers, nursery schools, family day care homes, and camps. It also follows up to help ensure successful child care. Bank of America's Family-Supportive program locates child care providers and provides relevant child/parenting information. John Hancock offers a special activity program called Kids-to-Go for employees whose child care arrangements do not extend to holidays and vacations. As of this writing, Hancock also planned an on- or near-site child care center. And Apple Computer has an employee-staffed child care center; as an extra "plus," Apple gives a "baby bonus" of $500 to new parents.

One of the most innovative corporate child care programs was established in September of 1989, by a consortium of seven New York-based employers: Consolidated Edison; National Westminster Bank USA; Time Inc.; Home Box Office; Colgate-Palmolive; Ernst & Young; and Skadden, Arps, Slate, Meagher & Flom. They pay for all or most of the cost of licensed home health care agencies who provide emergency at-home child care for the children of their more than thirteen thousand employees. This service is expected to reduce the absenteeism, lateness, and loss of productivity that frequently occurs when working parents are forced to tend to or arrange for the care of children who are ill.

Elder-Care Programs

One growing area of concern greatly affecting the relationship between work and family relates to the care of our nation's elderly population. According to the Older Women's League, elder care is the no. 1 workplace issue of the 1990s. As long as five years ago, the Travelers Insurance Company surveyed employees aged 30 and over and found that one in five cared for an elderly relative.

Workers who are responsible for the care of an elderly relative need both financial and emotional support from their employers. According to the National Council on the Aging, about three hundred companies have started to respond. International Business Machines Corp. pioneered one of the nation's first elder-care information and referral programs in 1988 after a survey revealed that 30 percent of its work force had some responsibility for older relatives. Other companies have also developed elder-care programs. Among them, National Westminster Bank USA works with Pathfinders/Eldercare, an organization providing elder-care information and counseling to NatWest employees. Remington Products, Inc., the electric-shaver manufacturer, offers its employees a "respite care" program, whereby the company pays half of the ten- to fifteen-dollar hourly cost for a health professional to come to the home and tend to an elderly family member so the employee can take some time off during nonworking hours. The Stride Rite Corp., a manufacturer and retailer of shoes, has gone even further with an on-site "intergenerational center" that, at full capacity, will accommodate twenty-four adults (it already accommodates fifty-five children). The center is available not only to relatives of Stride Rite employees, but also to people in the community. The company reportedly spent $700,000 to convert eighty-five hundred square feet of space for the center; operating expenses are estimated to be $600,000 a year. The center estimates that it costs $140 per week to care for an adult, $150 for a preschooler, and $170 for a toddler. Stride Rite employees pay anywhere from $20 to $130 per week for child care, depending on family income, and $85 per week for adult care. The balance is paid by a foundation set up by the company.

Companies such as NatWest, Remington, and Stride Rite recognize that employees torn between responsibilities to their loved ones and their jobs may be less effective on the job. In a 1984 study, the New York Business Group for Health found that employees caring for elderly relatives had on-the-job problems ranging from absenteeism to lateness and excessive use of the telephone.

Addressing employees' child care and elder-care needs can be a powerful recruiting tool in a tight labor market. As candidates size up and compare would-be employers, extra programs demonstrating management's commitment to employee well-being can often influence applicants to choose one employer over another.

Alternative Work Arrangements

As American businesses strive to both recruit qualified workers and accommodate changing work ethics, it is becoming increasingly evident that alternatives to the traditional workweek and work schedule must be considered if effective levels of productivity are to be maintained. Many of these alternative work arrangements, such as part-time employment, have found limited use for a long time; but now these options are being considered for different levels of employees and with some creative twists. Other work options, such as at-home work, are relatively new and will, no doubt, receive mixed reviews. And, of course, not all arrangements will work equally well in every environment. It is significant, however, that more and more organizations are willing to test different work options and are reporting positive results. A recent study conducted by Catalyst, a New York-based research and advisory organization that helps corporations foster the career development of women, reported that 85 percent of the managers who participated in the study felt that alternative work arrangements were well worth the effort. A copy of the report, "Flexible Work Arrangements: Establishing Options for Managers and Professions," may be purchased from Catalyst by calling 212-777-8900. Another useful resource is *Creating a Flexible Workplace* (AMACOM Books, 1989) in which authors Barney Olmsted and Suzanne Smith offer guidelines for selecting and implementing ten alternative work options.

As this trend toward varying work schedules continues, it is projected that by the turn of the century the typical American company will consist of workers from the lowest-paid entry level all the way up to the highest levels of management in several different work arrangements. In fact, it may very well be that at some point in the future regular, full-time employment will be the exception.

Regular Part-Time

Traditionally, candidates completing job applications have been asked to check off one of two boxes for their desired work schedule: full-time or part-time. The latter usually referred to schedules of up to twenty hours per week and meant ineligibility for benefits. It also generally applied to nonexempt-level employees—usually women with child care responsibilities and students.

As times have changed and continue to change, the term *regular part-time* has expanded in meaning and scope. The traditional part-timer, as described above, still exists in many industries, but now, more often than not, the term refers to varying levels of employees, male and female, on a reduced work-time schedule who are entitled to many of the privileges and benefits available to full-time workers.

The change in definition clearly indicates a redirection in thinking, as employers come to realize that there is a great deal of competition for good people. Companies such as Johnson & Johnson and Eastman Kodak now officially endorse reduced work schedules, recognizing that part-time schedules help today's workers balance family and job responsibilities. The trend is also spreading up through the ranks, as more professionals are requesting and being granted part-time work arrangements. For example, as of January 1990, the law firm of Skadden, Arps, Slate, Meagher & Flom had about forty lawyers working part-time.

Job Sharing

Job sharing may be defined as an arrangement in which two employees divide the responsibilities of one full-time job. It is distinguished from regular part-time employment in that it applies to positions that cannot be separated into two definitive part-time jobs. While the concept of job sharing has been around for about twenty-five years, it has only been since the mid-1980s that organizations such as Quaker Oats Co. and Levi Strauss & Co. have started viewing it as a viable alternative work arrangement. And, while initially it was viewed as a female-related issue, job sharing is now seen as a solution to the needs of many employees, including parents, older workers, and students.

Numerous employer benefits are reportedly derived from job sharing, including the broader range of skills brought to the position, valuable workers who might otherwise leave being able to stay on, a higher level of energy, and reduced absenteeism. In addition, job sharing virtually eliminates the need for employees to take care of personal business while on the job. Also, any time one partner terminates, the job is still half filled.

Naturally, there are some drawbacks: Twice as much payroll and personnel record keeping is required; an overlap in scheduling can create a logistics problem; and clients or customers may complain about not being able to deal with the same person consistently. The issue of benefits can also create some problems: Some employers offer full benefits to both partners, and others elect to divide a single package.

Organizations considering job sharing should conduct a full analysis, including consideration of the job's requirements and responsibilities; an assessment of each partner's skills, abilities, shortcomings, and interests; a clear definition of areas of accountability and lines of authority; a determination of how matters of salary and benefits are to be handled; and a schedule that is acceptable and workable for all concerned.

Flextime

The classic definition of flextime requires each worker to put in the same number of hours each day, with identical "core hours" and varying starting and quitting times. Employers may vary the amount of flexibility granted workers in establishing their schedules according to the specific needs of the organization and the employees concerned.

Flextime, the first alternative work arrangement to gain acceptance, was implemented at a Hewlett-Packard company plant beginning in 1972. Indications are that it is now gaining in popularity: As of 1985, according to a BLS survey, 12.6 percent of private-sector organizations and 11.3 percent of public-sector organizations were using flextime. Today, companies such as IBM and Pitney Bowes, Inc. use this form of scheduling with reported overall success.

Flextime allows employees to better balance work demands with those of home, school, and outside activities. It also helps relieve transit and commuting problems. In addition, given a voice in the scheduling of their workday, employees tend to feel involved in the company's decision-making process, which, in turn, may strengthen employer/employee relations. Employees are also able to schedule work more in tune with their own "biological clocks," that is, they can choose to work during those hours when their skill and response levels are most keen.

Benefits to the employer include extended hours of coverage or service, which reduces or eliminates the need for overtime; reduced tardiness, absenteeism, and turnover; an expanded and improved recruitment pool; and improved work performance that may be attributable to enhanced employee morale. As a system, it is also adaptable to many situations and can easily be implemented in most environments, although it tends to function best in work environments that promote independence and self-motivation and is least effective in assembly-line work or situations in which the work must be accomplished in a short time span.

As with any system, flextime has some drawbacks. The no. 1 problem appears to have less to do with the employees than with supervisors who are uncomfortable with having workers on the job, unsupervised, during non-core hours. A sufficient level of discomfort may compel some supervisors to put in longer hours in order to make certain work is being accomplished during non-core hours. Other concerns include difficulty in scheduling meetings, not always having key employees available when needed, and employee abuse of flextime. In addition, overhead costs are increased by keeping facilities open for longer periods of time.

Compressed Workweek

Following close on the heels of flextime in the early 1970s was the idea of the compressed workweek. This alternative arrangement allows employees to work the required forty hours in less than five days. The most popular schedule is four ten-hour days.

The compressed workweek has received a mixed reaction from both employees and management. Positive votes come from many employees who tend to react favorably to the longer periods of personal time the compressed workweek allows. They also seem to appreciate commuting during nonrush hours and saving money by not working a fifth day. In addition, many workers reportedly accomplish more in a given day during hours when phone calls from customers or clients are less likely to interrupt them. Employers have reported that the compressed workweek works well as a recruitment tool. Some improvement in rates of absenteeism, tardiness, and turnover has also been reported.

On the other hand, workers and managers alike have complained about excessive fatigue brought by the length of the workday. This is troublesome to older employees, young singles with active social lives, and employees with families. Long-term effects on health are also of concern. Both factors can adversely affect productivity.

While many long-term users of the compressed workweek have nothing but praise for the system, others have tried and abandoned it.

Companies that are considering this alternative work arrangement should make certain there are no state laws preventing a compressed workweek. Some states require the payment of overtime compensation for hours worked in excess of eight hours in any given day.

At-Home Work

While the concepts of working at home or in a satellite office have been around since the 1970s, they did not gain popularity until some ten years later with the growth of personal computers and facsimile machines. Today, the home-based work force is one of the fastest-growing components of the labor market. The U.S. Department of Labor estimates that by the mid 1990s there will be more than 15 million full-time and part-time at-home workers, as compared with approximately 5 million during the late 1980s.

This alternative work arrangement includes employees who are linked to their offices electronically—hence, the term *telecommuting*—and those who do paperwork. In January of 1989, the arrangement was extended beyond traditional office work, when the Labor Department determined that some garment industry work may now be done at home. It is projected that this will be especially welcomed by single mothers who will no longer have to contend with child care arrangements or travel costs. Unions are expected to challenge the decision, since organizing members who work at home is likely to be far more difficult.

Many companies, such as J. C. Penney and Pacific Bell, maintain that there are advantages to having some employees work at home, at least part of the time. (Pacific Bell reportedly started its program to reduce traffic congestion in Los Angeles during the 1984 Summer Olympics. By 1988 the company had between five hundred and one thousand regular at-home workers). Reduced utility and office space leasing costs as well as increased productivity were two of the most popular reasons cited for hiring at-home workers. Several employers also reported that this work option has proved to be an effective recruitment tool, not only because it attracts employees, but because it allows the employer to expand its recruiting base beyond the normal commutation area. In addition, organizations have been able to utilize the services of certain disabled and elderly individuals who are unable to travel to an office to work. Employers with at-home workers also report less absenteeism, since these employees will often work at home even if they are not feeling well.

Needless to say, many employees also appreciate the arrangement. In addition to disabled and elderly people, parents who want to work and care for their children can more readily do both. At-home workers also report being able to perform their duties without the typical office interruptions and enjoy the freedom of working during "off hours." Other benefits include not having to commute and being able to wear whatever they want while working.

But there are drawbacks, as well. For employers, there is the lack of direct control over an employee's work. In addition, when computers are involved, there is concern over unsupervised access to data and theft of equipment. And some employees complain of a sense of isolation and worry about being self-disciplined enough to meet deadlines.

Companies that are considering offering at-home work arrangements for some of their employees should consult with legal and tax experts regarding employee classifications, local zoning regulations, and insurance requirements.

Additional Alternative Work Arrangements

Part-time employment, job sharing, flextime, compressed workweek, and at-home work are the five primary alternative work arrangements available today. There are, however, some additional arrangements that may be deemed appropriate under certain circumstances:

1. *Temporaries* represent one of the largest areas of job growth in the United States today. This flexible work force, once almost exclusively clerical in composition and now consisting of a wide range of nonexempt and professional positions, is often used by small companies that cannot afford to hire regular employees and by large companies that have downsized or want to avoid overinflating their payrolls. Some organizations, such as Atlantic Richfield and Corning Glass, have established their own temporary pools staffed with former employees and retirees. The Travelers established a Job Bank, which allows company retirees to register for temporary work assignments as they become available. Temporaries

have grown so popular that some temporary agencies are beginning to offer benefits such as group health insurance to their workers.

2. *Sabbaticals* represent a less well-known but increasingly popular work arrangement, in recognition of our long-lived work force. Formal sabbatical programs offer employees periods of leisure or time to pursue other interests with a job guaranteed upon return. Actually, this is not a new idea, since academic sabbaticals are commonplace at colleges and universities. Though seldom utilized in business previously, they are now starting to catch on. Wells Fargo offers ten-year employees a fully paid, three-month personal-growth sabbatical. San Francisco newspapers that contract with the Newspaper Guild offer six-month unpaid sabbaticals to their workers. Dr. Ken Dychtwald reports in the February 1990 issue of *Training & Development Journal* that 14 percent of American companies currently offer sabbaticals and predicts that sabbaticals will soon become commonplace.

3. The *supplemental work force* is really a variation on an old theme. These are employees who are recruited and hired through conventional means and then trained in job and industry-specific matters. Now for the twist: They are then placed in a standby pool for work as needed, with the company committing to weekly or longer work assignments. This program provides a consistency and level of skill not usually available in temporary employees.

4. *Voluntary reduced work-time programs* allow full-time employees to become part-time for a certain period, usually six to twelve months. During their tenure as part-timers, salaries and benefits are adjusted accordingly. After the agreed-upon period of reduced work time is completed, the employees are able to return to their original full-time status. Full pay and benefits are also restored.

5. *Work sharing* is an alternative work arrangement generally employed by companies as a cost-reduction strategy and an attempt to avoid layoffs. It involves a reduction in the hours and salary of some or all of a company's employees until such time as regular pay and status can be restored. In some states, work sharing is combined with short-term compensation, whereby employees receive partial unemployment insurance payments to compensate for part of the decreased salary.

6. *Independent contractors* are self-employed workers in a variety of fields in exempt and nonexempt capacities. Companies may employ independent contractors for short- or long-term assignments, without any of the commitments or obligations that accompany an employer/employee relationship. Generally, there is a writ-

ten contract outlining the services to be provided, the approximate or specific period of time for said services, and the amount and schedule of payment. Conditions governing severance of the agreement may be outlined in the contract as well.

7. *Employee leasing* is a somewhat unique work arrangement used primarily by small and mid-sized companies in an effort to avoid some of the headaches of human resources administration. The system allows for an entire group of employees to be fired from a company, hired by a leasing agency, and then contracted back to the original employer. The leasing company handles all the paperwork, provides fringe benefits to the employees, and costs the employer approximately 20 to 35 percent above gross payroll.

Other Responses to Employee Needs

Besides the specific programs and techniques discussed above, what else can companies do to attract and motivate tomorrow's workers? To begin with, they can recognize that, unlike generations before, this new work force is more interested in opportunity than security. They are more willing to take risks and less concerned with financial security. Hence, employers need to provide challenging and varying work assignments. In addition, participative management, in which all employee levels are involved in at least some aspect of the decision-making process, is of greater importance to tomorrow's workers. Workers have also expressed the need to be recognized and rewarded for their specific contributions. Furthermore, they are seeking greater autonomy in a structure with fewer levels of management.

Flexibility will be a key element in the near future, with regard to both work schedules and work arrangements. Flexible benefits plans are increasingly being sought. Also growing in significance is an interest in promoting relationships among co-workers off the job. Managers will, therefore, need to plan more social activities and sponsor company outings. The continuing interest in physical fitness will also affect employment, as more and more employees seek out employers who provide workout rooms or gym memberships.

Summary

Recruitment at the turn of the next century will offer many challenges for employers. The work force is changing—young white male workers are no longer the representative population. Instead, we are seeing increasing numbers of older workers, the disabled, women, the homeless, and minorities enter the job market to compete for the available work. Competing, but not necessarily prepared. At present, 47 million adults in this nation are borderline illiterates, and $20 billion in profits are lost each year due to illiteracy. However, the fastest-growing industries require higher levels of skills and knowledge than ever before. This clearly means that greater attention must be paid to education and training.

The new work force also brings with it a new set of work attitudes, as well as on- and off-the-job requirements. Employers must become familiar with the needs of tomorrow's workers and be prepared to offer appropriate work assignments, provide suitable environments, and offer programs and benefits that are compatible with these needs in order to attract and retain qualified employees.

Finally, the traditional five-day workweek and nine-to-five work schedule must make room for alternative arrangements. Employees at all levels will require flexible scheduling to fit in with the other aspects of their lives. Hence, arrangements such as flextime, job sharing, and at-home work will become increasingly more commonplace.

For employers who accept these changes and prepare for them accordingly, the next few decades will be filled with many productive recruitment opportunities.

2

Familiarization With the Details of a Job

A commonly held but erroneous belief is that interviewing does not require any degree of preparation. The perception is that an interview consists of two people sitting down together, having a conversation. As they talk, one person—the interviewer—asks questions, while the other—the applicant—answers the questions. Whether or not a job offer is extended depends on just how well the applicant answers the questions.

Such an impression is largely based on observations of interviews being conducted by seasoned interviewers who certainly can make employment interviews seem like effortless conversation. It is, however, inaccurate because these interviewers have actually put a great deal of work behind this casual front by completing a number of preparatory steps before meeting the applicants.

The process of interview preparation begins with familiarization with the details of a job every time it becomes available. This includes reviewing the position's responsibilities, requirements, reporting relationships, environmental factors, exemption and union status, salary and benefits, growth opportunities, and special requirements. This important task provides necessary answers to four key questions:

1. Am I thoroughly familiar with the qualities being sought in an applicant?
2. Are these qualities both job-related and realistic?
3. Can I clearly communicate the duties and responsibilities of this position to the applicants?

4. Am I prepared to provide additional relevant information about the job and the company to the applicants?

Duties and Responsibilities

The first step in the job-familiarization process is a review of the specific duties and responsibilities of the position. If you are a human resources specialist, make it a point to spend time in the department where the opening exists. Observe and converse with incumbents as they perform various aspects of the job. Talk to the supervisor in charge for his or her perspective of the scope of work involved. If possible, seek out people who have previously held the position to see how the job may have evolved. Try to visit on more than one occasion so that you will be able to observe a typical day.

If a personal visit is not possible, have lengthy telephone conversations with several departmental representatives. Also request a job description and review its contents for a detailed description of the level and degree of responsibility. Job descriptions are an interviewer's most valuable tool. There are guidelines for developing maximally effective job descriptions at the end of this chapter.

It is extremely important for human resources specialists to learn as much as possible about the responsibilities of a given job. Not only will it prepare them for the face-to-face interview, but it will also help to establish a rapport between the human resources staff and a specific department. This is critical, since in many organizations there is some dispute as to who should recruit, interview, and select new employees: human resources experts, or department heads and other specialists in a given field. The argument against human resources grows stronger if the position in question is highly technical in nature, since human resources representatives are usually not technically trained. This is a difficult argument to resolve. On the one hand, it is quite true that human resources experts do not have the in-depth knowledge of a particular job that someone in the field possesses. On the other hand, they have a wide range of overall interviewing skills, which enables them to ascertain the information needed to make appropriate hiring decisions.

The ideal arrangement is a partnership between the human resources department and the department in which an opening exists. The human resources specialist should screen the résumés and applications and conduct the initial interview to determine overall job suitability. Referrals may then be made to the other department, where a more detailed, technical interview can be held.

As a final step, representatives from both departments should compare notes and reach a joint final decision.

Human resources specialists are cautioned not to consider themselves experts in a field other than their own simply because they learn certain jargon. If such expertise is assumed, one of two things is likely to occur: You will be convincing enough so that the applicant believes you know more than you really do and proceeds to ask technical questions beyond your realm of knowledge; or the applicant will see through your facade, particularly if key terms are misused. In either instance, the results are counterproductive.

Human resources experts are urged to learn as much as possible about the specific jobs they are trying to fill but should always concentrate on their human resources skills first and foremost.

Department heads and other departmental representatives should also thoroughly familiarize themselves with the degree and level of responsibility required for a given job. It is dangerous to assume that technical know-how and work experience within the department in which an opening exists automatically impart knowledge of the specific duties of that job. It is especially important that departmental representatives step back and objectively evaluate its scope. Are the required tasks realistic in relation to other factors, such as previous experience and education? Are they relevant to the overall job function? Do they overlap with the responsibilities of another job?

One final comment needs to be made about familiarization with the duties of a job. This process should take place *each time* that a position becomes available. Even if a position was filled six months ago and is now vacant again, the responsibilities of the job should be assessed to make certain that no major changes have occurred in the interim. This will ensure up-to-date job information and accuracy when discussing the position with potential employees.

Education and Prior Experience

The next step in the familiarization process concerns the role of educational credentials and prior work experience. Generally, the department head in charge of the area where a specific opening exists will describe the qualifications considered necessary to successfully perform the available job; human resources specialists will then comment on their appropriateness. Together, any educational and experience prerequisites are agreed upon and established.

This process is most effective when managers and human resources representatives ask these key questions:

1. What skills and knowledge are needed to successfully perform the primary duties and responsibilities of this job?
2. Why are these skills and knowledge necessary?
3. Why couldn't someone without these skills and knowledge perform the primary duties of this job?
4. Are the requirements consistent with the job duties and responsibilities?
5. Are we being influenced by the background of the present or last incumbent?
6. Are we subjectively considering our own personal expectations of the job?
7. Are we compromising because we are in a hurry to fill the job?
8. Are we unrealistically searching for the ideal candidate?
9. Are we succumbing to pressure from senior management as to what are appropriate job requirements?
10. Are the requirements in accordance with all applicable equal employment opportunity laws?

Arbitrarily setting high minimum standards in the hope of filling a position with the most qualified person possible can backfire. For example, suppose that you are trying to fill a first-line supervisor's slot and you decide that you want someone who not only has a great deal of hands-on experience, but is also well-rounded. To you, this translates into someone with at least five years of supervisory experience and a four-year college degree. If you asked yourself some of the questions just suggested, you would probably conclude that these requirements are too high for a first-line supervisory position. Also, for reasons of equal employment opportunity you would have to modify them. But even if there were no applicable employment laws, there is a good reason for setting more flexible standards: If you came across applicants who fell short of your experience and education profile, but who met other intangible or nonconcrete requirements and came highly recommended, you would not be able to hire them. It would be difficult to justify hiring someone who did not meet the minimum requirements of the job, especially if you also rejected candidates who exceeded them.

In addition to asking yourself these basic questions regarding experience and education, there is a way of setting requirements that does not paint you into a corner, but still allows you to be highly selective. By using carefully worded terminology in the job description, you can allow yourself room to choose the candidate who best combines concrete and intangible requirements. These phrases include the following:

- Demonstrated ability to _____ required.
- In-depth knowledge of _____ required.
- Extensive experience in _____ required.
- Knowledge of _____ would be an advantage.
- Proven ability to _____ required.
- We are looking for an effective _____ .
- Proven track record of _____ needed.
- Substantial experience in _____ essential.
- Familiarity with _____ would be ideal.
- Degree relevant to _____ preferred.
- Degree in _____ preferred.
- Advanced degree a plus.
- College degree in _____ highly desirable.
- An equivalent combination of education and experience . . .

These sample phrases all provide the latitude to select someone who, for example, may be lacking in one area, such as education, but who compensates with a great deal of experience. The use of such terms does not mean that hiring standards are compromised; rather, it means that care is being taken to avoid setting requirements that cannot be justified by the specific duties of the job, while at the same time offering the widest possible range of choice among applicants.

Intangible Requirements

In the previous section reference was made to intangible criteria and how they can help balance the lack of specific educational or experiential requirements. Intangible factors might include:

- Attitude
- Management style
- Ability to get along with co-workers, management, and subordinates
- Initiative
- Creativity and imagination

- Self-confidence
- Personality
- Temperament
- Responsiveness
- Appearance
- Maturity
- Assertiveness

These factors can be significant, but only when examined in relation to the requirements of the available job opening. That is, in addition to determining any relevant education and experience prerequisites and examining the scope and degree of responsibilities, you should explore the question of what type of individual would be most compatible with the position. This may best be determined by learning as much as possible about such factors as the amount of stress involved, the amount of independent work as opposed to closely supervised work, and the overall management style of the department. The combined information should translate into a profile of the ideal employee.

Keeping this profile in mind as candidates are considered can be helpful, particularly if two or more applicants meet the concrete requirements of the job. You can then compare intangible job-related criteria to help make the final decision. Intangibles can also be helpful in evaluating candidates for entry-level jobs for which there are few if any tangible educational and experience prerequisites.

Caution is advised when making comparisons based on intangibles, since the meaning of certain terms is highly subjective. For example, some of the more popular applicant evaluation phrases, that is, saying that an applicant has a bad attitude, a winning personality, a nice appearance, or a mature approach to work, may not always translate the same way for everyone. Furthermore, such descriptions really do not tell us anything substantive about what the person can contribute to a given job. Hence, be careful not to weigh intangible elements too heavily nor to select someone solely on the basis of any of these factors. If considered at all, such factors should be job related, not based on personal bias.

Reporting Relationships and Decision Making

Another facet of the familiarization process has to do with reporting relationships. In this regard, the following questions should be asked:

- What position will this job report to, both directly and indirectly?
- Where does this job appear on the department's organizational chart?
- What positions, if any, report directly and/or indirectly to this job?
- What is the relationship between this job and other jobs in the department, in terms of level and scope of responsibility?
- What is the relationship between this job and other jobs in the organization?

It is important to note that all these questions pertain to *positions,* as opposed to specific individuals. This eliminates the possibility of the answers being influenced by the personality or skill of a particular employee.

In addition to understanding reporting relationships, an understanding of the department's decision-making process is important to interviewers for two reasons: It gives them a more complete picture of the available position and prepares them to answer questions that applicants are likely to ask. Consider which positions in the department are responsible for decisions regarding:

- Salary increases
- Promotions
- Performance appraisals
- Transfers
- Disciplinary actions
- Vacations
- Leaves of absence

By being prepared with this information, you will be better able to describe the full scope of the decision-making responsibilities of the available position.

Work Environment

The next aspect of familiarization with a position concerns the work environment. In this regard, four different factors should be considered:

1. *Physical working conditions.* This encompasses such factors as sitting or standing for long periods of time, working in areas that

may not be well ventilated, exposure to chemicals or toxic fumes, working in cramped quarters, working in a very noisy location, and working with video display terminals for long periods of time. If the working conditions are ideal, few interviewers will hesitate to inform prospective employees of this. After all, this helps to sell the company and the job and might even make up for areas that are less ideal—perhaps the starting salary is not up to par with that of a competitor, or the benefits package is not as comprehensive. However, if the working conditions leave something to be desired, the tendency is to omit reference to them when discussing the job, in the hope that once an employee begins work and discovers the flaw in the work environment he or she will adjust rather than leave. Unfortunately, what frequently occurs is that a new employee resents the deception and either quits or develops a negative attitude.

The problems of high turnover and low morale as they relate to unsatisfactory working conditions can easily be prevented. In order to do this, you must first accurately describe existing working conditions to prospective employees. If an unpleasant condition is temporary, by all means say so, but do not make anything up. Be sure to ask candidates whether they have ever worked under similar conditions before and for how long. Also determine how they feel about being asked to work under these circumstances. When they respond to your questions, it is as important to watch as it is to listen to their answers. Often there is a contradiction between an applicant's verbal and nonverbal response. Your skill as an interviewer will in part be determined by how well you incorporate and evaluate each type of response to reach a decision. Chapter 6 deals with the issues of active listening and nonverbal communication more fully. For now, suffice it to say that if a candidate states that he does not mind standing eight hours a day, but you sense some resistance from his body language, you must pursue the subject until you are more certain of his true reaction.

Another accurate way to assess a potential employee's response to uncomfortable working conditions is to actually show the person where he or she would be working. Unless this is logistically impractical, a quick trip to the job site should be part of the interview. This way there are no surprises and a new employee knows exactly what to expect when reporting to work for the first time.

2. *Geographic location of the job.* As was already stated, if at all possible it is a good idea to show potential employees where they would be working. If recruiting from a central office for positions in satellite branches, be specific in the description of the job site. If

pamphlets or brochures are available illustrating the location where an opening exists, offer them to the applicant.

Occasionally, interviewers do not know exactly where a new employee will be assigned. For example, approval may have been obtained to hire a half-dozen security guards for different branches of a bank, but at the time of recruitment it may not be clear which branches the guards are to be assigned to. In this instance, describe all the possible locations and ask applicants for their preferences. Be certain to ask whether there are any branches where they would definitely not want to be assigned, and make a note of this. Do not make the mistake of assuming that someone will not want to work at a specific location because you deem it to be a lengthy or inconvenient commute. Likewise, it is unwise to assume that someone will find a certain site desirable just because it is close to his or her home. In other words, do not decide for yourself what the applicant wants.

Sometimes a position will call for rotation from one location to another. If this is the case, be prepared to describe the working conditions of each location and how long each assignment is likely to last. Be sure to solicit a reaction to the idea of job rotation. Many employees like to get settled into a work routine where they are familiar with the environment, the commute, and the other workers. On the other hand, some people like the variety offered by a rotational position.

3. *Travel.* Obviously, if it is known that a job requires traveling, this must be communicated to a prospective employee. Be sure to discuss the geographic span and the expected frequency of job-related travel. In the case of local travel, applicants will want to know whether they will be expected to provide their own means of transportation or whether a company car is to be provided. If the employee is to use his or her own car, how is reimbursement for mileage and any required maintenance handled? For long-distance trips, including those abroad, it is important to know how related expenses are to be reimbursed.

Often, a job does not currently require travel, but is expected to in the near future. This fact should be conveyed to applicants. Try to be as specific as possible, even though you cannot say exactly how much traveling is involved or where it will be done. Perhaps you can identify a percentage of work time that the employee can expect to spend traveling—say between 10 and 25 percent—and a general locale, such as the New England states.

4. *Specific schedule.* This is especially important for clerical and entry-level positions, where employees expect to be told when to

report to work each day and when they may leave. Although executives, managers, and supervisors generally assume that they will come in early and work late as required, they too need to know what the standard hours are. As described in Chapter 1, many companies have adopted alternative work arrangements. Hence, jobs are not necessarily on a traditional nine-to-five schedule.

Organizations also vary in the practice of how long a workweek is, generally ranging from thirty-five to forty hours. For an employee who must attend a class beginning at 6:00 P.M., leaving work at 5:15 P.M. instead of 5:00 P.M. could make a big difference.

Also be sure to know how much time is allotted for meals, as well as other scheduled breaks throughout the day. Conveying this information to applicants can prevent future disciplinary problems after they become employees.

Finally, when learning about a job schedule, do not omit the days of the week to be worked. Not all departments are on a Monday-through-Friday schedule. The job may require working alternate weekends or evenings. If this is the case, find out how days off are scheduled.

A work environment checklist appears in Appendix A.

Exemption Status

Another job facet requiring familiarity is its exemption status. As defined by the Fair Labor Standards Act (FLSA), the term *exempt* literally means exempt from overtime compensation; that is, an employer is not required to pay exempt employees for time worked beyond their regularly scheduled workweek. Although this generally pertains to executives, managers, and some supervisors, the Act does not prohibit companies from paying managerial staff for overtime. However, with the exception of strikes and other work-related emergencies, this is rarely done.

The term *nonexempt* literally means not exempt from overtime compensation. Nonexempt employees, such as clerical workers, must be paid for any time worked beyond their regularly scheduled workweek.

The actual work performed by an employee, not his or her job title, determines exemption status. With most positions there is no question as to the exemption status. However, some jobs, such as computer programming, fall into a grey area and are not as easily categorized.

To assist with exemption classification, the Department of Labor offers a series of requirements that must be met before classifying someone as exempt. These requirements appear in a short and long test that help evaluate the four employee classifications recognized by the FLSA: executive, administrative, professional, and outside salespersons. The tests include minimum salary requirements that are not frequently revised. Therefore, these should not be relied upon for determining exemption status. A more reliable gauge is the specific duties performed and level of a job's responsibility. Degree of independent judgment required and extent of managerial authority are two additional key criteria.

A copy of the Department of Labor's guidelines may be obtained by writing to the Employment Standards Administration, Wage and Hour Division, Washington, D.C. 20210.

Salary Ranges

The next aspect of familiarization with a position concerns salary ranges. Whether or not this information is disclosed to an applicant at the initial interview is a matter of company policy, but the interviewer should certainly know what a job will pay so that he or she can determine whether further consideration of a candidate is warranted. If, for example, there is an opening for an administrative assistant paying from $25,500 to $33,500 per year and an applicant is currently earning an annual salary of $27,000, there is no problem. If, on the other hand, a supervisory position becomes available offering a salary range of from $35,000 to $48,000 and an applicant is currently making $47,000, there are a number of areas to be concerned about. What is your company's policy regarding starting a new employee at the maximum of his or her salary range? If you offer the maximum, will this person want to accept an increase of just $1,000 a year? What about subsequent salary increases? Will he or she be "red circled" for being at the ceiling of the range and therefore remain frozen at $48,000 until either the salary structure is reevaluated or the position is reclassified?

Other salary-related issues may arise as well. An applicant may presently be earning considerably less than your minimum salary for what he or she maintains is comparable work. It could be that this person is underpaid by his or her present employer, or that the person is not being altogether forthright about the actual duties and responsibilities performed at his or her present job. Hence, a more thorough line of questioning regarding the level and scope of tasks presently being performed should be pursued during the interview.

Sometimes applicants indicate that they are currently earning considerably more than the maximum for an available position. Be careful not to automatically assume that this means that he or she is overqualified for the available position or will not remain long on the job. There are a number of possible explanations as to why someone would be willing to take a reduction in pay, including the opportunity to work for a specific company, the desire to learn new skills or enter a new field, or inability to find suitable work in one's own profession.

Related to the issue of salary is the "sign-on" or "hiring" bonus, a relatively new practice in businesses outside of sports or entertainment. Currently reserved for executive-level candidates and highly specialized, hard-to-fill positions, the bonus generally amounts to up to 10 percent of salaries not surpassing $100,000, and between 15 and 20 percent for salaries over $100,000. Depending on how difficult it may be to fill a given job or how desirable it is to attract a particular individual to your company, the bonus may reach as high as 25 percent.

The sign-on bonus enables employers to attract top-quality employees without disturbing the company's salary structure. Problems relating to salary increases in subsequent years may arise if the person's new salary is the same or only slightly greater than the combined starting salary and bonus.

It is projected that the sign-on bonus may become an increasingly popular means for attracting top college graduates.

Having salary information about a job opening before meeting with applicants can help the interviewer focus on the key areas during the interview. Employers should note, however, that the need for acquiring a job candidate's salary history is increasingly being challenged as concerns about pay inequities for men and women are voiced. (This is further discussed in Chapter 4.)

Benefits

An additional area of job familiarization concerns benefits. Describing your organization's benefits package can be an excellent "selling" point, especially for hard-to-fill positions. Interviewers are advised to prepare a brief presentation of approximately forty-five to sixty seconds in duration which includes a summary of company benefits, such as medical and disability insurance, dental coverage, life insurance, profit-sharing plans, stock bonus programs, vacation days, personal days, leaves of absence, holidays, and tuition reimbursement. This information may also be prepared in written form and distributed to all job applicants.

Be careful not to give the impression that describing your company's benefits means an applicant is being seriously considered for a job. Make it clear that providing this information is part of the interview process, and that whoever is selected will receive more comprehensive benefits information at the time of hiring.

Union Status

Interviewers should also be familiar with the union status of a job. Be prepared to tell applicants whether or not they will be required to join a union, which union it is, information relative to initiation fees or required dues, and essentially what being a union member entails. Exercise caution when discussing this subject: Do not express your personal opinions regarding unions; do not try to bias applicants, either for or against unions; avoid trying to find out their present views toward unions; and do not ask questions about past union involvement. Your job is to be informative and descriptive only. The National Labor Relations Act (Wagner Act) clearly states, "Employees shall have the right to self-organization, to form, join, or assist labor organizations, to bargain collectively, through representatives of their own choosing, and to engage in other concerted activities, for the purpose of collective bargaining or other mutual aid or protection."

Growth Opportunities

Another aspect of the familiarization process has to do with growth opportunities. Most people are interested in knowing whether they will be able to move up in an organization. In this regard, it is helpful for the interviewer to know about the frequency of performance appraisals, salary reviews, and increases; policies regarding promotions; relationship of a position's level and scope of responsibility to that of others within a job family (for example, the duties of a junior accountant compared with those of an accountant or senior accountant); policies governing internal job posting; likelihood of advancement; tuition reimbursement plans; and training and development.

Even if an applicant does not ask about growth opportunities, interviewers can volunteer the information as a means of making the company more attractive to prospective employees. If you, yourself, have been promoted since starting with the organization, briefly describe your experience. Likewise, recite any other known "success" stories.

It is important to provide an accurate account of growth opportunities, thereby precluding the possibility of morale problems developing later on. For example, if an applicant is applying for a position that is one step removed from the top position in a given job family and that top position has been occupied by the same individual for the past ten years, the opportunity for growth by way of promotion is unlikely. An applicant should be informed of this during the interview. There are, however, other ways to grow, such as an expansion of responsibilities that could, in turn, lead to the creation of a new job classification. In discussing such possibilities with an applicant, exercise caution: Your enthusiasm could be misconstrued as a commitment.

Special Requirements

Finally, interviewers need to consider any special requirements of the job. An example of this might be the wearing of a uniform. Applicants will want to know whether or not the company provides the uniform, who pays for the cost of cleaning and replacement, and whether lockers are provided.

Job Descriptions

At first glance, familiarization with the details of a job may seem like an overwhelming task. However, there is a single tool that can provide all the information needed. That tool is a job description— a formalized document of factual and concise information descriptive of the identity of the job, its responsibilities, and the work it entails. This multipurpose tool can be used in virtually every aspect of the employment process, including recruitment, interviewing, selection, job posting, training and development, performance appraisal, promotion, transfer, disciplinary action, demotions, grievance proceedings, employee orientation, work flow analysis, salary administration structuring, clarifying relationships between jobs and work assignments, exit interviews, and outplacement.

Since job descriptions can be used for so many different purposes, care should be taken to write them as comprehensively as possible. Initially, this will require a fair amount of time, but it will prove well worth the effort.

The task begins with a thorough job analysis. This is the process of gathering data that will later be used for preparing the actual job description. There are many ways to collect the required data. Following are some of the most successful methods:

- *Distributing questionnaires to incumbents, their managers, and anyone whose work is directly affected by the available position.* Questionnaires are considered especially helpful for identifying distinct categories of responsibilities and should be as job-specific as possible.
- *Asking incumbents and their managers to maintain logs over a period of time.* Work logs are considered effective tools for determining the frequency of time spent on different activities.
- *Directly observing incumbents as they work.* This method can be useful as long as the workers are not made to feel uncomfortable.
- *Interviewing incumbents, their managers, and others who interact with the incumbents.* Similar questions should be asked of everyone involved, focusing on what the job entails, as opposed to how they think it should be accomplished.

Ideally, a combination of methods should be employed for a maximally effective job analysis. That way, results from different methods can be compared and further data collection undertaken if discrepancies are found.

Once the job analysis stage is satisfactorily completed, it is time to prepare the written job descriptions. Job descriptions come in two different formats: *generic* and *specific.* Generic job descriptions are written in broad, general terms and may be used for several similar positions in different departments of the same organization. When preparing generic job descriptions, care must be taken to combine only those duties that all positions of the same title have in common. Specific job descriptions define the duties and tasks of one particular position. They are written when a given position requires the performance of unique or distinct responsibilities, thereby separating it from other jobs.

Here are fifteen guidelines for writing effective job descriptions:

1. *Arrange duties and responsibilities in a logical, sequential order.* Begin with the task requiring the greatest amount of time or carrying the greatest responsibility.

2. *State separate duties clearly and concisely.* This way anyone can glance at the description and easily identify each duty.

3. *Try to avoid generalizations or ambiguous words.* Use specific language and be exact in your meaning. To illustrate: "Handles mail" might be better expressed as "sorts mail" or "distributes mail."

4. *Do not try to list every task.* Use the phrase "primary duties and responsibilities include . . ." at the beginning of your job description and proceed from there. You may also choose to close with the phrase "performs other related duties and responsibilities, as required."

5. *Include specific examples of duties wherever possible.* This will enable the reader to more fully understand the scope of responsibility involved.

6. *Use nontechnical language.* A good job description explains the responsibilities of a job in terms that are understandable to everyone using it.

7. *Indicate the frequency of occurrence of each duty.* One popular way of doing this is to have a column on the left of the list of tasks with corresponding percentages that represent the estimated amount of time devoted to each primary duty.

8. *List duties individually and concisely, rather than using narrative paragraph form*; a job description is not an English composition.

9. *Do not refer to specific people.* Instead refer to titles and positions. Incumbents are likely to change positions long before the positions themselves are revamped or eliminated.

10. *Use the present tense*; it reads more smoothly.

11. *Be objective and accurate in describing the job.* Be careful not to describe the present incumbent, yourself when you held that particular job, someone who may have just been fired for poor performance, or someone who was recently promoted for outstanding job performance. Describe the job as it should be performed—not as you would like to see it performed.

12. *Stress what the incumbent does, instead of attempting to explain a procedure that must be used.* To illustrate, use *records appointments* rather than *a record of appointments must be kept.*

13. *Be certain that all requirements are job-related and are in accor-*

dance with equal employment opportunity laws and regulations. This will preclude the likelihood of legal problems developing later on.

14. *Eliminate unnecessary articles,* such as *a* and *the.* Do not make the description too wordy. Most job descriptions can be completed in one or two pages. The length of a job description does not increase the importance of the job.

15. *Use action words.* This means any word that describes a specific function, such as *organizes.* Action words do not leave room for confusion. Within a sentence one word should stand out as most descriptive, a word that could really stand alone. This action word will also convey to the reader a degree of responsibility. For example, compare *directs* to *under the direction of. . . .* Try to begin each sentence with an action word; the first word used should introduce the function being described.

Here is a list of action words that may be referred to for writing job descriptions:

accepts	constructs	files
acts	consults	fills in
administers	coordinates	fines
advises	corrects	follows up
allocates	correlates	formulates
analyzes	counsels	furnishes
anticipates	creates	generates
approves	decides	guides
arranges	delegates	identifies
ascertains	deletes	implements
assigns	designs	informs
assists	determines	initiates
audits	develops	inspects
authorizes	devises	instructs
balances	directs	interprets
batches	disseminates	interviews
calculates	documents	investigates
circulates	drafts	issues
classifies	edits	itemizes
codes	ensures	lists
collates	establishes	locates
collects	evaluates	maintains
compiles	examines	manages
conducts	facilitates	measures
consolidates	figures	modifies

monitors	provides	selects
negotiates	pursues	signs
notifies	rates	specifies
observes	receives	studies
obtains	recommends	submits
operates	records	summarizes
organizes	refers	supervises
originates	renders	tabulates
outlines	reports	trains
oversees	represents	transcribes
participates	requests	transposes
performs	researches	troubleshoots
places	reviews	types
plans	revises	utilizes
prepares	routes	verifies
processes	schedules	writes
proposes	screens	

Considering certain questions before actually writing the job description can be helpful:

- Does the job holder supervise the work of others? If so, give job titles and a brief description of the responsibilities of those supervised.
- What duties does the job holder perform regularly, periodically, and infrequently? List these in order of importance.
- What degree of supervision is exercised over the job holder?
- To what extent are instructions necessary in assigning work to the job holder?
- How much decision-making authority or judgment is allowed to the job holder in the performance of the required duties?
- What are the working conditions?
- What skills are required for the successful performance of the job?
- What authority does the job holder have in such matters as training other people or directing the work force?
- At what stage of its completion is the work of the job holder reviewed by the supervisor?
- What machines or equipment is the job holder responsible for operating? Describe the equipment's complexity.
- What would be the cost to management of serious mistakes or errors that the job holder might make in the regular performance of the required duties?

• What employees within the organization and customers or clients outside the organization will the job holder interact with on a regular basis?

The exact contents of a job description will be dictated by the specific environment and needs of an organization. What follows provides the fifteen basic categories of job information required for most positions:

1. Date
2. Job analyst (person who wrote the job description)
3. Job title
4. Division and department
5. Reporting relationship
6. Location of the job
7. Exemption status
8. Salary grade and range
9. Work schedule
10. Job summary
11. Duties and responsibilities, including extent of authority and degree of independent judgment required
12. Job requirements, including education, prior work experience, and specialized skill and knowledge
13. Physical environment and working conditions
14. Equipment and machinery to be used
15. Other relevant factors, such as degree of contact with the public or customers and access to confidential information

A job description form containing these categories appears in Appendix B.

Once a job description is written, review it on a semiannual or annual basis to make certain the nature of the job has not changed substantially.

Summary

In this chapter the steps that should be taken before recruiting job applicants have been examined. These steps are:

1. Reviewing the specific job duties and responsibilities
2. Assessing the role of prior work experience and relevant educational credentials

3. Considering intangible requirements
4. Understanding reporting relationships and decision-making roles
5. Becoming familiar with various facets of the work environment, including working conditions, location of the job, travel, and schedule
6. Knowing the exemption status
7. Assessing the salary range
8. Reviewing the benefits
9. Knowing the union status
10. Being aware of growth opportunities
11. Considering any other special requirements

These steps are generally best accomplished, and the information best imparted to applicants, by human resources specialists who may then share the information with those managers involved with the interviewing process.

It was further explained that the most comprehensive and expeditious way of accomplishing these steps is via a job description. Having completed the job-familiarization stage, the interviewer is now ready to explore and compare various recruitment sources.

3

Recruitment Sources

Once you have become thoroughly familiar with the details of an available job, it is time to begin screening qualified applicants. Numerous sources may be utilized, and care must be taken to select the ones that are most appropriate for a given opening.

Several factors should be taken into account before embarking on a recruitment campaign:

1. *Your budget.* The amount of money you have allocated for recruitment can reduce your options considerably. However, spending a great deal of money does not always ensure a substantial number of qualified candidates. In fact, some of the most effective recruitment sources, such as job posting and employee referrals, cost very little or nothing at all.

2. *The likelihood that a source will yield immediate results.* If you are anxious to fill the position as soon as possible, recruitment sources more likely to yield immediate results should be explored. In this regard, newspaper ads and your own personnel files are among the most effective recruitment sources.

3. *The need to reach a wide audience.* Some positions are highly specialized and more difficult to fill. Consequently, you will need to reach as many people as possible. Also, you may not be certain as to the type of individual you are seeking and will, therefore, want to interview many applicants. Employment agencies and search firms may be helpful in these instances.

4. *The exemption level of the job opening.* Recruitment sources that produce qualified exempt candidates do not always work as well for nonexempt applicants. For example, most walk-in and call-in candidates are interested in nonexempt employment. Direct mail recruitment, on the other hand, is targeted more for professionals.

5. *Your company's affirmative action goals.* Certain sources, such as job fairs and government agencies, can help you as you strive to attain your objectives in this area.

Each time a position becomes available, all possible recruitment sources should be reviewed with consideration of these five factors. After becoming familiar with the details of the job, you should be able to quickly identify the source most likely to produce qualified applicants. A word of caution: Avoid using the same recruitment source every time an opening is available for a similar position. Aside from the possibility that market conditions and certain internal factors may have changed, thereby rendering that source less effective, there is also the possibility that this practice could lead to charges of systemic discrimination. This term refers to the denial of equal employment opportunity through an established business practice, such as recruitment, as opposed to a specific action against an individual. Even though inadvertent, the disparate effect produced by systemic discrimination may develop into a prime area of vulnerability for employers. Relying on the same recruitment source each time a particular position becomes available could have an adverse impact on members of certain protected groups not having the same access as others to that source. This, in turn, could translate into the denial of equal employment opportunity.

The following discussion includes some commonly used recruitment sources, as well as some relatively new methods for filling positions. Each of them has advantages and disadvantages (summarized in Table 3-1 at the end of this chapter) that should be weighed each time there is a job opening.

Job Posting

Almost without exception, the first recruitment source that should be explored is your own organization. Promoting or transferring employees from within offers several advantages:

1. It usually creates an opening at a lower, easier-to-fill level.
2. The company saves considerable time and money by transferring someone who is already familiar with the organizational structure and methodology.
3. Employee morale is boosted.
4. Hidden talent may be uncovered.

The process by which internal recruitment is accomplished is called *job posting*. With this system, every time a position becomes available it is offered to present employees before recruitment via outside sources. A simplified job description citing the department, location, exemption status, salary grade and range, work schedule, requirements, primary duties and responsibilities, and working conditions is literally posted in one or more centrally located places. Also included is a closing date by which time all applications must be submitted. The standard period of time for this is generally from one to two weeks. Some organizations require that interested employees receive permission from their existing supervisors before applying, others require notification, and still others respect the confidentiality of the process until a decision has been reached. A sample job posting notice form appears in Appendix C, and a sample job posting application form is shown in Appendix D.

All applicants are considered in the same manner as any outside candidate would be. If an appropriate person is found, arrangements for a starting date in the new position are made between the existing department head, human resources, and the new department head. Anywhere from two to four weeks is generally allowed for finding a replacement to fill the position being vacated.

Some organizations have a policy of posting all openings; others post only nonexempt positions. Some steer clear of job posting altogether. Reasons for this include the following:

1. Supervisors and managers sometimes want to promote someone they have groomed for a position. Therefore, they do not want to even consider other candidates.
2. Some members of management get upset with employees who apply for jobs outside of their department and tend to take any such move personally.
3. Losing an employee to job posting may mean having to wait for a replacement who may not be as good.
4. Some companies believe that it is better to bring in "new blood" rather than to recycle existing employees.

The success of a job posting system depends largely on how well it is designed and monitored. For example, an organization may choose to stipulate that employees must be with a company for at least one year and in their current position for at least six months before they may utilize the job posting system. The number of jobs that an individual may apply for within one year is also limited, generally to three. In addition, employees must have received a rating of satisfactory or better on their most recent performance appraisal in order to use the job posting system. These guidelines help prevent the problem of the "revolving door" employee who may opt to apply for virtually every job posted. It also treats the process in a serious manner and lends it credibility, thus increasing its effectiveness.

Employee Referral Programs

One of the most expeditious recruitment sources is a company's own employee referral program, also known as word of mouth. In basic terms, this method entails "spreading the word" as soon as a position becomes available. The department head in charge of the area with the opening tells other department heads; employees talk to one another; word may be carried outside the organization to family, friends, and acquaintances. To make this method more effective, incentives of varying worth are offered to encourage employees to refer qualified candidates.

Employee referral programs work most effectively when everyone understands the prevailing ground rules. Certain restrictions generally apply, such as not referring either individuals already working for the company in another capacity or relatives to work in one's own department. Also, human resources employees and company officers are usually precluded from participating. The granting of awards is customarily conditioned upon the new hire satisfactorily completing a predetermined period of employment.

These awards or bonuses are often in the form of cash, generally ranging from twenty-five dollars for a nonexempt hire to several thousand dollars for a top-level executive. They may, however, take other forms. Growing in popularity is the concept of a drawing. In addition to cash bonuses, employees who successfully refer a new hire may enter for the chance to win even bigger prizes. A drawing is held after a certain number of referral-based hires. The greater the number of referrals, the grander the prizes, which may include vacations or trips, over and above accrued vacation time, and cars, including taxes and the first year's insurance.

Most employers agree that employee referral programs work well. Employees respond favorably to the incentives offered, usually costing the company considerably less than expenditures for other recruitment sources, such as advertising or search firms and employment agencies. Caution must be exercised in their use, however. Because it has been shown that "like tends to refer like" (for example, white males tend to refer other white males), women and minorities may not receive equal employment opportunities if they are not proportionately represented in your organization. Indeed, employee referral programs are one of the primary sources of systemic discrimination. Hence, they should be used only in conjunction with other recruitment sources.

Newspaper and Magazine Advertising

One popular and often effective means for soliciting applications is advertising in both newspapers and professional publications. Careful planning in terms of content, timing, and location can generate a large response, usually resulting in a hiring.

Consider those you want to reach when designing the contents of an ad. If you are looking for individuals with very specialized skills, the ad should clearly stipulate those skills. If on the other hand you are scouting for talent, the wording of your ad should be less specific. The same holds true for the extent to which you spell out the job's duties and responsibilities. Some employers want applicants to know virtually everything about a job before they apply for it. Others prefer to learn about the candidates and establish interest before describing the details of the job. When advertising, make certain that enough information is provided for applicants to determine whether or not it is worth their while to apply. Also be sure to include how you want to be contacted: résumé, telephone call, or walk-in. A sampling of ads illustrating the range of information offered appears in Appendix E.

Regardless of how explicit you plan to be, it is generally best to be direct and straightforward in your wording. Job hunters should not be expected to wade through cute, nondescriptive, or unprofessional jargon to determine what positions are available or the employee qualities being sought. While this kind of language may succeed in catching the reader's eye, it is not likely to generate the kind of response you are seeking.

This is not to say that you should avoid designing an ad that will stand out. Using creative graphics, color, clever job-related language, and tasteful humor can accomplish this objective and still project an appropriate image. Keep in mind that the way your ad looks and reads is a reflection of your organization. Consider the image you wish to project, and proceed accordingly.

If you have not developed ads before, consider enlisting the services of an agency to help write the copy, select the categories under which an ad should appear, and determine the most effective combination of spacing, boldness and size of letters, layout, and other graphic elements. Agencies may also be able to provide advice as to the best day of the week to run an ad for a specific job category. The issue of timing can make a substantial difference in the number of responses received. Not only can specific days of the week be significant, but the time of year can also influence responsiveness. Ads running just before Christmas, for instance, generally do not do well, except, perhaps, during times of high unemployment. February, on the other hand, is traditionally the time when soon-to-be college graduates begin thinking about employment opportunities.

Where you choose to advertise will also have an effect on responsiveness. It is a good idea to begin by scouting a variety of newspapers both in and outside your area. Note the frequency with which certain jobs appear in specific publications. Consider papers that have broad appeal, as well. This becomes especially important if you are seeking to attract candidates for a hard-to-fill position. In addition, consider publications that are read mainly by women or minorities. Ads placed in these publications can reach highly qualified applicants and, at the same time, help your company meet its affirmative action goals.

If you are not in a hurry to fill a position and can wait for the issue carrying your ad to be published, you may choose to advertise in a bimonthly or monthly business magazine. Most professional journals have a classified section that reaches a wide audience of specialists in a given field and is generally not costly.

Researching the circulation and readership of publications that may carry your ads also makes sense. In addition to contacting the publication directly, review standard media guides, which are available in most public libraries. These list national and regional newspapers and various professional magazines, along with information relating to their audience profile and circulation.

Advertising can be a costly means of recruitment. Generally, if you are seeking candidates for a highly competitive field, you may need to compete visually with other ads. This often means eye-catching display ads with large type, logos, and borders. If you are going to spend a great deal of money, make certain that the ad says exactly what you want it to say. In order to outshine competitors, brag about your company's standing in the industry, outstanding benefits package, and any other perks offered. Commenting on some key attractions within striking distance of your company can also draw applicants.

Some organizations like to run blind ads. These are ads that do not reveal the company's identity, instead giving a box number to which a résumé may be forwarded. This is usually done to avoid having to respond to a flood of phone calls. On the other hand, with hard-to-fill positions where the number of responses will probably be limited, you will want interested individuals to get in touch with you as soon as possible. Blind ads sometimes discourage people from applying altogether. Without knowing who is running an ad, there is always the danger of someone applying to his or her own company for a new job.

As a final comment with regard to advertising, make certain that the language used does not violate equal employment opportunity laws and regulations, specifically Title VII of the Civil Rights Act of 1964. Such language would include indicating an age preference via terminology such as *young man* or *mature woman;* using certain other subjective terms, such as *attractive, pretty,* or *handsome;* or stating a preference for either sex. With regard to the latter, it is significant to note that masculine or feminine terms do not automatically constitute a violation of Title VII. In April 1990, the Equal Employment Opportunity Commission (EEOC) issued a policy statement regarding sex-referent language in employment advertising, noting that terms such as *patrolman* or *meter maid* have become "colloquial ways of denoting particular jobs rather than the sex of the individuals who perform those jobs." The statement continues that therefore ". . . the use of sex-referent language in employment opportunity advertisements and other recruitment practices is suspect but is not a per se violation of Title VII." The EEOC goes on to urge employers to clearly indicate their intent to consider applicants of both sexes whenever sex-referent language is used. A statement in a recruitment ad confirming nondiscriminatory intent such as "equal employment opportunity employer, male/female" should, therefore, be included.

Employment Agencies and Search Firms

Two popular recruitment sources are employment agencies and search firms. Generally speaking, search firms handle only professional openings, while employment agencies recruit for all other types of jobs. Sometimes a minimum dollar figure is used to determine the level of job a search firm will recruit.

There are two primary reasons why agencies and search firms are frequently used. First, they have access to a large labor pool and can readily scout the market for qualified candidates. This includes seeking out applicants who may seemingly be content with their present jobs. Second, they can often help fill a position more quickly than a company could on its own.

The most significant reason for not retaining the services of an agency or search firm is the cost. While the fee structure of each employment service varies somewhat, most work on a contingency basis; that is, they do not collect the fee until a referred applicant is hired. The cost then ranges from one percent per $1,000 of salary, all the way up to a straight 25 percent of the annual salary. Executive search firms may charge more, ranging from 25 to 30 percent of the new employee's salary for the first year. For example, at 30 percent, an employee earning $50,000 would cost a company $15,000 in fees. There may be additional charges for related out-of-pocket expenses. It should be noted that fees charged for sales positions may or may not take into account incentive or bonus compensation.

Before agreeing to register an opening with either an employment agency or a search firm, consider these five guidelines:

1. *Be certain that the agency will evaluate applicants and refer only those who meet the standards stipulated.* Too often agencies merely forward résumés to a client, expecting the company's interviewer to do the screening.

2. *Be firm about the job's requirements and refuse to consider anyone who does not meet them.* In this regard it is a good idea to forward a copy of the job description for the available position.

3. *Ask for a written agreement regarding the fee arrangement, including how much, when it is to be paid, and any other conditions.* For instance, some search firms will refund a percentage of the fee paid if employees placed as a result of their efforts are terminated within the first three to six months of work.

4. *Be selective in determining which agencies and search firms will receive your business.* Meet with and interview representatives in advance to make certain that they clearly understand your objectives. Establish their degree of knowledge in the area for which they will be recruiting, and make certain that you feel comfortable working with them. Ask for information regarding their methodology, experience, and track record. Do not hesitate to ask for references and consider their reputation in the field. Also be sure that the person with whom you meet is the person who will actually be handling your company's account.

5. *Formally notify all agencies and search firms with whom you will be working that you are an equal opportunity employer.* Also, share information regarding your organization's affirmative action plan. Make it very clear that you expect them to comply fully with all equal employment opportunity and affirmative action laws and regulations and that you will terminate your relationship if they should violate these laws at any time.

Once you have decided to work with a particular employment agency or search firm, allow agency representatives to learn as much as possible about both your organization and the specific job opening. The more information the agency has, the better able it will be to meet your needs effectively and expeditiously.

Employers should note that private employment services may be regulated by state and federal laws. Federal coverage is by Executive Order 11246; Title VII of the Civil Rights Act of 1964; the Fair Labor Standards Act of 1938, as amended; the Fair Credit Reporting Act of 1971; and the Truth-in-Lending Act. Coverage varies among the states and may regulate such facets as annual licensing, fees, and certain practices, such as misrepresenting a job or advertising without identifying the source as an employment service.

With an estimated seventeen to twenty thousand placement agencies in the United States, employers can afford to be selective when choosing an employment service. Recommendations from satisfied clients can assist in the process, as can publications such as *The Directory of Executive Recruiters,* published by *Consultants News.* It lists over sixteen hundred firms, providing a brief description of each one's services and location.

Personnel Files

Sometimes the expense of an agency or ad can be avoided simply by referring to the company's personnel files. It is quite possible that someone applied for a similar position not too long ago. If the person was not hired, this does not mean that he or she was a poor candidate. It may have been that there were several qualified applicants at the time among whom only one could be chosen. Or perhaps there were no suitable openings when this individual filed his or her application. It is also possible that the applicant's salary requirements exceeded the amount then being offered.

When scanning personnel files for existing applications, carefully compare background and skills with the requirements of the available position. Also, review the notes of the previous interviewer and, if possible, talk to him or her in person. The previous interviewer may recall the individual well enough to provide you with additional information.

Walk-Ins, Call-Ins, and Write-Ins

Three other closely related, valuable recruitment sources that do not cost anything are walk-ins, call-ins, and write-ins. Walk-ins and call-ins usually consist of nonexempt applications; write-ins are usually professionals. These unsolicited applications can often result in the hiring of outstanding employees. Too often, however, walk-ins, call-ins, and write-ins are not treated seriously. Walk-ins are automatically told by the receptionist that there are no openings at the present time. If they are permitted to complete an application, these forms are quickly filed away without an interviewer ever seeing them. Call-ins are generally told to apply in person. When they do, they are told that there are no openings. Likewise, unsolicited résumés are given a cursory glance at best and then filed. Sometimes letters of acknowledgment are sent, but more often than not there is no communication whatsoever.

A simply monitored system for handling these types of applicants can yield excellent results. Make certain that the receptionist in the human resources department has an up-to-date list of job openings, accompanied by a simplified job description for each one. Every time a walk-in applies for a job, this list should be referred to. If the individual has expressed an interest in a position that appears on that list, an interviewer should be informed of this. If possible, an interview should be conducted at this time. If time does not permit for an immediate meeting, arrangements should be made for the applicant to return at a specified time.

Call-ins can be treated in a similar fashion. The receptionist can check the list of openings and refer callers to the interviewer in charge of a particular job. A brief telephone interview can usually be conducted on the spot to establish further interest. An appointment can then be scheduled.

Unsolicited résumés can also be reviewed with the list of openings in mind. Possible job matches can then be pursued, either by telephone or by mail.

These three recruitment sources can be especially valuable when you are trying to meet the requirements of certain hard-to-fill positions.

School Recruiting

School recruiting is not what it used to be. Not so long ago, many companies would visit selected campuses, or high schools and trade schools, for certain positions and select the names of candidates to interview from the placement office's résumé book. If mutual interest was established, follow-up interviews at the company would be arranged. Other companies would conduct an open house on campus to promote the benefits and advantages being offered. Letters would then be sent to promising graduates, inviting them to apply for jobs. On-campus recruiting has always required careful planning and preparation, because of the high degree of competition for those graduating from the nation's top schools. But now a subtle shift has developed in bargaining position: Today's graduates, knowing that they are in greater demand, expect to be courted and can be even more selective.

This change in attitude is attributable, for the most part, to those changes in the work force described in Chapter 1. Specifically, it is due to an increased number of positions requiring higher levels of education, a decline in the number of potential new hires from known populations, and a general national shift to a service economy prompting companies to rely more on the quality of management than on the quality of manufactured goods.

These factors have resulted in new forms of school recruitment. For example, an increased number of organizations are now promoting educational assistance programs. By offering scholarships, low-interest loans, internships, and work-study programs, these companies hope to nurture the educational and professional development of students as early on as the beginning of high school.

"Professor programs" are another relatively new method of school recruitment. Professors not only identify students who are high-potential candidates, but also take information about a company back to their students after having spent time meeting with management and observing company employees at work. A variation of the professor program occurs when company executives teach courses at selected schools. This gives them direct access to students with demonstrated potential.

Moreover, the traditional company recruiting brochure, used to describe the organization in terms of its origins, product, and objectives, is being updated. Today's students want to know more about career paths, training programs, and specific benefits. They also want details about the city in which they would be living and working.

While printed brochures identifying these and other aspects of employment are still the norm, there are other means of communicating this information. Some companies have developed intriguing videotapes, emphasizing the positive aspects of employment with them, in order to attract students. Also, while the recruitment method of distributing computer diskettes to selected students is still in the experimental stages, it is starting to catch on. As an example, Bristol-Myers Squibb Co. prepared "The MBA and Squibb" diskette in 1989 and mailed it to approximately one-thousand students attending some of the nation's top schools. Production of the master diskette cost about $35,000 with an additional cost of seventy-five cents to two dollars for each copy.

None of these techniques, however, should be considered a substitute for effective interviewing skills. Managers and human resources representatives involved in school recruiting should have the ability not only to ask questions and evaluate answers, but also to disseminate appropriate information.

School recruitment, it should be noted, can prove to be costly, and if the end result is the hiring of only a few students, the cost per hire may not be economical. While there are no standard cost-per-hire figures within which companies should try to stay, the following rule of thumb may be helpful: If an organization is spending up to two-thirds of its recruitment budget on students who never become employees, then the recruiting program should be revamped.

Not all employers have abandoned traditional school recruitment methods. Because of their excellent reputations, many companies are able to rely on the submission of unsolicited résumés from students. Other companies continue to conduct back-to-back on-campus interviews of approximately fifteen to thirty minutes in duration. These interviews, however, often fail to attract the top students, who have already been targeted by organizations using some of the newer recruitment methods described above.

Employers unable to compete for the top students from prestigious schools are urged to recruit from less well-known schools. For many jobs, even at a management level, a person's educational credentials may take a back seat to those other skills and job-related knowledge not necessarily acquired through formal education.

Aside from cost, there is another major disadvantage of school recruiting: Because most students have had limited work experience, interviewers are faced with the difficult task of making decisions based almost exclusively on intangible factors. Although examining a student's chosen field of study is helpful, recruiters must still concentrate on evaluating potential. They must judge the likelihood of a particular student becoming an asset to their organization. If effective recruiting and interviewing skills are applied, however, many candidates selected through school recruiting efforts will develop a keen sense of company loyalty and go on to become valued, long-term employees.

Job Fairs

An increasingly popular recruitment source is the job fair. This is where organizational representatives gather to interview several applicants over a period of one or two days, often in a specialized field such as engineering. These job fairs may also specialize in placing women, minorities, or disabled people. Companies conducting these fairs vary somewhat in their approach, but essentially operate in a similar fashion. Advertisements announcing the location and date of a job fair appear in newspapers. Organizations are invited to call for additional details. Upon doing so, company recruiters are informed that they will receive a notebook filled with résumés of prescreened, qualified candidates for specifically designated positions. Candidates' names are omitted, but all other pertinent information, including salary history and requirements, is included. After reviewing the résumés, recruiters contact the hosting company, identifying the candidates they wish to interview by number, and set up appointments to be held during the job fair. The fairs are usually held over a weekend in a hotel or conference center. For a flat fee, recruiters can interview and hire as many people as they choose.

To get the most for your money, you should conduct brief interviews during the fair. Make them in-depth enough to establish further interest, but not so detailed as to make a hiring decision. In this way, a maximum number of candidates can be seen and potential employees may be called to the company for a full interview at a later date.

If all goes well, you may be able to hire several people for what it would cost to hire one employee if you used a search firm. It is also possible that you may not find anyone suitable. Even if this should occur, however, your efforts should not be considered wasted. Job fairs usually have social functions in the evenings; this is a wonderful opportunity to meet and exchange information with recruiters from other organizations. This type of networking among recruiters often leads to a sharing of résumés and information for hard-to-fill positions later on.

Open House

Another type of recruitment effort occurring outside of the company is the open house. Organizations generally place ads in newspapers throughout various geographic locations. The ads announce a recruitment drive in these areas on specific dates. Unless the companies are very well-known, a somewhat lengthy description appears of the company's product and its reputation in its field. Statements regarding the excellent starting salaries and benefit packages are also included. All available jobs are listed as well.

A more expensive, but very effective, medium for advertising a company's open house is television. Organizations such as Los Angeles County/U.S.C. Medical Center and Walt Disney World ran successful thirty-second TV commercials in 1988, announcing their recruitment drives.

On the advertised date of the open house, company recruiters gather to greet and interview anyone expressing an interest in working for them. Either decisions are made during this recruitment drive or arrangements are made to have the applicants return to the company at a later date for additional interviews.

An open house is usually a risky proposition in terms of cost and time. It is difficult to predict with any certainty whether there will be a large turnout, resulting in the filling of several openings, or whether very few qualified people will show up. Prescreening applicants by telephone or asking them to submit résumés in advance are two ways to safeguard against this occurrence.

Government Agencies

Another recruitment source is the state or federal employment agency. These agencies are cost-free; they screen and refer many applicants, usually for entry-level or nonspecialized positions. Because they keep such careful equal employment opportunity records, government agencies can be counted on to help your organization meet its affirmative action goals.

An additional advantage is that candidates referred by government agencies are all currently unemployed, which means that anyone you select can usually begin work right away. If the person were currently working, anywhere from one to four weeks' notice to his or her current employer would be in order. When you have deadlines to meet and work to get out, those four weeks can seem like an eternity.

While government agencies can be very helpful, they are frequently known to refer unqualified job applicants in spite of the requirements stipulated. In addition, they often challenge the reasons given for rejecting a candidate. Therefore, it is important that recruiters learn appropriate rejection language. This is covered in Chapter 9.

Direct Mail Recruitment

A recruitment source that is less frequently used but that can be effective is the direct mail campaign, whereby specific individuals are contacted by a company with an opening, hoping for a job match.

The first step in this type of recruitment is determining whom to contact. Since the expected response rate is between 0.5 and 2 percent, you will need several different mailing lists to begin with. These lists and list information may be obtained through professional associations, business directories, trade groups, and magazine subscription lists. *Direct Mail List Rates and Data,* published by Standard Rate and Data Service, Inc., 5201 Old Orchard Road, Skokie, Illinois 60077, can offer additional assistance. You may also opt to hire the services of direct mail specialists or consultants to help you plan and implement your mail campaign.

If you are embarking on an extensive mailing effort, it is advisable to have a mailing house help you fold, stuff, seal, and mail everything. If, however, your mailing list is rather small, you can do everything yourself. Obtain a copy of the *Mailer's Guide* from your local post office for guidance.

Direct mail campaigns often fail because recipients do not even open the envelope. Sometimes this problem can be circumvented by putting some sort of attention getter on the envelope. Teasers, such as "we want to give you $50,000!" are not advisable because they are unprofessional. Instead, you may print "personal" or "confidential" on the outside. Not only is it more likely that the addressee will open the envelope, but others, such as clerks or secretaries, are less likely to do so. The letter should contain a clear, brief, easy-to-read message. The first sentence should inform the reader of your purpose and interest. Include information about the requirements of the job, its duties and responsibilities, and its benefits. Try to anticipate any basic questions an applicant might ask and provide answers for these. Enclose a response card (see section on "Response Cards" later in this chapter) or ask to be contacted by telephone. If possible, also provide a flier or brochure about your company.

One final suggestion is to ask for a referral; in the event that your initial prospect is not interested in the position, he or she may know of someone who is.

Radio and Television

There are two main advantages to using radio or television advertising to fill an opening. First, you will appeal to a large audience in a short period of time. Second, you can reach and tempt prospects who are not actually looking for a job. This can be a real plus when you have a hard-to-fill position.

In the past, employers have had a tendency to shy away from radio and television advertising as a recruitment source primarily because of the cost. While there is no doubt that these are still among the most costly recruitment sources, radio and television have become more accessible media. For example, radio spots in communities outside of major metropolitan areas are far more affordable by comparison and still reach a good-sized audience. This is illustrated by Rockwell International's radio advertising campaign in Huntsville, Alabama. Between September 19 and October 19, 1988, Rockwell ran a series of three one-minute ads on four of the area's top radio stations for a total cost of less than $5,000. This included hiring professional actors to read the ads. The radio campaign resulted in approximately three thousand applications.

Since advertising on television no longer necessitates dealing with the major networks, it has become more affordable. The growth of independent stations and cable television has created more opportunities for employers with limited budgets. For example, "CareerLine," a half-hour program describing job opportunities at various companies, appeared until recently on cable TV's Financial News Network. Companies could choose among different "packages," ranging in cost from $3,500 to $14,000, for the opportunity to reach a national audience of potentially one-half million viewers. Other television stations, such as WFBO-TV, Channel 66 in Chicago, offer a series of thirty-second want ads and job-search suggestions on Television Employment Network, making television a viable recruitment option.

Proponents of radio advertising emphasize that radio often reaches people when "their guard is down," that is, when they're not necessarily thinking about job hunting. For example, they may have the radio on while getting ready for work in the morning or sitting in traffic, commuting to and from work. Television advertising receives high marks from supporters because aspects of the job can be demonstrated as well as described. Done well, this can compel job seekers to respond.

To get your money's worth, make certain that your radio or television message is believable. The speaker's voice should be sincere and pleasing to the ear. The appearance and attire of your television spokesperson should set an appropriate tone and reflect the image your company wants to project. No matter how short your ad may be, make it a point to repeat the name of your company and how you may be reached. If possible, your phone number should be particularly easy to remember in the event that the viewer or listener does not have a pad and pen handy. As with newspaper or magazine advertising, consider those you want to reach and prepare the contents of your ad accordingly. Your objective is to capture their attention within the first few seconds, keep them listening and/or watching, and then get them to call or write in. Be careful, however, not to throw too much at your audience—you want them to be able to retain what you have said. This usually means limiting the contents of the ad to no more than three key statements or ideas.

Computerized Systems

Another source of potential employees is computer-based recruitment. This type of system matches jobs with viable candidates. Computers can be very helpful in finding qualified applicants, often in much less time than any of the other means described. Some of these systems put candidates directly in contact with prospective employers; others act as a liaison, contacting companies as applicant representatives. To utilize this method of recruitment, employers will need both hardware and appropriate software.

In considering a computerized recruitment system, you should review certain factors:

- How up-to-date the information on candidates is.
- How many candidates are generally available for each job field (databases of about five hundred applicants per job field are considered to be good).
- How efficient the system is in terms of distinguishing the most qualified candidates.
- How cost-effective the system is in relation to other recruitment sources.
- How much time will be saved by using a computerized system.

In this regard, look for services that offer on-line access twenty-four hours a day.

- How difficult the system is to operate.
- Confidentiality of information for both the employer and the applicant.
- How adaptable the system is to existing equipment.

Some organizations choose to develop a computerized recruitment system in-house. They usually purchase a predeveloped package from an outside vendor and then proceed to implement and monitor it internally. However, most companies utilize the services of an outside organization. Payment for services is on either a monthly or an annual basis for limited or unlimited use of the system. The actual cost varies greatly. If you believe that your company might benefit from this service, take time to examine exactly what you will be getting for your money.

Some computerized systems offer specialized services. For example, Career Counselling Network uses a computer to help companies link thousands of students to information about job openings within the students' scope of preference and interest. By viewing job listings at computer workstations located at career placement centers on campus, students may effortlessly review job opportunities and then pursue those of interest. While there is no fee for students, as of fall 1989 companies were reportedly paying a base fee of $500, entitling them to maintain a company profile on the system for one year, in addition to two job listings appearing for thirteen weeks each.

Research Firms

Research firms may be described as abbreviated versions of full-service executive search firms, providing essentially one-half the services. Their primary function is to provide organizations with information about potential high-level professional employees; the interview and evaluation is then up to the employer. Research firms generally charge by the hour, as opposed to a percentage basis, although some offer flat-rate fees.

Most research firms begin by ascertaining the specifications of available positions within the company. Then, "target companies" are identified, that is, companies likely to have employees who might meet the job's specifications. Following this, specific employees within the target companies are researched, with any relevant information being turned over to the client company in written form. Contacting well-established persons within a given industry to request personal recommendations of potential employees is a variation on this procedure.

At this point, most research firms terminate their services, although, on occasion, the client company may ask the research firm to make the initial contact with the targeted candidates. This phase is intended to clarify qualifications and to determine mutual interest.

Research firms are considered most useful when a company is looking for a cost-effective way to recruit top-level professionals or when more hands-on involvement in the interviewing process is desired.

When evaluating the services of a research firm, consider whether or not the company serves a wide range of industries or specializes in one particular field. Also, determine its "success rate" and reputation. Ask for references from satisfied clients to determine the extent to which the research firm provided client companies with candidates whose qualifications reflected the job's specifications. In addition, find out how long it took for a firm to produce the candidates. Finally, ask how many job offers were extended to applicants as a result of the research firm's efforts.

Preemployment Training

Preemployment training is a means for employers to ensure the hiring of those candidates who are "guaranteed" to possess the basic knowledge and skills needed to perform a given job. This may be accomplished through advertising a program that offers, free of cost to participants, various skills training. Such prospects are not necessarily being trained for specific jobs; nor are they being offered employment. The emphasis is on preparation, so that when jobs do become available, the individuals who have been trained will be considered first.

Pretraining programs usually include a companywide orientation. A tour of the premises is conducted; the history, products, and goals of the company are described; and salary/benefits information is provided. Interviews are scheduled for those who are still interested.

Throughout the process, it should be stressed that the successful completion of the pretraining program does not imply or guarantee a job; rather, it ensures eligibility when an appropriate opening becomes available.

Selecting employees from a pool of pretrained candidates generally works best in plant or manufacturing environments requiring the operation of equipment or machinery. Employers benefit by having an available work force of skilled individuals from which to choose, without having to waste time screening a group of unknown applicants. In addition, upon selection for hire, program graduates will not have to devote the first several days, or in some cases weeks, to learning their jobs. Program participants benefit by acquiring marketable skills and being first in line for employment opportunities. Of course, there is no guarantee that they will not apply the acquired skills to another company. In this regard, pretraining may not be cost-effective.

Outplacement Firms

Outplacement firms are generally retained by companies to help higher-level managers and executives find new employment after termination. Lower-level management and nonexempt workers who have lost their jobs through plant closings or other major work-force reductions may be provided with partial or group outplacement services.

While outplacement firms can be very helpful for those seeking advice and guidance in finding new employment, they can also be a valuable recruitment source. To begin with, most of these firms are staffed with generalists who do not specialize in placing people in particular occupations or fields. Therefore, they may know of a number of candidates meeting your various jobs' specifications. In addition, the immediate availability of candidates referred by outplacement firms is a big plus. Since most recipients of outplacement services are at a professional level, this translates into a savings of at least two to four weeks in starting time.

Another benefit in dealing with a reputable outplacement firm has to do with the degree of information that can be provided about a candidate. Part of the firm's responsibility is to become thoroughly familiar with a terminating person's skills and interests. Some may even conduct career or psychological assessment testing to confirm information acquired through multiple interviews with the individual, his or her peers, supervisors, and subordinates. Having a thorough profile of a job candidate can assist an employer in deciding whether or not to pursue employment possibilities.

Once they have obtained a complete picture of a job candidate, employers may still be concerned with the accuracy of the representations. One of the most difficult areas to evaluate is why people leave a job; indeed, it is often very difficult, if not impossible, to determine the true reason for termination. Reference checks, explored in Chapter 9, cannot always be relied upon to reveal the actual set of circumstances surrounding a person's termination; the candidate may also be an unreliable source. Outplacement firms, however, usually have access to this information.

One significant disadvantage of interviewing outplacement firm referrals is that these candidates may not project a clear overview of their intangible qualities. The traumatic experience of losing a job, in some cases after twenty or more years of service, and the stress of having to market oneself, added to the pressure of finding new employment, can greatly impact an applicant's self-image. This, in turn, affects how the applicant comes across and is perceived.

Full-service outplacement firms receive a fee from the candidate's former employer in the range of 10 percent to 25 percent of annual salary, with most averaging around 15 percent.

Billboard Advertising

Billboard advertising is a relatively new and virtually unexplored recruitment source. In a study conducted by Globe Research Corp. for *Personnel Journal* in the early part of 1989, only 4 percent of the respondents reported having used it.

Since most people view billboards while driving, often at high speeds, they will not have much time to take in the details (unless, of course, they are stuck in traffic). Therefore, an effective billboard ad must catch the eye and offer a limited amount of information that the average person can both understand and remember (it is unlikely that a pad and pen will be handy). This usually limits a company to a statement about employment advantages, available jobs, an enlarged logo, company name, and phone number in an easy-to-recall format.

Billboard ads seem to work most effectively for hotel/motel chains, restaurants, and airlines and are generally targeted toward nonexempt-level workers.

Response Cards

Response cards may be viewed as a takeoff on direct mail recruitment in that cards are mailed to the homes of targeted candidates.

The language on the card is designed to pique the interest of even those not interested in seeking new employment. After a brief description of the job opportunities available, potential applicants are invited to complete a brief questionnaire that can easily be detached from the informative portion of the card and mailed, postage-paid.

Recruitment Today's Fall 1989 issue described a response card campaign launched by Union Special, an industrial sewing machine manufacturer. In June 1989, the company mailed postage-paid response cards to the homes of thirty-three hundred engineers in anticipation of filling ten positions for project and design engineers. The card carried a simple, direct message and invited interested candidates to send in a brief description of their current employment status and areas of interest. Approximately one hundred engineers responded, among whom thirty were selected for follow-up.

Response cards may also be attached to ads appearing in magazines or other publications. General information about the company and available jobs is provided; those interested are invited to complete the card and mail it in.

An example is illustrated in Figure 3-1. Hyundai reported, in *Recruitment Today*, August 1988, that it ran this ad one Sunday in September of 1987, in the *Los Angeles Times* special "Job Market" section. Hyundai received over fifteen hundred responses and, as of *Recruitment Today*'s August 1988 publication date, had hired five people as a result of the response cards. A spokesperson for the company reported that one year after the ad ran inquiries were still being received.

IBM initiated a five-month response card recruitment campaign at the end of 1988 that was very subtle and reportedly very successful. The company distributed a series of four posters, illustrating technological achievement, to colleges and universities throughout the country. The posters did not mention IBM employment, but invited students to return an accompanying coupon entitling them to receive a free 1989 calendar with the same picture appearing on the poster. The coupon asked for the student's name, address, university, year of graduation, degree, major, and grade point average. The result: five thousand names for IBM's data bank.

Military

Mention the military and words like *self-disciplined, traditional, structured, orderly, organized, adaptable,* and *responsive* come to mind. While

Figure 3-1. Sample response card ad.

▶ Title: "The Great Career Rip-Off"
▶ Company: Hyundai
▶ Agency: Ad Masters, Orange, CA
▶ Creative: Audre Braggins, Dolf Dela Rosa
▶ Media: *Los Angeles Times* "Job Market"
▶ Insertion: September 20, 1987

The Great Career Rip-Off
is at the bottom of this ad!

At Hyundai, we believe no one should be ripped off. Not in cars, not in careers. Fill out the bottom of this ad and mail (with a resume if you wish) to us for a follow-up on potential opportunities with us. Current areas of growth in our company include:

Automotive
Sales
Service
Parts
Port Operations
Marketing
Distribution

General Business
Finance
Administration
Data Processing
Legal
Human Resources
Marketing

Hyundai offers an exciting and professional environment, excellent salaries and benefits. Hurry! Send this coupon or your resume to Attn: SA-LL-JM at Hyundai, P.O. Box 2669, Garden Grove, CA 92642-2669. An Equal Opportunity Employer M/F/H/V.

HYUNDAI
Careers that make sense.

NAME_____

ADDRESS _____

CITY_____ STATE_____ ZIP_____

JOB TITLE _____

Source: Steven Antonoff of Hyundai Motor America.

these are qualities many employers seek in their workers, few have considered the military as a recruitment source.

However, with the changing job market compelling employers to explore different recruitment sources, more companies are starting to turn directly to military recruiting firms, military career conferences, and military job fairs for many future employees.

Military personnel frequently have a great deal of hands-on experience in a variety of tasks but lack general business knowledge. For this reason, they often start in entry-level sales, technical, or staff positions, although some do go directly into management.

Newspaper Inserts

Newspaper inserts represent a relatively untapped recruitment source. Arguments against their use include the possibility that they will fall out of the paper or will be overlooked as job hunters head straight for the classified or special employment sections. Others fear that inserts will not be taken seriously.

Proponents, on the other hand, view newspaper inserts as a refreshing approach to advertising and believe that the fact that this is not a frequently used medium is a plus. In addition, unlike ads that must be cut or torn out, insert ads can easily be slipped out of the rest of the paper. The higher quality of the paper used for inserts as well as the absence of newsprint on one's clothing and hands might also appeal to job seekers. Also, because they are generally larger than standard newspaper ads, inserts are less likely to be misplaced. Finally, newspaper inserts may use several colors, making them more appealing visually.

Professional Associations

Most employers agree that the primary benefit of joining a professional association is the opportunity to network with people from other organizations who work in the same field.

For human resources specialists this can mean exchanging information about selected job applicants and sharing the résumés of those candidates deemed unsuitable for specific openings in your company. These candidates may, however, be well suited for positions in other organizations. The process is simple: Working with two or three other human resources representatives belonging to your association, agree to review, on a monthly basis, a list from within your company of those job openings for which you are responsible, accompanied by abbreviated job descriptions. If the list indicates some viable candidates whom you have either interviewed or whose résumé/application you have reviewed, this information can be shared with your colleagues. They will do the same for you. In addition to the cost-effectiveness of these exchanges, you may also benefit from someone else's impressions of a candidate.

A variation on this approach is to join professional associations in those fields related to your recruitment responsibilities. The associations' membership directory, mailing list, placement service, and publications can provide the names of your company's future employees.

Consulting Firms

Consider this scenario: One of the department heads in your company has submitted a requisition to you, a human resources specialist, for an addition to staff. The reason given is an increase in work because an employee is out on extended disability (no one is quite sure of his status). In addition to the difficulty of managing the normal day-to-day work load, the department head is feeling the added pressure of an impending deadline for a major project. The nature of the position is deemed too complex for a temporary employee, and asking others in the department to work overtime to pick up the slack does not seem to be helping. The only solution, it appears, is for you to hire a full-time expert to fill the gap.

Not so. This situation and others like it may call for retaining the services of a consultant until such time as the crisis caused by the project deadline is over and the situation of the employee on leave is resolved.

Many employers shy away from hiring consultants because of anticipated costs. In fact, consultants may actually be an economical alternative. While their hourly rates—which may range anywhere from $50 to $200 an hour—are likely to be considerably more than what would be paid to an employee, a consultant's services are terminated when the specific task is completed. Depending on the nature and projected duration of the work, many consultants will agree to a "per project" fee, resulting in additional savings.

More than helping an employer save money, consultants may offer other benefits: They can usually devote greater time to a specific assignment than a staff member can; they often bring to the task a wide range of experience and knowledge; they can be more flexible with regard to the hours and days they are willing to work in order to complete a task; and they can accomplish the work without worrying about internal protocol or politics.

However, while consultants can generally devote more time to a specific project than can an employee, those in demand are likely to be working on other assignments for other clients at the same time. This could result in their inability to focus enough attention on your particular project. Hence, before agreeing to retain a consultant's services, find out about any other short- and long-term commitments.

Consultants may be hired to perform any one of a number of assignments. Frequently, they are asked to write various manuals, such as user manuals for a new product, or personnel policies and procedures manuals. Other tasks might include setting up various systems, designing and conducting training and development programs, or acting as a liaison between managers and employees to help resolve employer/employee conflicts. Consultants are also increasingly being hired as contract recruiters when a backlog of job openings needs immediate attention.

Finding a qualified, reliable consultant can be a challenge. Acting on the referral of someone who has experienced a problem similar to yours is your best bet. Former employees or associates provide another possible source of consultants. In addition, various directories, such as the annual *Buyer's Guide & Consultant Directory* of the American Society for Training and Development, which lists hundreds of products and services available for human resources professionals, or the *National Directory of Personnel Consultants by Specialization,* published by the National Association of Personnel Consultants, can prove helpful. Selection of a consultant should be based on several factors, including experience with similar projects, reputation, and cost.

In order to establish a maximally effective working relationship with a consultant, be certain you have clearly agreed to what is to be accomplished *before* any work begins. That and resources required should be determined, as well as the consultant's methodology. The consultant should be allowed access to as much information about the company as possible, including its policies, procedures, and politics. Key personnel should be available to the consultant for additional information, as needed.

Temporary Help Agencies

"Temps" are historically thought of as fill-ins for clericals who miss a day or more of work. While they may still be called upon for that purpose, the categories and functions of temporary employees will be changing dramatically in the 1990s.

In addition to clerical positions, the temporary work force now includes many other exempt and nonexempt classifications, such as computer operators; engineers; lawyers; accountants; researchers; nurses; laboratory technicians; factory, warehouse, and construction workers; security guards; telemarketers; sales clerks; mailroom personnel; and cafeteria workers. Even CEOs have been recruited for temporary assignments, while the company searches for a new permanent executive officer.

This dramatic expansion in available temporary positions has arisen as temps are being called upon to provide human resources in many diverse circumstances. In addition to filling in during emergency situations, peak business periods, and hiring freezes, temporary employees are also being asked to accomplish specific one-time tasks, such as helping an office relocate or processing a particular report. Indeed, the duration of a temporary assignment can range from one day to as long as two years.

The concept of using temps in a variety of work situations obviously appeals to many businesses. According to the U.S. Department of Commerce, the annual temporary payroll in 1980 was $3.5 billion; just seven years later, that number had increased to more than $8.6 billion. It is further reported that the temporary industry continues to grow at a rate of approximately 18 to 20 percent annually.

There are several reasons for the tremendous growth and increased popularity of the use of temporary employees. To begin with, temporary agencies can save employers a great deal of money. These savings may come from costs associated with various aspects of the employment process, including recruiting, testing, and benefits (many temporary agencies provide their workers with health and life insurance, paid vacations, and paid holidays; some even have employee referral programs and offer bonuses to workers who bring in other good workers). Agencies can also save employers the time it takes to launch a recruitment campaign, screen, interview, test, and finally hire. In addition, they are ultimately assured of a proper job match; and if an employer should be dissatisfied with the work performed by the referred temporary employee, a phone call to the agency will result in a replacement.

Other benefits of hiring temporary workers include their immediate availability (unless, of course, you have requested a particular individual and he or she is on another assignment) and your chance to evaluate a person's performance before extending an offer of permanent employment (policies on "temp-to-perm" vary with different agencies).

When considering the services of a particular temporary agency, ascertain performance record; policies regarding rates; placement fees, if any, for "temp-to-perm" arrangements; types of temps available; staff training and background; and the variety of services offered. Obtain and verify references. Contacting referrals from colleagues may prove useful, as well.

A growing number of employers, who are enthusiastic about the idea of temporary help but want more control over temporary workers, have developed what essentially amounts to *in-house temporary agencies*. These are pools of trained workers able to work when a regular employee is unavailable or when there is a special assignment requiring immediate, short-term attention. Companies that hire many seasonal workers also tend to favor in-house temporary programs. Such in-house operations often require one or more full-time permanent individuals to oversee and monitor job performance, although some companies try to manage by delegating this responsibility to existing staff.

The use of in-house temporary agencies can be especially beneficial for retirees who want to work but require flexible scheduling. Many working mothers also favor this arrangement, as do students and new workers who are getting a feel for the job market before committing to any particular field or employer.

Employee Leasing

Employee leasing involves the on-paper transfer of a company's work force from its payroll to that of a leasing firm. The employees are all "fired" from their company and then immediately "hired" by the leasing company, which in turn leases them back to their original employer. The employees are not affected by the paper transfer; they still continue to do the same work at the same location for the same rate of pay. The company, however, benefits in that it no longer has to deal with various human resources tasks; the leasing company now handles the payroll; pays all taxes, insurance, and health premiums; and processes all benefit claims. The fee for relieving a company of these administrative burdens is generally 20 to 35 percent above gross payroll.

While employee leasing has been around since the early 1970s, it has gained popularity only in the past five years or so. In an article in *Management Review* (April 1989), Joseph Honick, executive director of the National Staff Leasing Association, states that once employee leasing caught on, it showed gains of between 30 to 40 percent per year. Employee leasing is most popular among small and mid-sized companies that do not qualify for the benefits premium discounts that larger organizations receive. Small companies are also less likely to have a highly computerized operation or full-time professionals to handle all of the payroll and benefits paperwork.

With more than 450 employee leasing firms across the country, employers are urged to select carefully. It is wise to select a company that is a member of the National Staff Leasing Association, which reportedly has strict membership requirements. Credit and reference checks can also be conducted to determine the financial status and reputation of firms under consideration.

Voice Ads

If you are looking for a truly innovative way of finding job applicants, try one of the newest recruitment sources: telephone voice ads. This enables employers to register voice ads of varying duration with a company such as CareerLine in San Francisco, California. By using a touchtone phone, applicants are able to review the employer's ads, usually for professional jobs, and, if interested, may leave a phone message in the company's "RSVP" mailbox.

While still too new to be evaluated effectively, voice ads are certainly an easy recruitment tool for both employers and applicants.

On-Site Recruitment

On-site recruitment, while limited to the types of businesses that attract large numbers of people to their locations each day, can be quite effective, usually for various nonexempt-level positions. For example, railroad companies may place pamphlets describing employment opportunities on car seats at various times of the day; airlines might do the same with seats on planes; department stores might attach fliers to packages at cashier stations; and fast-food chains, as well as family restaurants, might describe job openings on tray liners and table tents. The brief message, which usually describes the benefits of working for the company, is often framed by bright, eye-catching colors and graphics. Interested candidates are invited to see or call the employment manager (or equivalent) to obtain an application form. In some instances postage-paid applications are attached to the message; anyone who is interested can simply complete the form for submission.

Summary

This chapter explored twenty-six different recruitment sources. Table 3-1 summarizes the advantages and disadvantages of these sources.

(Text continues on page 82.)

Table 3-1. Advantages and disadvantages of the various recruitment sources.

Recruitment Source	Advantages	Disadvantages	Level of Positions
Job posting	• Creates openings at lower, easier-to-fill levels • Saves time and money • Boosts employee morale • Reveals hidden talent	• Managers feel they can no longer select persons of their choice • Managers resent employees who want to post for jobs outside of their department • Time may be lost waiting for replacement	• Nonexempt and exempt
Employee referrals	• Inexpensive • Expeditious • Related bonus boosts employee morale	• May result in charges of systemic discrimination if not used in conjunction with other recruitment sources	• Nonexempt and exempt
Newspaper and magazine advertising	• Reaches a wide audience • Can solicit responses via blind ads • Magazine ads zero in on specific occupation categories	• Can be very costly • Can delay filling of a position	• Nonexempt and exempt
Employment agencies and search firms	• Access to large labor pools • Can help fill position quickly	• Can be very costly • Can refer unqualified applicants	• Employment agencies nonexempt; search firms exempt

(continued)

Table 3-1. (continued)

Recruitment Source	Advantages	Disadvantages	Level of Positions
Personnel files	• No cost • Good public relations	• If on a manual system, can be time-consuming • Poor notes taken by the previous interviewer may misrepresent applicant	• Nonexempt and exempt
Walk-ins, call-ins, and write-ins	• No cost • Good public relations	• Poorly monitored system can result in lost applications • Interviewing walk-ins and talking with call-ins can disrupt interviewers' work schedule	• Walk-ins and call-ins nonexempt; write-ins exempt
School recruiting	• Opportunity to groom and develop future management of a company • Opportunity to select top graduates	• Can be costly • Must evaluate potential, as opposed to concrete work experience	• Exempt
Job fairs	• May fill many openings in a short period of time • Opportunity to network with other recruiters	• Can be costly • Usually means working on a weekend • Fatigue	• Exempt
Open house	• Good public relations • May fill several openings at one time	• Can be costly • Time-consuming	• Exempt

Source	Advantages	Disadvantages	Status
Government agencies	• Cost-free • Can result in referral of many applicants • Can help with affirmative action goals • Can help fill positions quickly	• May send unqualified applicants • May challenge reasons for rejection	• Nonexempt
Direct mail	• Personalized form of recruitment • Selective	• Time-consuming • Can be costly	• Exempt
Radio and television	• Reaches a wide audience • Can help fill positions quickly	• Can be costly	• Nonexempt
Computerized systems	• Can help fill positions quickly • Extensive database	• Requires specific hardware and software • Can be costly	• Exempt
Research firms	• Cost-effective • Allows for more involvement in the interviewing process	• Services end upon research firms' contacting of candidates	• Exempt

(continued)

Table 3-1. (continued)

Recruitment Source	Advantages	Disadvantages	Level of Positions
Preemployment training	• Creates trained work force prepared for times when targeted jobs become available	• Time-consuming • May not be cost-effective	• Nonexempt
Outplacement	• Can result in referral of many applicants • Can help fill positions quickly • Can provide a thorough profile of job candidates	• Incomplete picture of intangible qualities	• Exempt and sometimes nonexempt
Billboard advertising	• Can be eye-catching	• Can only offer a limited amount of information	• Nonexempt
Response cards	• Personalized form of recruitment • Selective	• Time-consuming • Can be costly	• Exempt
Military	• Applicants with desirable intangible qualities • Applicants with extensive hands-on experience	• Applicants who lack general business knowledge	• Nonexempt and exempt
Newspaper inserts	• Easily removed from the paper • Less likely to be misplaced • Eye-catching	• Easily lost • Easily overlooked • May not be taken seriously	• Exempt and nonexempt

	Pros	Cons	Status
Professional associations	• Able to obtain résumés and information about applicants without direct solicitation • Can be cost-effective	• Time-consuming • Can be supplied with applicants with no marketable skills	• Exempt and nonexempt
Consultants	• Can be cost-effective • Provide wide range of experience and knowledge • Flexible scheduling	• May not be able to devote sufficient time to your project	• Exempt
Temporaries	• Can be cost-effective • Can save time • Can assure proper job match • Can lead to permanent hires	• Constant change in personnel can be disruptive	• Exempt and nonexempt
Employee leasing	• Relieves employer from performing certain human resources/administrative tasks	• Can result in incomplete or improper handling of payroll and benefits	• Exempt and nonexempt
Voice ads	• Easy	• So new, applicants may be "gun shy"	• Exempt
On-site recruitment	• Can reach a wide audience • Can save time • Good public relations	• May not be taken seriously	• Nonexempt

With all the different recruitment sources available, you should never find yourself in the position of saying, "I can't find anyone to fill this job." If this occurs, it is probably because the job expectations are unrealistic. Nor should you ever feel pressured into taking the first person who applies for an opening because you feel desperate. This often backfires when the person hired quits or is terminated for poor performance in a short period of time. You are then in a position of having to recruit all over again.

By exploring the various sources described in this chapter, you can afford to be selective. The investment in time and money will pay off when you find the best person for the job.

4

Preparing for the Interview

In Chapter 2, it was stated that there are a number of preparatory steps to be completed before meeting a job applicant for the face-to-face interview. The process begins by familiarizing yourself with various aspects of the job and continues by exploring different recruitment sources. If done properly, these steps should lead to the identification of one or more job candidates possessing suitable qualifications. The groundwork has been laid.

At this point, many interviewers feel prepared to meet their applicants. They should not, for there are still several preinterview activities to complete. In some instances, the preinterview process may include telephone screening to determine whether, in fact, there is sufficient reason to proceed any further. When there is continued mutual interest, and when telephone screening is not done, there are additional steps to take before meeting the job candidate. Preparing for the actual interview is a multifaceted process that includes reviewing the application and résumé, allocating sufficient time for the interview, planning an appropriate interview environment, reviewing your objectives, planning basic interview questions, anticipating how the applicant may be feeling, and taking into account the role of perception.

None of these steps should ever be omitted; careful attention to this important phase of the employment process should result in a smoother, more effective meeting with an applicant and is more likely to ensure selection of the best possible employee.

Telephone Screening

While it may not be feasible to screen all job applicants by telephone, this should be done in as many instances as possible. In fact, with the exception of applicants who come via a third-party employment agency or search firm, internal job posting, school recruiting, job fairs, and open house situations, telephone screening is appropriate in virtually every instance. In particular, telephone screening is considered an essential preinterview activity for professional candidates who will be traveling some distance, usually for a series of face-to-face interviews taking up the better part of a day.

Telephone screening is intended to accomplish one of two objectives: to establish continued interest in a job candidate and result in the scheduling of an appointment to meet in person for an in-depth interview or to determine that a candidate's qualifications do not sufficiently meet the job's specifications. Under no circumstances should telephone screening be viewed as a substitute for the face-to-face interview.

Successful telephone screening depends on establishing and following a certain format. To begin with, it is usually wise to contact a candidate at his or her home during nonworking hours. Identify yourself and explain the purpose of your call. Also, confirm the individual's interest in the specific job. To eliminate any possible thoughts of misrepresentation on the part of the candidate, request that he or she call you back at a mutually convenient time. If it is a long-distance call, offer to accept the charges. Suggest that the candidate allot approximately fifteen to forty-five minutes for the call, with fifteen to twenty minutes being considered sufficient for a nonexempt-level candidate and thirty to forty-five minutes being set aside for a professional.

When the specified time arrives, be prepared to describe the available position, being careful not to identify the qualities being sought in the desired candidate. Encourage the applicant to ask any questions related to the specific opening or the company. Have ready a series of questions to assist you in determining whether continued interest is warranted. These questions should prompt some responses that, by themselves, will indicate whether this is a viable candidate. For example, if not already known, the person's salary expectations can help you decide whether or not a potential job match is possible. The level and nature of the job opening should suggest other questions.

Some questions to ask nonexempt-level applicants are:

- Why they are leaving their present (or last) employer
- What they do (or did) in a typical day
- What they like (or liked) most and least about their present (or last) job
- Why they are applying for this particular position

In addition, ask questions relative to any significant aspects of the job. For example, if it requires standing for long periods of time, ask applicants to describe jobs where they have had to do this. In addition, describe a typical situation that is likely to occur with this job and ask the candidates to describe how they have handled similar situations in the past.

Appropriate questions to ask exempt-level applicants include:

- Why they are leaving their present (or last) employer and why they are applying for this particular position
- What they know about your organization
- What they have contributed in past positions
- What contributions they anticipate being able to make in this position
- What they expect from your company
- How this position fits into their long-term goals

Then, based on the particulars of the job, ask a series of questions regarding how they have handled certain situations in past positions.

As candidates respond to your questions, remind yourself of the purpose of the call: You are deciding whether a face-to-face interview is in order, not whether they should be hired. Take notes as they talk; if the conversation itself is not determinative, reviewing their responses to your questions after the call is completed can help you decide whether to schedule an interview. If you do decide to bring them in for an interview, the notes can be used as a point of reference and comparison as you repeat some of the questions asked on the phone, seeking more in-depth information.

Be careful not to judge the quality of a candidate's telephone presentation if effective verbal communication skills are not a job-related criterion. On the other hand, some people, especially those in sales or marketing, do very well communicating on the phone; consequently, you must be able to separate style from substance.

Before concluding the conversation, go over a brief checklist:

- Does the applicant understand the job?
- Did you ask questions that will enable you to determine whether or not further interest is warranted?
- Did the applicant ask pertinent questions?
- Has the applicant expressed interest in the job?
- Does the applicant meet the basic qualifications for the job?
- Is there consistency between the information on the résumé (or application) and what the applicant has told you?

- Are the applicant's salary expectations consistent with the range for the available position?

If there is no doubt in your mind that the person should be invited in for an interview, do so before the conversation is completed. If you are not certain and want to review your notes before making a decision, thank the candidate for his or her time, describe the next step, and estimate when he or she may expect to hear from you. If you are absolutely certain that the candidate is not suitable for the job—that is, you've screened the person out—you have one of two choices: You may be honest and say that his or her qualifications are not suitable or that there is a lack of specific expertise or knowledge necessary for the performance of the job, or you may say that you will be reviewing the results of your conversations with all of the candidates before taking any further action. If you do reject the candidate outright, be certain to explain your policy on keeping applications and résumés on file and encourage him or her to apply again in the future for other openings. If you have handled the situation tactfully, the person can hang up the phone feeling good, even though no job interview is forthcoming.

Telephone screening offers numerous benefits. The process enables you to weed out those candidates not qualified, thereby allowing more time to devote to viable potential employees. It is also an impartial process; that is, neither party can be influenced or distracted by such visual factors as appearance, clothing, or grooming. While these can be important job-related intangibles (discussed later in this chapter under the section entitled "Reviewing Your Own Perceptions") they are irrelevant at this screening stage.

Reviewing the Application and Résumé

Never omit reviewing the completed application form and/or résumé, even if you are interviewing walk-ins or are running behind schedule. Take the time necessary to review all applicants' backgrounds and qualifications before seeing them. Experienced interviewers find that they can review the application as they walk from their office to the reception area to greet the candidate.

There are two reasons for doing this. First, you will become familiar with the person's credentials, background, and qualifications as they relate to the requirements and responsibilities of the position; second, you will be identifying questions to ask during the interview.

Each organization should have an application form that reflects its own environment and individual needs. For example, the application form for a highly technical company will differ from one used by a nonprofit organization. Some companies have more than one form: One is used for professional or exempt positions and another for nonexempt positions.

Appendix F contains a sample job application form with questions that might be used in most organizations. Review its contents with your own organization in mind, modifying it as required.

When designing an application form, it is important to remember that all categories must be relevant and job-related. This is critical from the standpoint of compliance with equal employment opportunity laws. Interviewers should note that familiarity with federal laws is not sufficient, since many state laws are more stringent. Therefore, compliance with federal regulations could still mean violation of state regulations. Where there is a difference, the stricter law prevails. Oversight or ignorance of the law does not provide immunity.

Even the simplest application form has numerous categories that should be reviewed before a face-to-face interview. The same holds true for résumés. As you review these categories, keep in mind that a completed application form or résumé that deviates from the acceptable format does not automatically mean that the candidate should not be considered for the position. The way in which people present themselves on paper is only one of the factors that you should consider when making your hiring decision.

Be aware that résumés differ somewhat from applications, in that people start with a blank piece of paper, as opposed to a form with specific questions to be answered. Consequently, on their résumés people offer whatever data they choose. Generally speaking, the same basic information should appear on a résumé as appears on an application form. This includes work history (i.e., employer, location, duration, duties, and special accomplishments), educational degrees, and scholastic achievements. Career objectives may be cited and a list of the applicant's publications may also be included. Usually, professional candidates who submit résumés are also asked to complete an application form, although not until after a hiring decision has been reached.

Following are ten key areas to focus on when reviewing an application or résumé. A completed application form illustrating these areas appears in Appendix G. Remember, these are guidelines only. Deviation from any one of the standards described should not, in and of itself, result in the dismissal of a candidate. Nor should a specific standard in this list be considered at all if it is not relevant to the responsibilities of the position in question:

1. *Scan the overall appearance of the application or résumé.* Check to see that it is neat and easy to read. The handwriting on applications should be legible. Résumés should be typed and then printed up as opposed to photocopied. The contents of applications and résumés should be grammatically correct and the language easy to understand. Résumés are generally one to two pages in length and sometimes have writing samples attached. They should be professional in appearance and not made to capture your attention with garish colors, clever phrases, or scented paper. Although they are not essential, cover letters usually accompany résumés and show added interest on the part of the applicant.

2. *Look for any blanks or omissions.* This is easy with an application form; with a résumé, check to see that basic information (work and educational history) has not been excluded. Make a note of any missing information so that you can ask the applicant about it. Some employment application forms are poorly designed, causing candidates to inadvertently overlook certain questions. Or it may be that an applicant purposely omitted certain information. If this is the case, it is up to you to find out why and to determine the importance of the missing data during the interview.

3. *Review the applicant's work history and make a note of any time gaps between jobs.* If an applicant indicates that he or she took some time off between jobs to travel throughout Europe, make a note of it. Be careful that you do not pass judgment, deciding that this was a frivolous and irresponsible pursuit. Fill in the gaps and worry about drawing conclusions after the interview process is completed.

4. *Consider any overlaps in time.* For example, the dates on an application may show that the candidate was attending school and working at the same time. Of course, this is possible, but not if the school happens to be in California and the job was in New York (unless it was a correspondence school). Even if the locations are consistent, you need to verify the accuracy of the dates.

5. *Make a note of any other inconsistencies.* To illustrate let's say there is an applicant with an extensive educational background who has been employed in a series of nonexempt jobs. This may be because he or she has degrees in a highly specialized field and cannot find suitable work, or it may be that his or her educational credentials are misrepresented. It is up to you to find out.

6. *Consider the frequency of job changes.* People voluntarily leave jobs for many reasons, including an inaccurate description of the work at the time of hire, an improper job match, personality conflicts on the job, inadequate salary increases, limited growth opportunities, and unkept promises. Some employees who know that they are doing poorly will voluntarily terminate their employment just prior to a scheduled performance evaluation. Then there are instances when an employee is let go. This may occur when a company shuts down for economic reasons, when major organizational changes cause the deletion of several positions, or when a temporary assignment has been completed and there is no additional work to be done. Of course, employees are also terminated for reasons such as poor performance or excessive absenteeism.

When reviewing a candidate's employment record, you should not draw premature, negative conclusions regarding the frequency of job changes. To determine what constitutes a frequent change is highly subjective. Too often interviewers set arbitrary guidelines, sometimes patterned after their own work history. You may decide that changing jobs more often than once every two years is too frequent and that this translates into unreliability. However, at this stage of the interview process, you simply do not have enough information to make such a decision. After all, you have not even met the applicant yet. Make a note that you want to discuss his or her pattern of job changes, and move on to the next category: salary history.

7. *Be objective when evaluating a person's salary requirements.* In our society it is assumed that everyone wants (and needs) to make more money. Indeed, it is one of the most commonly cited reasons for changing jobs. However, you will undoubtedly come across applicants who are willing to take a job at a lower salary than they were previously or are presently earning. The reasons for this vary. Sometimes an individual wants to move from one area of specialization to another and recognizes that his or her lack of expertise in the new field will mean less money—something he or she is willing to contend with in order to make the change. Sometimes people want to work for a particular company and are willing to earn less in order to do so. Then again, some people simply do not care about money all that much. They only want to have enough to meet their basic expenses and are not concerned with luxuries. For them, job satisfaction is of paramount importance. Then there are those individuals who have been unemployed for a long period of time and cannot find work at their old rate of pay. They may be willing

to work for less until they can get back on their feet. Once again, you must be careful not to draw conclusions.

It is significant to note that, while not apparently illegal, requesting that applicants provide information relevant to salaries earned in past positions may be a violation of the Equal Pay Act of 1963, which prohibits paying women less than men for performing substantially equal work (see Chapter 5). This could occur, for example, where an employer learns that a woman applicant has been earning considerably less in previous jobs than has a male candidate with a comparable background of skill and experience. If both are hired for the same job, will be performing substantially equal work, are offered starting salaries that are, say, $5,000 above their previous salaries, and perform at comparable levels of effectiveness during their respective terms of employment, the pay differential between the two will widen that much more. Consider, for example, a male candidate who is hired at a starting salary of $40,000 per year and a woman candidate who is hired to perform comparable work at a salary of $35,000. Both receive an "above average" evaluation at the time of their first performance evaluation, resulting in a 7 percent increase. The original $5,000 gap between their respective salaries has just increased to $5,350, as the male employee's annual earnings rise to $42,800, and the woman employee's salary increases to only $37,450. If their performance levels remain comparable at the time of their next review, warranting another 7 percent raise, the gap will increase to $5,724.50, since the man will now be earning $45,796 and the woman will only be making $40,071.50 (little more than the man was offered at the time of hire). Such a pay difference that is based on past earnings could be a violation of the Equal Pay Act because it is, in effect, a differential based on sex.

For this reason, reference to salaries in past positions does not appear in the sample application forms in Appendixes F and G.

8. *Carefully review the candidate's reasons for leaving previous jobs.* Look for a pattern. For example, if the reason given for leaving several jobs in a row is "no room for growth," it may be that this person's job expectations are unrealistic. This explanation for leaving could also be a cover-up for other, less acceptable, reasons. Of course, it may also be perfectly legitimate. Whatever the explanation may be, this is a key area to explore in the face-to-face interview.

9. *If the person's duties are not clearly described on the application or résumé, make a note to ask for elaboration.* Job titles may also require explanation. Some titles are not functional or descriptive in nature and, therefore, do not reveal an incumbent's general realm of

responsibility. Examples of such titles include *administrative assistant* and *vice-president*. Sometimes titles sound very grand, but upon probing, you may discover that they carry few responsibilities.

10. *Review the application or résumé for any "red-flag" areas.* This is any information that does not seem to make sense or that leaves you with an uneasy feeling. A classic example is the response to the category "Reason for Leaving Last Job." The popular answer "personal" should alert you to a possible problem. Many interviewers assume that they have no right to pursue this further—that to do so would be an invasion of the person's privacy. This is not true. You have an obligation to ask the applicant to be more specific. Of course, if people begin to volunteer truly personal information about their home life and personal relationships, then you must interrupt and ask them to focus on job-related incidents that may have contributed to their decision to leave. Also note that "personal" is frequently a cover-up for "fired." Many applicants count on interviewers not going any further upon seeing the explanation "personal" and, therefore, use this term instead of revealing that they were asked to leave their last job.

Applications and résumés are full of information for you to pursue during the course of the interview. Because they are the foundation of the selection process, it is critical that you take time before meeting with a candidate to clearly identify those areas that need to be investigated further.

Keeping Applicant Data Records

Employers required to take affirmative action in hiring practices may want to analyze applicant flow by implementing a system of applicant record keeping. This information should have no bearing whatsoever on the hiring decision. Accordingly, it has no place on the employment application. However, many companies do distribute separate forms to applicants along with the employment application. The completed form is then placed in a separate box or basket and later put in a confidential file. At no time should the form be viewed by anyone involved in the selection process, or any other aspect of employment, if the individual is hired.

The form should offer anonymity, clearly indicating that the information is provided strictly on a voluntary basis and is requested for the preparation of statistical analyses for further compliance with governmental affirmative action requirements. Categories of information may pertain to source of referral, disabled person status, Vietnam era veteran or disabled veteran status, age, sex, and race/ethnic group. Categories of the latter are generally identified as white, black (including people who identify themselves as African-American, Afro-American, Haitian, Jamaican, West Indian, etc.), Hispanic (including people whose origin is Mexico, Puerto Rico, Cuba, or any other Spanish-speaking country of the Caribbean or Central or South America, or Spain), American Indian/Alaskan Native (tribal affiliation is not necessary), Asian/Pacific Islander (including people who identify themselves as, for example, Laotian, Vietnamese, Cambodian, Pakistani, Bangladeshi, Sri Lankan, Burmese, Fijian, or Indonesian).

Allowing Sufficient Time for the Interview

The next step in the interview preparation stage has to do with the amount of time allotted for each interview. Think about the entire interview process and not just the portion devoted to the face-to-face meeting. Time is needed *before* the interview to review the application and/or résumé, as already described. Time is also needed *during* the interview for you to ask questions of the applicant, provide information about the job and the company, and allow the applicant to ask questions. Finally, time is needed *after* the interview to write up your notes, reflect on what took place, set up additional appointments, and check references. Additional time may also be needed before or after the interview for testing.

Considering all that must be done, just how much time should be set aside for each interview? There is no single correct answer. Much depends on the nature of the job; that is, whether it is nonexempt or exempt. Generally speaking, more time is needed for interviewing professionals: usually a total of ninety to 120 minutes. This amount of time should be sufficient for you to ascertain the necessary information about a candidate's qualifications and to get a good idea of job suitability and applicant interest. If the actual face-to-face interview runs much beyond ninety minutes, it becomes tiresome for both the applicant and the interviewer. A ninety-minute interview leaves approximately thirty minutes to be divided between the pre- and post-interview activities previously mentioned.

In the case of interviews for nonexempt positions, approximately forty-five to seventy-five minutes should be allotted, with thirty to forty-five minutes for the face-to-face meeting. More concrete areas are usually probed at this level (i.e., specific job duties, attendance records, and the like). These take less time to explore than do the numerous intangible areas examined at the exempt level, such as management style, level of creativity, and initiative.

The time frames discussed here should only be used as guidelines. Be flexible in the actual amount of time allotted, but also be aware of these general parameters because they can help you to ascertain sufficient information and to avoid discussing irrelevant factors. For example, if you find that your interviews are over within fifteen minutes, you may not be phrasing your questions properly; that is, you are asking yes/no questions as opposed to open-ended questions (see Chapter 6). It may also be that you are not adequately probing suspicious areas, as described earlier in the chapter, or perhaps you simply do not know what questions to ask. If, on the other hand, your interviews last much beyond forty-five minutes for a nonexempt position or ninety minutes for an exempt position, it is likely that the applicant has taken control of the interview. When this occurs, interviewers often find themselves describing their own career with the company at some length. They may also find themselves discussing the contents of books on their shelves or explaining photos on their desks. It is not unusual for inexperienced applicants to try to steer interviewers away from questions regarding their job suitability. By diverting the interviewer's attention and talking a blue streak about irrelevant matters, applicants hope to cloud the real issue of whether or not they are qualified for the job. Of course, some people simply like to talk a lot and do not intend to be devious. Regardless of the motive, however, interviewers are cautioned against allowing applicants to take control of the interview. This is less likely to happen if you are aware of the appropriate time frame for an interview.

To help maximize the time set aside for meeting applicants, consider the three scheduling guidelines that follow:

1. *It is best to interview only during the time of day when your "biological clock" is at its peak—that is, when you are most alert.* If you tend to slow down around midmorning, but then pick up again around 1 P.M., it would be best to schedule interviews during the afternoon hours. Likewise, if you are at your best first thing in the morning, late-afternoon appointments would be unwise.

2. *When you have a number of positions to fill and several candidates remain to be seen, try to take a ten-minute break in between interviews.* The time can be used for just about anything, including taking a short

walk, getting a drink of water, stretching, making a few short phone calls, or doing other work. The break will help you feel more in control of your interview schedule and also allow you to focus more clearly on your next applicant.

3. *Try not to conduct more than four or five interviews in one workday.* Obviously, this may not always be possible, particularly when you have a number of openings to fill. If, however, you can space your interviews with other work, you will find that your attention level during the interviews and for your other work is likely to improve.

Planning an Appropriate Environment

Once you have blocked the necessary amount of time for your interview, plan the environment in which it will be conducted. Here are some guidelines to consider:

1. *Ensure privacy.* This is very important if applicants are expected to talk freely. They must be assured that what they are saying cannot be overheard by others. This is particularly important when they are discussing sensitive matters, such as why they are being asked to leave their present jobs.

While not everyone may have a private office, everyone does have access to privacy. This may mean borrowing someone else's office when it is not being used, using the company cafeteria or dining room during off-hours, or sitting in a portion of the lobby that is set apart from those areas receiving the most traffic. Such options may be preferable if, for example, your own office has partial partitions instead of full floor-to-ceiling walls. Sounds can easily carry over and around partitions; depending on their height, people can also easily peer over the tops.

2. *Ensure a minimum number of distractions.* More obvious distractions include your phone ringing without someone answering it for you, people walking into your office while you are interviewing, or papers requiring attention left exposed on top of your desk. Some interviewers claim that such distractions are actually beneficial in that they allow for an assessment of how the applicant handles interruptions. This is unlikely. Distractions and interruptions waste valuable time for both the applicant and the interviewer. Moreover, the applicant may be left with an unfavorable impression of the interviewer in particular, and possibly the organization overall.

A more subtle distraction, but one that can interfere as much as a phone ringing or someone barging in during the interview, is the interviewer's own thoughts. Thinking about all the work that needs to be done not only may prevent you from focusing fully on the applicant but may even result in your resenting him or her for keeping you from it. To guard against this, remind yourself just prior to meeting an applicant that interviewing is an important part of your work. It might also help if you cleared off your desk before the applicant enters.

3. *Make certain that the applicant is comfortable.* It is a simple fact that if the applicant feels comfortable, you will be assured of a more productive interview. Comfort level is not determined by how much furniture you have in your office, whether or not you have rugs on the floor, or a scenic view outside your window (or whether you even have a window!). It is your behavior and general approach to the interview that will largely determine the comfort level of the applicant. If you come across as friendly, appear genuinely interested in what the applicant has to say, and have made an effort to ensure privacy and prevent interruptions, what the interview surroundings look like is not going to matter a great deal. If you can offer the applicant a choice of seats, that's fine. If, however, space is limited, and there is only one chair in addition to yours, that is all right too. What matters is that the applicant feel welcome.

4. *Consider the seating arrangement.* The most common office seating arrangements between an interviewer and an applicant include: the applicant and interviewer seated on either side of a desk; the applicant's chair on the side of the desk; the applicant and the interviewer sitting across from one another, away from the desk; the applicant and the interviewer seated at a table, either next to each other or across from each other; the applicant and the interviewer seated at opposite ends of a sofa; and the applicant or interviewer seated on a sofa with the other person seated on a chair across from the sofa.

There is no one proper relationship between your seat and the applicant's seat. Some interviewers feel that desks create a barrier between themselves and the applicant. If this is how you feel, then the desk does indeed become a barrier. Also, some interviewers want to be able to see as much of the applicant as possible so they can better assess his or her nonverbal communication. However, if you are comfortable seated behind your desk, then by all means sit there. The applicant is likely to feel comfortable at the other side of the desk in this instance.

The only arrangement that is not desirable is for either the interviewer or the applicant to be standing while the other sits. This can occur with interviewers who favor stress interviews; that is, creating an uncomfortable environment for the applicant to see how he or she handles matters. For the interviewer to remain standing or to "half sit" on the desk while asking questions of the applicant is unprofessional and will undoubtedly be perceived as such. Likewise, to begin firing questions at applicants as soon as they enter your doorway, without first offering them a seat and attempting to put them at ease, is counterproductive. The interviewer cannot learn anything job-related about the applicant under these circumstances and, hence, cannot possibly make an effective hiring decision.

Being Clear About Your Objectives

As part of the interview preparation stage, it is important that you remind yourself of exactly why you are conducting these interviews. What are your objectives? Always start by examining the large, overall picture and consider your organization's goals. Ask yourself: What kind of place do I work in? What is the atmosphere like? What is the image that my company wants to project? What kind of employee does this organization want to hire?

Next consider the divisional and departmental goals, both short- and long-term. Consider what type of employee is going to be of help in achieving these goals. Also carefully consider the personalities of the manager and the other employees in the department where the opening exists. While skill and experience are the main factors used to evaluate an applicant, an individual's style of working can clash with that of others in the department. For example, someone who works best independently and without direction would not fare well in a unit with a hands-on supervisor who not only wanted to know what his or her employees were doing at all times but also wanted to be actively involved in the actual work.

This step only takes a few moments yet is all-important, especially when you have a number of closely qualified candidates to choose from. Recalling your objectives can help you focus more clearly during the interview on the most relevant skills and characteristics.

Planning Your Basic Questions

Next consider the basic questions to be asked. In addition to reviewing the completed application and/or résumé for areas to be pursued and developed, you should plan a handful of general questions. These will serve as the foundation for your interview. The job description is an excellent source for this type of question. By reviewing the job description, you can easily identify what skills are required. Then proceed to formulate the questions you will need to ask in order to determine whether or not applicants possess these skills and are capable of performing the required duties and responsibilities. Hypothetical situations can also be developed from this, which can then be presented to candidates to enable them to demonstrate their skills and potential.

Be careful not to list too many questions or become very specific during this stage of preparation. If you have an extensive list of detailed questions, the tendency will be to read from that list during the interview. This will result in a stiff, formalized session, which could conceivably make the applicant feel ill-at-ease. In addition, with a lengthy list of questions, interviewers feel compelled to cover the entire list and often end up being redundant. Again, this can result in the applicant feeling uncomfortable and wondering whether or not you are really listening to his or her responses.

Limit yourself to about a half-dozen general questions. Once you get into the interview, the other questions that need to be asked will follow as offshoots of the applicant's answers. In fact, if your first question is a good, open-ended question, the applicant's response should provide you with numerous additional questions to ask. An example of an effective first question might be, "Would you please describe your activities during a typical day at your present (or most recent) job?" As you listen to the applicant's response, note any areas that he or she mentions that you want to pursue further during the course of the interview.

This one question alone will yield enough information to fill an entire interview if you listen closely to the applicant's answer and use portions of it as the basis for additional questions. Consider, for example, the applicant who is currently working as a customer service representative. Upon asking him the question "Would you please describe your activities during a typical day at your present job?" the applicant provides a rather scant response: "Well, let's see. Each day is really kind of different since I deal with customers and you never know what they're going to call about; but basically, my job is to handle the customer hot line, research any questions, and process complaints."

If you were to leave this answer and go on to another question, you would be overlooking a wealth of information. The applicant has handed you four valuable pieces of data worthy of exploration:

1. His job requires dealing with a variety of people and situations.
2. He "handles" a customer hot line.
3. He "researches" questions.
4. He "processes" complaints.

Here are some of the questions that may now be asked based on these data:

"Describe the nature of some of the situations you are asked to deal with."

"Who are the people who call you?"

"What is the process that someone with a complaint is supposed to follow?"

"What is your role in this process?"

"Exactly what is the customer hot line?"

"When you say that you 'handle' the hot line, exactly what do you mean?"

"Who else works the hot line?"

"What do you say to a customer who calls on the hot line?"

"What do you say to a customer who calls with a specific question?"

"What do you do when you do not have the answer being sought by a customer?"

"What do you do when a customer is not satisfied with the answer you have given him or her?"

"How do you respond to customers who are extremely angry?"

"How would you respond to a customer who demands to speak to someone else?"

"How would you handle several demanding customers at the same time?"

"Describe a specific situation in which a customer repeatedly called, claiming his or her problem had still not been resolved. How did you handle it?"

"How much of your time is devoted to researching questions?"

"Describe the research process, including the resources you use."

"How do you prepare for each day, knowing that you will probably have to listen to several people complaining about a variety of problems?"

These are just some of the questions triggered by the applicant's response to one broad, open-ended question. Each of these is also likely to result in additional answers and further inquiries that will ultimately provide you with a clear picture of the level and scope of this individual's responsibilities at his present job. As the interview progresses, this well-established base will allow you to apply his present experience to the opening in your company.

This one question is so comprehensive that it, alone, could suffice as the only prepared question you have before beginning the interview. However, most interviewers feel better prepared if they have some additional questions planned; furthermore, some applicants not having any prior work experience cannot provide information about a typical workday. Here, then, are some questions that may be prepared prior to the interview. Note that all are open-ended and broad enough so that the answers will result in additional questions; there will then be no need to prepare more than a few:

For Applicants With Prior Work Experience

1. What [do/did] you like most and least about your [present/most recent] job? Why?
2. Describe a situation in your [present/most recent] job involving _____; how did you handle it?
3. What [are/were] some of the duties in your [present/most recent] job that you [find/found] to be difficult and easy? Why?
4. Why [do/did] you want to leave your [present/most recent] job?
5. How do you generally approach tasks you dislike? Please give me a specific example relative to your [present/most recent] job.

For Applicants With Formal Education but No Prior Work Experience

1. What were your favorite and least favorite subjects in [high school/college/other]? Why?
2. Describe your study habits.
3. Why did you major in _____?
4. How do you feel your studies in _____ prepared you for this job?

For Applicants Without Formal Education or Work Experience

1. Here are a series of hypothetical situations that are likely to occur on the job. How would you handle them?
2. What has prepared you for this job?

Considering the Applicant's Feelings

Another aspect of preparing for the interview is to anticipate how applicants may be feeling just prior to being interviewed. It is not uncommon for candidates to experience emotions such as anxiety, fear, nervousness, and intimidation as they sit waiting to be evaluated. This may be particularly true when someone has a sketchy employment record or anticipates being asked about a particularly sensitive aspect of his or her work history. Even applicants who feel completely qualified for the available position and confident in their skills and knowledge may experience a certain degree of discomfort considering the fact that there are probably a number of other equally qualified candidates.

It is very difficult to assess job suitability when an applicant is experiencing self-doubt or other negative feelings. Therefore, make every effort to start the interview punctually. If you have allotted sufficient time for each interview, as discussed earlier, you should succeed frequently; however, other work-related matters can occasionally prevent you from adhering to your schedule. When this happens, and it appears that you are going to be delayed by more than a few minutes, go out to where the applicant is waiting and explain the situation. If you anticipate being able to begin the interview shortly, you may want to suggest that the applicant read some company literature and have a beverage while waiting. If, however, the delay is going to be rather lengthy, say more than half an hour, then perhaps someone from the department with the job opening might take the applicant on a tour of that department. Another option is to ask someone else to begin or even conduct the interview. If at all possible, do not suggest that the applicant leave and return later in the day or on a different date.

Reviewing Your Own Perceptions

One last area to consider before you actually conduct an interview is the role of perception. This is a critical phase in the objective evaluation of job candidates. Before meeting an applicant, interviewers should briefly review the five primary ways in which we formulate our perceptions and ideas about people:

1. *First impressions.* This is the most prevalent and often the most damaging way of formulating our ideas about people, since we often form first impressions without even realizing it. Interviewers

who are unaware of the importance of perception frequently boast, "The minute he/she walked in the door, I could tell he/she was right/wrong for the job."

This is a mistake. You cannot determine job suitability by sizing someone up in a split second based on his or her appearance. Of course, appearance, which consists of many components including clothing, colors, and grooming, does play a role in the selection process. After all, employees represent an organization, and therefore the image that they project is a direct reflection on that company. The problem is that interviewers have a tendency to form preconceived notions of how employees in certain job classifications should look. An accountant, for example, conjures up a different image than does a mechanic. If a person applying for a mechanic's opening came to an interview dressed in a suit, you would be surprised but probably not turned off. However, if an accountant appeared in your office wearing overalls, it is far more likely that you would form a negative first impression. This is true because we tend to have very specific impressions of how an employee in a particular job category should look. We also fail to consider that the applicant may have a reason for dressing a certain way. It is possible that at the applicant's former place of employment a casual style of dress was acceptable.

First impressions should play a role in your decision-making process, but not at the exclusion of all the other factors to be examined. Do not allow them to act as a substitute for judgment. Try not to form a complete impression until after you have conducted the interview. You may find that the applicant's attire or grooming is the only problem. The person's job skills may be superior to those of all other candidates. At this point you can talk to the applicant about the desired image of your organization. Then schedule a brief follow-up interview to see if your message was clearly received.

2. *Information from others.* An applicant who comes highly recommended by someone for whom you have high regard can elicit a positive response from you prior to the actual face-to-face meeting. On the other hand, someone you dislike may make a referral to you and thereby automatically create a negative bias toward the person being recommended. In both instances you are allowing yourself to be influenced by information from others. Instead of assessing the applicant on his or her own merits, you are assessing the person making the recommendation, thereby transferring your opinion from the referral source to the applicant. Like first impressions,

information from others does play a role in the decision-making process. Anything that might supplement the data on an application or résumé can be helpful, but it is premature to make an evaluation based on this highly subjective aspect of perception at this stage of the employment process.

3. *Single statements.* Suppose an applicant's response to one of your questions rubs you the wrong way. If you are not aware of the impact that a single statement can have, it could bother you to the extent that you eliminate the person from further consideration. This might occur even though the comment does not constitute a valid reason for rejection. You must be particularly careful if this should happen during the initial stage of the interview, when you are trying to put the applicant at ease and establish rapport. This is commonly accomplished through a few minutes of small talk (see Chapter 6). During this portion of the interview, you might comment about some political news that caught your eye in the morning newspaper. The applicant might then express his or her views on the subject, which happen to be contrary to yours. If you are not careful, you could allow this difference to influence your objectivity in assessing the applicant's job suitability. You will then have taken a single statement—one that is totally irrelevant to the decision-making process—and allowed it to affect your judgment.

Even single statements that *are* job-related must be weighed in relation to other qualifying factors. Keep in mind that it is usually a combination of factors that results in the rejection of a candidate.

4. *Nonverbal communication.* Nonverbal communication, commonly referred to as body language, is a vital aspect of the employment process. Often an interviewer can learn as much about an applicant through his or her nonverbal messages as can be learned from verbal ones. This topic will be additionally explored in Chapter 6. However, it is important at this point to recognize body language as one of the components of perception. Nonverbal messages that are misinterpreted by the interviewer can result in poor selection or rejection decisions. This usually occurs when body language is interpreted according to the interviewer's own gestures or expressions. For example, just because you have a tendency to avoid eye contact when you are hiding something does not mean that the applicant is avoiding your eyes for the same reason. It may very well be a sign that he or she is deep in thought.

Each of us has our own pattern of nonverbal expression, attributable to a combination of cultural and environmental factors. These factors influence such elements of body language as gesture, posture, touching, and the distance we maintain from one another. With regard to the latter, referred to as *proxemics,* our culture recognizes a distance of from two to five feet as being an appropriate distance between interviewer and applicant. A candidate from a culture that regards this as too much distance might immediately pull his or her chair up much closer to the interviewer. This might be interpreted as a violation of space or as an act of aggression or intimacy, leaving the interviewer with feelings of discomfort, hostility, or intimidation. Some interviewers may go so far as to move their chairs back or actually get up during instances of excessively close proximity.

Another aspect of nonverbal communication—*chronemics*—has to do with the amount of time that passes between verbal exchanges. In our culture we expect people to respond to our questions immediately. In other cultures people deliberately wait before answering. An applicant who does this might be perceived by his or her interviewer as being bored, inattentive, confused, or nervous.

Be careful not to draw conclusions too early in the interview process, based on an applicant's nonverbal messages. Allow time for the individual's patterns to emerge, and then relate these patterns to the other factors involved in making a selection.

5. *Ethnocentrism.* This is the final aspect of how our perception of others is formed. Ethnocentrism means that we use our values, standards, and beliefs to judge or evaluate others. Overall, this is a perfectly natural result of the cultural conditioning process that we are all exposed to. In our early years we are taught by well-intentioned parents, teachers, and religious leaders to think and act according to certain standards and values. At the age of five or six, few of us question the validity of these standards. Unfortunately, many people grow up believing that these are the only acceptable standards. This results in stereotypical thinking. Consequently, we assign specific attributes and roles to others, based on surface characteristics, such as sex, age, or ethnic origin.

Other factors come into play. For example, the interviewer sees from a résumé that the applicant graduated from the same college that he or she attended. On the basis of the interviewer's fond memories and high regard for the school, certain positive qualities about this candidate may erroneously be assumed. Or perhaps the résumé shows that the applicant attended Harvard. The interviewer's general assumptions about Harvard graduates could lead him or her to hastily conclude that the person would fit in.

Negative reactions may also occur. For instance, a candidate may presently be working for an organization from which your brother was recently fired. This negative association could bias your assessment of the applicant's job suitability. When perceptions are based on ethnocentric thinking, objectivity falls by the wayside. The chances for open, effective communication are blocked whenever an applicant's response or nonverbal messages deviate from the interviewer's preconceived notions. Keep in mind that ethnocentrism does not pertain to work-related standards established by the company; rather, it comes into play in the intangible areas of an individual's style and approach. It is in direct opposition to objectivity, which is an interviewer's no. 1 obligation.

The five aspects of perception—first impressions, information from others, single statements, body language, and ethnocentrism—together become a valuable tool in the preparation stage of interviewing. Briefly reviewing them just prior to meeting with an applicant can help you avoid hasty hiring or rejection decisions based on nonfactual, subjective factors.

Summary

This chapter has outlined the steps required to prepare for the face-to-face interview. In summary, they are as follows:

1. Conduct telephone screening interviews whenever possible.
2. Review the completed application form and/or résumé.
3. Distribute applicant data record forms to job candidates.
4. Block sufficient time before, during, and after the interview.
5. Establish an appropriate environment for the interview.
6. Be clear about your objectives.
7. Plan your basic questions.
8. Consider how the applicant may be feeling.
9. Consider the role of perception.

Taking the necessary time to go through this process will yield excellent results as you approach each interview prepared to select the best possible candidate.

5

Employment and the Law

By now you must be thinking, "Surely there can't be anything else that has to be done before conducting the face-to-face interview!" But there is: familiarization with equal employment opportunity (EEO) and affirmative action-related laws and regulations. These exist, generally speaking, to ensure all individuals the right to compete for all work opportunities without bias because of their race, color, religion, sex, national origin, age, or disability. Those of you who are not human resources professionals should not skip over this chapter, thinking that EEO and affirmative action are not your concern. Anyone having anything to do with any aspect of the employment process is expected to have a basic knowledge of EEO and affirmative action. Unintentional violations caused by ignorance of the law are not excusable.

The information in this book is current as of this writing. However, it is important that you keep abreast of developments in this ever-changing field. There are several ways to accomplish this: Read about recent EEO cases and related developments in human resources journals and newsletters; scan major daily newspapers for articles on recent changes in legislation; contact your local offices of the Equal Employment Opportunity Commission (EEOC) and the Deaprtment of Labor (DOL) for recent literature; review various legal newspapers and periodicals for summaries of recent court cases; network with people responsible for EEO and affirmative action in other organizations and exchange information; attend workshops and seminars on the subject; and consult with legal counsel experienced in matters of EEO and affirmative action.

The information contained herein is not intended to represent legal advice.

EEO Legislation and Affirmative Action: Categories of Discrimination

The following fair employment laws and categories of discrimination represent federal statutes, rules, and regulations. As previously mentioned, state laws may differ and should also be considered. Failure to comply with these laws could result in costly litigation. Readers are urged to consult with in-house or outside counsel in the event their organization is charged with discrimination.

Civil Rights Act of 1866

Many people are surprised to learn that employment-related laws have been around for about 125 years. One of the earliest and most significant pieces of legislation was the Civil Rights Act of 1866. The most relevant portion for today's employers is Section 1981, Title 42, which ensures all people the same "equal rights under the law . . . as is enjoyed by white citizens . . . to . . . make and enforce" contracts.

Essentially, this has been interpreted to mean that discrimination against nonwhites in the making of written or implied contracts relevant to hiring and promotions is illegal. This law was originally intended to support charges of race discrimination and was expanded in 1982 to include national origin discrimination. It applies to all employers regardless of the number of employees.

Over the years, this early civil rights act has been a significant weapon against employers in that it permits the person suing to seek punitive damages in addition to compensatory damages such as back pay. Moreover, it allows a jury trial.

It should be noted that while the awards for violation of this Act can be substantial, the claimant must establish intent to discriminate on the part of the employer. That is to say, it is necessary to prove that the employer deliberately denied an individual an opportunity for employment or promotion on the basis of his or her race or national origin. This is to be distinguished from establishing effect, which means that while one or more representatives of an organization did not intend to deny someone equal employment opportunity on the basis of his or her race, the effect of a certain employment practice, i.e., exclusively using employee referrals as a recruitment source, was discriminatory. It is usually more difficult to establish intent to discriminate than it is to show effect.

Civil Rights Act of 1964

This is probably the best known piece of civil rights legislation and the most widely used, in that it protects several classes of people and pertains to so many employment situations. Title VII of this Act prohibits discrimination on the basis of race, color, religion, sex, or national origin in all matters of employment, from recruitment through discharge. The criteria for coverage under Title VII includes any company doing business in the United States that has fifteen or more employees. Title VII does *not* regulate the employment practices of U.S. companies employing American citizens outside of the United States. Violations are monitored by the EEOC.

Violators of Title VII are generally required to "make whole"— this includes providing reinstatement, if relevant, and back pay. Jury trials are not allowed.

Plaintiffs in Title VII suits generally do not have to prove intent; rather, they may challenge apparently neutral employment policies that cause a discriminatory effect.

Employers will find it significant that many claimants sue for violations of both Section 1981 and Title VII.

The EEOC's 1980 guidelines on *sexual harassment* have become an important aspect of the Civil Rights Act of 1964. Defined as unwelcome sexual advances, requests for sexual favors, or other unwanted verbal or physical conduct of a sexual nature, sexual harassment is considered a violation of Title VII if submission to, or rejection of, such conduct is made a term or condition of employment; substantially interferes with a person's work performance; or creates an intimidating, hostile, or offensive working environment. Examples of such behavior include: verbal abuse, sexist remarks, dirty or sexual jokes, sexually suggestive cartoons, suggestive or insulting sounds, constant talk of sexual experiences, repeatedly asking an employee for a date, patting, leaning over or brushing up against someone, suggestive looks or gestures, leering, whistling, obscene gestures, pinching, and physical assaults. Men or women may be victims of sexual harassment; consequently members of both sexes may sue for violation of Title VII.

The EEOC guidelines state that employers are absolutely responsible for acts of sexual harassment if they are committed by a supervisor; if the acts are committed by rank and file employees or nonemployees, such as customers or vendors, employers are liable only if they knew or should have known about the situation and failed to take action.

Following the Civil Rights Act of 1964, acts of discrimination continued. The excuse most commonly offered by employers was that while they certainly did not intend to discriminate, they simply could not find women and minorities for their job openings. The result of this frequently repeated statement was a revamping of recruitment sources. Up to this point the most popular, cost-effective means of recruitment was word of mouth. The inherent problem with this method was that whenever there was an opening at a supervisory or managerial level—the level at which women and minorities were so few in number—the existing managers, predominately white males, spread the word among close friends and colleagues: other white males. Not surprisingly, the candidates referred were more white males. Therefore, the word-of-mouth system was inherently discriminatory when it was the only method of recruitment used. Recruitment sources were subsequently expanded to include many of those identified in Chapter 3.

Even after recruitment sources were expanded, discrimination continued. However, employers no longer claimed that they could not find women and minorities to hire. The problem, they now claimed, was that they could not find *qualified* women and minorities. A close examination of most educational and experiential requirements revealed unrealistic standards that were not necessary for the successful performance of the job. It was also true that because of the limited educational and employment opportunities afforded women and minorities, few individuals who fell into these two categories possessed the stipulated qualifications.

The result of this close examination of position qualifications was a revamping of job requirements. An employer could no longer arbitrarily decide that a degree was necessary for a given position. It now had to be shown that a person without a degree could not do the job. Individuals with an equivalent combination of education and experience had to be considered. Likewise, an arbitrarily set number of years of prior experience was eliminated and replaced with more realistic requirements.

Affirmative Action

Because Title VII did not immediately have the desired effect against discrimination, a series of Executive Orders was issued by the federal government, first by President Kennedy in 1961, and later strengthened by President Johnson in 1965. The best known, E.O. 11246, contained an EEO clause that required companies doing business with the federal government to make a series of commitments. Three of the most significant commitments with regard to employment are as follows:

1. The first obligation concerns nondiscrimination in employment. When a company does business with the federal government, it is on the basis of a contract; should the company discriminate in employment practices, it would effectively be violating its contract. The ramifications of this could be severe, including contract cancellation and debarment, meaning that the government would no longer do business with that company.

2. The second obligation of a company doing business with the federal government is to obey the rules and regulations of the Department of Labor. This agreement extends to allowing periodic checking of its premises by labor representatives to ensure compliance with the other two commitments listed here.

3. The third obligation has to do with a company attaining its affirmative action goals. This commits a company to hiring, training, and promoting a certain percentage of qualified women and minorities. The actual percentage is based on the number of women and minorities in a specific geographic location, referred to as a Standard Metropolitan Statistical Area (SMSA). Employers should contact the Office of Federal Contract Compliance Programs (OFCCP) to determine the most recent requirements for separate affirmative action plans pertaining to different establishments. The OFCCP has also recently published a new Compliance Manual that outlines the specific steps its field staff follow in reviewing and monitoring affirmative action plans.

Affirmative action is a way of ensuring minimal compliance with EEO. Franklin A. Thomas, the first black president of the Ford Foundation, said in a speech he gave at the 1982 Granada Lecture Series in England:

> Affirmative Action is really a way to introduce us to each other. . . . One day our descendents will think it incredible that we once made so much out of such small things as the amount of melanin in our skin or the shape of our eyes or the single element of gender in the complex human being.

Increasing numbers of employers are adopting formal, written affirmative action plans, even where these are not required, in an effort to correct racial and sexual imbalances in the workplace. In the absence of a written plan, it is more difficult to provide credible evidence that the employer is making a bona fide effort to correct real or perceived problems. To assist employers with the process of establishing a plan, the OFCCP has issued a list of eight basic factors for them to consider:

1. What percentage of the population in the SMSA is composed of minority groups?
2. What percentage of minority and women workers in the SMSA are unemployed?
3. What percentage of the SMSA's civilian work force is composed of minorities and women?
4. What percentage of the minority and women workers in the SMSA have the required skills for available jobs?
5. What percentage of minority and women workers in a "reasonable recruitment area"—larger than the local labor market—have the required skills for available jobs, especially higher-paying ones?
6. What percentage of minority and women workers already within the company are promotable or transferrable to various job groups?
7. What are the minority and female enrollments at local educational institutions that might provide skilled workers for the company?
8. What percentage of women and minority employees are enrolled in the company's own training courses?

Based upon these considerations, a written affirmative action plan may be prepared, encompassing seven key elements: a policy statement; internal dissemination of the policy; external dissemination of the policy; positive utilization efforts; a review of internal procedures; implementation, development, and execution; and the establishment of a complaint procedure.

In addition, any plan should be temporary only, to be abandoned once workplace equity has been achieved.

Having a written plan and a proven commitment to achieving its goals is often viewed as an important effort in precluding discriminatory practices. Some cases involving employment discrimination do not develop beyond the initial stages because of the existence of such a demonstrated effort. The plan must actually be practiced, however, and not merely written.

The Equal Pay Act of 1963

The Equal Pay Act of 1963 requires equal pay for men and women performing substantially equal work. The work must be of comparable skill, effort, and responsibility, performed under similar working conditions. This law protects women only. Others who felt they were being discriminated against in matters of pay would claim violation of Title VII of the Civil Rights Act of 1964. Criteria for coverage is at least two employees.

Unequal pay for equal work is permitted in certain instances, for example, when wage differences are based on superior educational credentials or extensive prior experience. It should be noted that coverage applies to all aspects of the employment process including starting salaries, annual increases, and promotions.

Despite this law, the federal Department of Labor reports that the average pay of women nationwide is still only about 70 percent that of men's. Experts contend that this is due to several factors: More women than men work at lower-level jobs; more men than women enjoy seniority at work, since many women interrupt their careers to raise children; and the stereotype of men being their families' primary wage earner still persists, thereby leading many employers to believe that men should be paid more than women.

An important issue related to equal pay is *comparable worth.* Several states have implemented programs for comparable worth pay whereby employers are required to compare completely different job categories. Those held predominately by women (e.g., nursing and secretarial) must be compared with those occupied predominately by men (e.g., truck driving and warehouse work). Point systems determine the level of skill involved in the job, as well as the economic value of each position. If the female-dominated jobs are deemed comparable, pay adjustments are made to reduce the difference in wages.

The important distinction between comparable worth and equal pay is that in order to claim violation of the Equal Pay Act identical job classifications must be compared. Therefore, if a woman accountant believes that she is not receiving an equal rate of pay to that of her male counterpart—a male accountant who is performing substantially equal work—she could conceivably have sufficient cause to claim violation of the Equal Pay Act. On the other hand, comparable worth requests or argues for comparison between different job categories. For example, if a clerk-typist believes that her work is of comparable worth to her employer as that of a male custodian working for the same employer, she might sue on the basis of sex discrimination. Since there is presently no federal law regarding comparable worth, she would sue for violation of Title VII of the Civil Rights Act of 1964.

Companies are urged to voluntarily assess their hiring practices and work toward minimizing specifically female or male categories.

The Age Discrimination in Employment Act of 1967

The federal Age Discrimination in Employment Act of 1967 (ADEA), as originally written, protected workers from ages 40 to 70. A 1978 amendment permitted jury trials, which gave claimants more power. Effective January 1, 1987, Congress unanimously approved, and President Reagan signed into law, H.R. 4154, amending the ADEA by extending the protection of the Act to workers beyond the age of 70. Now, most private sector and federal, state, and local government employees cannot be discriminated against in matters of pay, benefits, or continued employment regardless of how old they may be. The law also pertains to employees of employment agencies and labor organizations, as well as to U.S. citizens working outside the United States. A seven-year exemption for state and local government employers whose employees deal with public safety was granted by Congress, pertaining to such job classifications as police officers, firefighters, and prison guards.

The ADEA also contains an exemption for bona fide executives or high-level policymakers who may be retired as early as age 65, if they have been employed at that level for the preceding two years. To be exempt, executives or policymakers must also be eligible to receive immediate aggregate annual retirement benefits of at least $44,000.

The EEOC, which administers the ADEA, has provided the following guidelines for defining bona fide executives:

- Those who exercise discretionary powers on a regular basis
- Those who direct the work of at least two employees on a regular basis
- Those whose primary duty is the management of an entire organization, department, or subdivision
- Those who are authorized to hire, promote, and terminate employees
- Those who devote less than 20 percent of their time to activities other than those described above

Each of these elements must be met in order for the exemption to be valid.

High-level policymakers are defined as those "who have little or no line authority, but whose position and responsibility are such that they play a significant role in the development of corporate policy and effectively recommend the implementation thereof."

The general criterion for coverage under this Act is employment of at least twenty employees. Labor organizations employing at least twenty-five workers are required to comply. Part-time employees are included when calculating coverage.

Age discrimination is currently the fastest-growing workplace bias charge. According to *Fair Employment Practices: Summary of Latest Developments* (BNA), December 1987, there were almost twenty-seven thousand age discrimination complaints in 1986—more than twice as many as there were in 1980.

The following guidelines should help you avoid age discrimination suits:

- Language in personnel policies and procedures manuals, employee handbooks, orientation publications, and any other company-issued written material should be age-neutral.
- Employment advertisements should avoid any reference to age-related criteria, since age is rarely a legitimate qualification.
- Employment application forms should not require the applicant to provide his or her date of birth.
- Some state laws prohibit listing of graduation dates on the application form.
- Interviewers should ask only age-neutral questions, except in those rare instances where age is considered a bona fide occupational qualification (BFOQ). For example, formal apprenticeship programs may limit participation to individuals between the ages of 20 to 25. However, this practice is being challenged by groups such as the American Association of Retired Persons (AARP). Age is also considered a BFOQ for police officers, firefighters, and airplane pilots.
- Apply the same salary guidelines when hiring older workers as you would when hiring anyone else. Do not try to justify a lower salary because an older worker is receiving a pension or Social Security.
- Do not deny older workers training, promotional, or transfer opportunities.
- Make certain that poor work performance, supported by comprehensive written performance appraisals and documentation or other "good cause"—and not age—is the basis for all disciplinary action, including termination.

The Rehabilitation Act of 1973

This law protects qualified handicapped individuals against discrimination in employment. The term *qualified* means capable of performing the essential functions of the job. The term *handicapped,* now more preferably replaced by *disabled,* is defined by the Act as "any person who (1) has a physical or mental impairment that substantially limits one or more of the person's major life activities, (2) has a record of such an impairment, or (3) is regarded as having such an impairment."

Included in this definition are drug addicts and alcoholics. However, this Act does not pertain to current abusers whose drug or alcohol use prevents them from performing the duties of the job in question or whose employment, by reason of such drug or alcohol abuse, would constitute a direct threat to the property or safety of others.

Victims of acquired immune deficiency syndrome (AIDS) and AIDS-related conditions may also be considered disabled. Because of particular concerns surrounding this illness, AIDS will be discussed later in this chapter as a separate topic.

The Act applies to the federal government, federal contractors, or recipients of federal funding. Section 501 of the Act requires affirmative action in the hiring and promoting of qualified handicapped or disabled individuals. Section 503 stipulates that employers who hold contracts with the federal government for dollar amounts in excess of $2,500 must take affirmative action to employ qualified disabled individuals. A written affirmative action plan is required of employers with fifty or more employees and more than $50,000 in contracts. And, according to Section 504, employers receiving federal financial assistance are obligated to take affirmative action in hiring and promoting qualified disabled individuals.

An employer's obligation with regard to a qualified disabled applicant or employee is to make a reasonable effort to accommodate the person's disability, as long as such accommodation does not create an undue hardship. Undue hardships are determined by considering such factors as the size of the organization, the type of work involved, and the nature and cost of such accommodation. For example, job restructuring might be required if the disabled person can perform the essential functions of the job, but requires assistance with one remaining aspect of the work, such as heavy lifting. Other aspects of job restructuring may be developing new career paths for disabled individuals, relocation, modification of procedures, providing readers or interpreters, or modification of equipment. Any adjustment that does not create an undue hardship may be required.

Alterations to facilities (e.g., the installation of ramps, special parking, and new means of access to buildings) may also be required. Compliance with the *American National Standard Specifications for Making Buildings and Facilities Accessible to, and Usable by, the Physically Handicapped,* published by the American National Standards Institute, Incorporated, is required.

Many resources are available to assist in modifying facilities and equipment to accommodate disabled individuals. State vocational rehabilitation agencies are a good place to start, as is the Job Accommodation Network (1-800-526-7234). In addition, employers may want to contact their local Governor's Committee on Employment of People with Disabilities.

With regard to positions requiring tests (see Chapter 8 for detailed information), generally speaking, if the disabled applicant cannot take a required test, he or she must be allowed to demonstrate the ability to perform the essential functions of the job through alternative means.

Also relevant to the subject of the disabled is the issue of preemployment physicals. Generally speaking, if your organization has been conducting preemployment physicals as a matter of past practice, then there is no problem with continuing to do so. However, if this has not been the case and you want to start requiring physicals, you must prove necessity. In addition, physicals must be required for everyone; you cannot require physicals only for the disabled. Furthermore, the physical cannot be the first step in the application process. Either it may be the last factor evaluated or it may be required after a conditional job offer is made.

Determining an individual's physical fitness for work must be done by a qualified physician. Any negative findings should be phrased in specific, objective, job-related terms. The results of the examination must be shared with the applicant. If the applicant can do the job that he or she is interviewing for, but you fear that employment will aggravate an existing condition, you are on weak ground if you deny that person employment. You are on stronger ground if the condition is degenerative. If the applicant can do the present job but can probably not do the next job in the promotional chain, you may be able to deny employment if you can document that promotion is the normal pattern in a particular job family.

The Americans with Disabilities Act of 1990

In July 1990, President George Bush signed landmark legislation prohibiting all employers, including privately owned businesses and local governments, from discriminating against disabled employees or job candidates. Exempt are the federal government, government-owned corporations, Indian tribes, and bona fide tax-exempt private membership clubs. Religious organizations will be permitted to give preference to the employment of their own members. In addition, the law requires every kind of establishment to be accessible to the disabled and usable by them. This legislation, entitled the Americans with Disabilities Act of 1990 (ADA), pertains to employers with fifteen or more employees and is monitored by the EEOC. The Act affects an estimated 43 million Americans who have some type of disability.

Title I of the Act prohibits any employment practice that may prevent a disabled person from work or work advancement. Such employment practices typically include interviews inquiring about the existence of a disability as opposed to inquiring about a person's ability to perform a given job, and assigning disabled workers to positions that lack opportunities for growth or promotion.

In the ADA, the term *disability* is defined the same as in the Rehabilitation Act of 1973, that is, as a physical or mental impairment that substantially limits an individual's major life activities. The definition also encompasses the history of an impairment and the perception of having an impairment. Examples of disabilities that are covered include: impaired sight and hearing; muscular conditions such as cerebral palsy and muscular dystrophy; diseases like cancer, AIDS, diabetes, and epilepsy; cosmetic disfigurements; emotional disturbances; exceptionally low IQs; stuttering; smoke sensitivity; tension; and depression. In fact, there are over one thousand different impairments that are covered by this Act. It is important to stress that individuals may have certain disabilities, and are therefore protected by the ADA, even though they may not be limited in performing significant life activities. On the other hand, current users of illegal drugs or alcohol are not protected by the ADA. Also, people with contagious diseases or who pose a direct threat to the health or safety of others are not covered by this Act. In addition, ADA specifically excludes homosexuals, bisexuals, transvestites, transsexuals, individuals with sexual behavior disorders, compulsive gamblers, kleptomaniacs, and pyromaniacs.

Under the ADA, employers are required to make a "reasonable accommodation" for those applicants or employees who can perform the "essential" functions of the job with reasonable proficiency. Reasonable accommodation includes: job restructuring, allowing part-time or modified work schedules, reassignments, hiring additional workers to aid disabled employees in the performance of their jobs, and installing new equipment or modifying existing equipment. Such equipment or modification might include adaptive computer hardware, Braille devices or audio recordings (for the visually impaired), and amplifiers or hearing aids (for the hearing impaired). An accommodation is considered unreasonable only in those instances where undue physical or financial hardship is placed on the employer. Such hardship is determined according to the overall size of an organization in relation to the size of its work force, its budget, and the nature and cost of the required accommodation. Generally speaking, large organizations are expected to make greater accommodations than are small or mid-sized companies.

Essential functions are loosely defined as tasks that are "fundamental and not marginal," according to the Senate report on the ADA. Employers are encouraged to conduct a detailed review of each job to determine just which functions are essential. This should include an assessment of the amount of time devoted to each task.

The ADA also refers to what an employer may require in the way of preemployment physical examinations. According to the Act, employers cannot single out disabled individuals for medical exams. If they are shown to be job-related and consistent with the requirements of the business, medical examinations are permitted after an offer of employment has been made to a job applicant, prior to the start of work. In this instance, an employer may condition an offer of employment on the basis of the results of the examination.

Title III of the Act prohibits discrimination against the disabled by private businesses that provide public accommodations. This includes: hotels, restaurants, theaters, stadiums, convention centers, museums, libraries, schools, recreational facilities, all sales and service establishments, banks, hospitals, and other medical facilities and law offices. Unlike Title I, which takes an organization's size into consideration when determining hardship, Title III requires even the smallest business to accommodate disabled customers, clients, and patients. This means removing all architectural and communication barriers. To do so, businesses might have to install ramps, widen doorways, modify rest rooms, install elevators, and provide additional help and services as needed by anyone disabled.

Businesses failing to comply with the ADA's requirements face civil penalties of up to $50,000 for the first violation and $100,000 for subsequent infractions. In addition, the ADA provides for equitable remedies, including job reinstatement, back pay, and payment of attorneys' fees. Moreover, compensatory and punitive damages and the right to jury trials may also be available.

The ADA's employment discrimination provisions will go into effect on July 26, 1992. At that time employers with twenty-five or more employees will be covered. Employers with fifteen or more workers will be expected to comply by July 26, 1994. For assistance with compliance employers may contact several resources, including: the Job Accommodation Network (1-800-526-7234), the United States Architectural and Transportation Barriers Compliance Board (1-800-USA-ABLE), Mainstream, Inc. (202-898-1400), Industry-Labor Council on Employment and Disability (516-747-6323), and the President's Committee on Employment of People with Disabilities (202-653-5044).

AIDS

As the number of AIDS cases increases, so does the number of employment conflicts involving workers having or suspected of having this disease. Testing individuals for AIDS or AIDS-related ailments will be covered in Chapter 8. The legal considerations relating to AIDS in employment are as follows: Individuals with AIDS are protected by federal, state, and local legislation governing discrimination against disabled employees. As previously discussed, federal protection is provided by the Rehabilitation Act of 1973 and the Americans with Disabilities Act of 1990. In addition, in accordance with Section 510 of the Employee Retirement Income Security Act of 1974 (ERISA), it is unlawful for any person to discipline, suspend, or discharge a plan participant for exercising his or her rights according to the provisions of any employee benefits plan. This includes employees with AIDS. Hence, ERISA prohibits employers from discharging AIDS employees for the purpose of denying them earned benefits. Also, the Comprehensive Omnibus Benefits and Retirement Act (COBRA) extends an AIDS-afflicted employee's eligibility for continued medical benefits to eighteen months after termination. Furthermore, because it is generally accepted that AIDS is not transmitted by casual contact and thus does not constitute a risk in the workplace, the employment of a person with AIDS does not violate the Occupational Safety and Health Act (OSHA).

Accordingly, employers should treat employees infected with AIDS the same as employees suffering from other serious illnesses.

As with other disabilities, employers are required to make reasonable accommodations for AIDS-afflicted employees. In addition, these individuals should be permitted to continue working as long as they are able to perform their jobs without adversely affecting the health or safety of others in the workplace.

While the controversy over how to deal with AIDS-afflicted employees continues, there is little disagreement that more education is needed regarding this disease. A number of educational programs have been designed specifically to help employers deal with the issue of AIDS in the workplace. For example, the Professional Development Program of Rockefeller College, State University of New York (518-442-5731), has developed an AIDS Education Project that provides organizations with custom-made programs on AIDS and its impact on the workplace. The San Francisco AIDS Foundation (415-864-4376) can also offer assistance with its video and management guide entitled "The Next Step," a package that addresses problems occurring after AIDS policies have been implemented. In addition, an abundance of AIDS information is available in *Learning AIDS*, a directory of over seventeen hundred books, brochures, films, and programs, published by the American Foundation for AIDS Research.

The Vietnam Era Veterans Readjustment Act of 1974

This Act protects veterans who either incurred a disability or had a disability aggravated in the line of duty against employment discrimination. Under this Act, a "veteran of the Vietnam era" means a person who served more than 180 days of active duty, any part of which was during the period of August 5, 1964, through May 7, 1975, and who was discharged with other than a dishonorable discharge or released because of a service-connected disability. "Special disabled veteran" means a veteran entitled to compensation for a disability rated at 30 percent or more, or rated at 10 percent or 20 percent if determined to be a serious employment disability, or a person discharged or released from active duty because of a service-connected disability.

All companies doing business with the government and holding contracts in excess of $10,000 are required to take affirmative action to employ and promote qualified veterans of the Vietnam era and special disabled veterans. Depending on the nature and extent of the disability, reasonable accommodations might be required.

Pregnancy Discrimination Act of 1978

The Pregnancy Discrimination Act (PDA) of 1978 recognizes pregnancy as a temporary disability and prohibits sex discrimination based on pregnancy, childbirth, or related conditions. Women must be permitted to work as long as they are able to perform the essential functions of their current job. Likewise, pregnant applicants may not be denied equal employment opportunities if they are able to perform the essential functions of the available job. The Act prohibits mandatory pregnancy leaves of any duration unless a similar requirement is imposed on male employees with disabilities impairing their job performance. If an employer insists on establishing special rules for pregnancy, such rules must be dictated by business necessity or related to issues of safety or health. The PDA further stipulates that an employer must permit an employee on maternity leave to return to her job on the same basis as other employees returning to work following an illness or disability leave.

The provisions of the PDA seem fairly straightforward; however, a U.S. Supreme Court ruling in 1987 may have broadened its intent somewhat. In January of that year, the Supreme Court upheld a California amendment to its Fair Employment and Housing Act requiring all employers covered by Title VII of the Civil Rights Act of 1964 to provide up to four months of pregnancy leave. The Supreme Court determined that this state law did not conflict with the PDA requirement of equal treatment for pregnancy-related disabilities and any other disability, even though the California statute seemingly requires preferential treatment of pregnancy leave by mandating up to four months' leave. The Court supported its decision by stating that the California statute does not preclude employers from extending the same benefits accorded pregnancy to all other employees for all other disabilities.

As of this writing, twenty-two states, in addition to California, have enacted some form of pregnancy leave statute. They are Colorado, Connecticut, Hawaii, Iowa, Kansas, Kentucky, Louisiana, Maine, Maryland, Massachusetts, Minnesota, Montana, Nevada, New Hampshire, New York, Ohio, Oregon, Rhode Island, Tennessee, Texas, Washington, and Wisconsin. These statutes cover several child-related issues, including parental leave, adoption, mandatory leave, health benefits, and reinstatement policies. It should be noted that when a state law expands upon a federal law but is consistent with its intent, there is no conflict and state law controls.

An important concern related to pregnancy discrimination has to do with fetal protection. Whether or not an employer may bar women of childbearing age from jobs that involve toxic substances, X rays, lead exposure, or the like is an issue that has been addressed by the EEOC in a set of fetal protection guidelines. The guidelines require employers to first determine if there is substantial risk of harm to an employee's potential offspring from exposure to a workplace hazard. To accomplish this, employers should rely on scientific evidence of the risk of fetal or reproductive harm from exposure and the minimum period of time required for exposure to cause harm. Then, the employer should assess its policy and determine whether there is a reasonable alternative that would be less discriminatory than exclusion, such as a temporary transfer to another nontoxic job or wearing a personal protection device.

The matter of fetal protection extended beyond EEOC guidelines to the Supreme Court when the Court agreed to decide a case challenging the "fetal protection policy" of Johnson Controls Inc., a Milwaukee-based manufacturer of car batteries. The company's policy bars women under the age of 70 who cannot provide medical proof of infertility from work involving exposure to lead regardless of their childbearing plans. This includes most of the company's production jobs, including many that are high-paying. Proponents of the policy maintain that its purpose is to protect the health of the unborn child. Opponents, however, argue that the policy is sexually discriminatory because absorption of lead by the body is a known hazard to all adults as well as to fetuses, and both men and women should be protected. If the Supreme Court accepts this argument, this case may have occupational health and safety consequences beyond fetal protection.

International Union v. Johnson Controls reached the Supreme Court after the United States Court of Appeals for the Seventh Circuit in Chicago upheld Johnson's policy. In its 7-to-4 decision, the Court of Appeals found that even though the company's prohibition singles out women for special treatment, such treatment is justified as a business necessity and is "well reasoned and scientifically documented" given the known dangers of exposure to lead. The United Automobile Workers, which represents many of Johnson's employees, is seeking a reversal of this decision.

The Supreme Court ruling in this case, which is expected by July 1991, could affect as many as 20 million women workers in circumstances similar to the Johnson situation. Until then, employers are encouraged to follow the EEOC's guidelines, except in those states (Illinois, Wisconsin, and Indiana) where lower court rulings currently prevail.

Religious Discrimination

In regard to religious observances in employment, the EEOC guidelines define religion and religious practices as "moral or ethical beliefs as to what is right and wrong which are sincerely held with the strength of traditional religious views. . . ." In 1972 Congress amended that portion of Title VII of the Civil Rights Act of 1964 pertaining to religion in the workplace by expanding the definition to include an individual's right to "all aspects of religious observance and practice, as well as belief, unless an employer demonstrates that he is unable to reasonably accommodate an employee's or prospective employee's religious observance or practice without undue hardship on the conduct of the employer's business." It is generally accepted that the laws and guidelines prohibiting religious discrimination also protect nonreligious employees from being discriminated against or forced to participate in religious activities.

Essentially, this means that applicants or employees need not be affiliated with large, popular, well-known religious sects in order to justify a claim that some aspect of a company's employment practice interferes with their religious beliefs. Moreover, the 1972 amendments place the burden on employers to prove their inability to reasonably accommodate an individual's religious practices.

The issue of religion may come up during the course of an employment interview, often in conjunction with a requirement to work on Saturdays or Sundays. All preemployment inquiries concerning availability on these or any other days must be job-related, dictated by business necessity, and worded in such a way that availability is stressed, as opposed to specific questions about religion. Therefore, if a given position requires working on Sunday, you might phrase your inquiry in this way: "This job requires working on Sunday. Is there any reason you would not be able to meet this job requirement?" Or, "Will you be able to meet this job requirement?" If the applicant responds by saying, "No, I cannot work on Sunday, because of my religion," then a number of things should follow. First, it is recommended that you confirm his or her response by repeating your original question: "Are you then saying that you cannot meet one of the requirements of this job, which is to work on Sundays?" When the applicant repeats his or her response, document this as part of your interviewing notes by writing in very simple and clear language, "Applicant is unable to meet the job requirement of working on Sundays." Do not make any reference to the reason given, which is religion.

Your next step is to try and make a reasonable effort to

accommodate this person's religious practices as long as they do not create an undue hardship for you, the employer. Reasonable efforts might include finding voluntary substitutes for the period of time when this individual would be unavailable; flexible scheduling of hours so that his or her religion could be accommodated; consideration of another position with comparable salary, responsibilities, working conditions, location, and growth opportunities; or perhaps hiring a temporary employee to cover the person's duties during the time when he or she would be unable to work. As with accommodating the disabled, just what would constitute an undue hardship depends on a number of factors, including prohibitive cost. Generally speaking, the larger the company, the more you are expected to be able to spend for accommodation. Undue hardship must be provable. The size of your organization is again taken into consideration—the larger the company, the harder it is to prove hardship in terms of time, resources, and money.

In instances where employees able to meet a job's work schedule at the time of hire may, upon subsequently becoming involved with a particular religious practice, no longer be able to do so, good-faith attempts should be made by the employer to accommodate religious-based scheduling requests such as time off to observe the Sabbath or prayer breaks. Such accommodation might include adjusting work schedules, implementing flexible working hours, or responding to other viable employee suggestions that will integrate the employee's religious needs with the needs of the company.

Certain work assignments might also require some adjustment if an employee raises a religious objection. For example, a foreign work assignment to a country whose prevailing religious practices conflict with the beliefs of an individual might be the basis for that individual's request to work at a different location. Every effort should be made to accommodate such a request.

Balancing an employee's religious beliefs with an organization's dress and grooming practices may also become an issue. When the safety of the employee or others is at stake, the employee may be required to conform to company policy in spite of any religious convictions. If, on the other hand, safety is not a factor, the employer should make a reasonable effort to accommodate religious-based attire and grooming.

In addition to work schedules, assignments, and attire, union membership is another variable in the context of religious beliefs. As long as an employee's religion meets the EEOC definition cited above, he or she may refuse to join a union or pay union dues. In such instances, the employee may be exempted from union membership; however, he or she may be required to donate to a charitable fund a sum equal to the union dues.

Religion and work should be kept separate, meaning that employers have the right to require "quiet and unobtrusive" observance.

National Origin Discrimination and the Immigration Reform and Control Act of 1986

The EEOC's "Guidelines on Discrimination Because of National Origin" preclude denial of equal employment opportunity because of an individual's ancestry; place of origin; or physical, cultural, or linguistic characteristics. There are four main areas of concern pertaining to employment:

1. Citizenship requirements may not be valid if they have the purpose or effect of discrimination on the basis of national origin.
2. Selection criteria that appear to be neutral on first glance may have an adverse impact on certain national groups.
3. Speak-English-only rules may be considered discriminatory when applied at all times.
4. Ethnic slurs may be considered national origin discrimination and must not be tolerated.

Related to the issue of national origin discrimination is the Immigration Reform and Control Act of 1986 (IRCA). This Act requires employers to certify that all employees hired after November 6, 1986, are eligible to work in the United States. Each employee's identity must also be verified. This may be accomplished by examining certain documents and then completing the I-9 form. Some of the documents that establish both identity and employment eligibility are a U.S. passport, certificate of U.S. citizenship or naturalization, alien-registration receipt card ("green card"), and temporary-resident card. If the applicant does not have a single document that satisfies both needs, he or she must produce a document establishing identity, such as a driver's license, in addition to a document establishing employment eligibility, such as a Social Security card or a birth certificate. What constitutes acceptable documents are defined by the Immigration and Naturalization Service (INS). Currently, seventeen different documents may be used.

The required documents must be produced within three days

of a new hire's starting date. If the documents are unavailable, the employee is entitled to an extension of twenty-one business days from the date of hire to obtain them.

Failure to properly complete and maintain the I-9 forms may result in a warning letter for a minor violation, to fines ranging from $100 to $1,000 per employee. Penalties for hiring unauthorized employees range from $250 to $2,000 per unauthorized worker for a first violation, and $2,000 to $5,000 per unauthorized worker for a second violation. Subsequent violations range from $3,000 to $10,000 for each unauthorized employee hired. Where a pattern of intentional hiring of undocumented workers is established, penalties may include six months in prison.

According to the General Accounting Office, the investigative and auditing segment of Congress, many of the documents that may be used to verify American citizenship or alien-authorization to work in the United States are being counterfeited. This has reportedly produced widespread hiring discrimination against people with a "foreign appearance or accent." Because of this, the possibility of reducing the number of documents proving worker eligibility from seventeen to perhaps two or three and issuing more secure versions of them has been suggested. In addition, creating a simpler, more secure method of identification, a "national I.D. card," has been proposed. Proponents of such a document believe that it would make it easier for employers to verify the eligibility of job applicants and consequently reduce hiring discrimination. Opponents maintain that a national I.D. card would violate individual privacy rights.

The question of whether it is legal to hire a U.S. citizen over an equally qualified authorized alien is frequently asked. The answer, according to the INS, is "On an individual basis, the employer may prefer a United States citizen or national over an equally qualified alien." This is not to say, however, that bias against qualified aliens may be practiced with impunity or that charges of national origin discrimination may not result if a hiring decision is based on factors other than job qualifications. The U.S. Justice Department has an Office of Special Counsel for Immigration Related Unfair Employment Practices that handles charges of discrimination on the basis of national origin or citizenship status. The EEOC also has jurisdiction over some cases.

Additional information regarding IRCA and related issues may be obtained by contacting the INS hot line at 1-800-777-7700. The Office of Special Counsel for Immigration Related Unfair Employment Practices may be reached by calling 1-800-255-7688.

The Employee Polygraph Protection Act

Effective December 27, 1988, an employer's right to use lie detectors in various preemployment and postemployment situations is strictly limited by the Employee Polygraph Protection Act. The specifics of the Act, the few exceptions to it, and the penalties for employers who violate the Act are discussed in detail in Chapter 8 in the section "Polygraph Tests."

Reverse Discrimination

Charges of reverse discrimination by nonminorities are usually brought by white males, who maintain that they have been denied equal employment opportunities because of favoritism shown to minorities and women. Such claims are often the result of affirmative action plans that inherently limit employment, promotional, and training opportunities for nonminorities.

Consider, for example, the landmark case of *Regents of the University of California v. Bakke* (1978). Allan Bakke, a white male, sued after he was denied admission to a University of California medical school because sixteen of the one hundred available openings were set aside for minorities. In a 5-to-4 decision, the Court ordered Bakke admitted, stating that while it was appropriate for the school to take steps toward ethnic diversity, the numerical quota was too rigid.

Other U.S. Supreme Court rulings have addressed the issue of reverse discrimination in affirmative action hiring. In *Wygant v. Jackson* (1986), by a 5-to-4 vote, the Court held unconstitutional a negotiated labor contract that sought to preserve recent gains in the hiring of minority teachers in Michigan by requiring the layoff of white teachers with more seniority.

Employers are, however, afforded a certain degree of protection against charges of reverse discrimination by the EEOC. According to 1979 guidelines, employers who can demonstrate that they have conducted a reasonable self-analysis and have, accordingly, developed a sound basis for concluding that affirmative action is appropriate may be immunized from reverse discrimination complaints filed with that agency.

The Civil Rights Act of 1990

On October 22, 1990, President George Bush vetoed the Civil Rights Act of 1990, a proposed law that would have expanded Title

VII of the Civil Rights Act of 1964 by allowing jury trials, compensatory damages, and punitive damages for intentional discrimination. Employers would also have been liable for a greater amount of attorney and witness fees. Title VII remedies are currently limited to make-whole remedies such as back pay, reinstatement, and some attorneys' fees. If the Act had been passed, applicants and employees could have established that an organization's employment practices, as a whole, caused a disparate impact on women and minorities by showing statistical evidence that the work force did not match their availability in the community. A claimant could also have challenged the discriminatory impact of a group of employment practices, requiring the employer prove that each practice did not cause the impact. Currently, to establish unlawful discrimination, a claimant must identify a particular employment practice and show that there is a "causal connection" between that practice and a lower-than-average percentage of minorities and women employed. Employers must then respond by demonstrating that the employment practice is necessary.

The Senate passed the bill in July 1990; two weeks later, the House of Representatives passed a somewhat modified version of the bill. Revisions included a statement that "Nothing in this act should be construed to require an employer to adopt . . . quotas" as a basis for hiring, and a limit was set of $150,000 for punitive damages required of companies with fewer than one hundred employees. In spite of the fact that the bill was ultimately vetoed, supporters are confident that it will be reintroduced and voted into law in the near future.

The Uniform Employment Termination Act

The Uniform Employment Termination Act (UETA) is, as of this writing, a proposal likely to be voted on by the National Conference of Commissioners on Uniform State Laws in August 1991, at the earliest. After that, it would be up to each individual state's legislatures to adopt the proposal on a state-by-state basis. Although it will clearly be some time before the details of the Act are finalized, employers should begin to familiarize themselves with its content and understand its ramifications.

Essentially, the Act would allow workers and employers to create contracts at the time of hire; these contracts would give employers the right to terminate, at any time without cause, a worker's employment, without incurring legal liability. The Act would also establish severance pay obligations on the part of the employer. This means that employers will have the right to terminate an employee without good cause, but only if there is a written employment agreement, signed by both the employer and the employee. Instances of at-will termination include the elimination of a position, retirement, and an employee quitting a job because of unacceptable conditions set by his or her employer. What would happen in instances of economic layoffs is unclear. When an employee is terminated without cause, employers must provide for severance pay tied in with the worker's number of years of service according to the following scale:

Number of Years of Service	Amount of Severance Pay
Less than one	None
One through five	One month's pay for each full year of employment after the first year
Six to sixteen	An additional one-and-one-half months' pay for each full year of employment from the sixth year on
More than sixteen	An additional two months' pay for each full year of employment from the sixteenth year on

The maximum total severance pay under the proposal is four years' wages. Calculation of the amount due will be based on the wage level in place at the time of termination, including the value of any fringe benefits, such as vacation, medical insurance, pension, and sick leave. Employees must have worked an average of twenty hours a week during the six months prior to termination to qualify.

For workers who do not have a written contract allowing for termination-at-will, discharge for cause only will be permitted. This would include instances of theft, fighting on the job, destruction of company property, alcohol or drug abuse, insubordination, excessive absenteeism or tardiness, incompetence, or negligence. In such instances, employers should follow their organizations' progressive steps of discipline, which might result in termination.

The Impact of EEO and Affirmative Action on the Employment Process

It is important to understand just how all of these EEO and affirmative action laws affect recruitment, hiring, and selection. As the employer you have the right to select whomever you believe is best qualified to perform the duties and responsibilities of a given job.

You are not required to select the *most* qualified person; rather, you are required to select someone who meets the minimum requirements of the job. Your responsibility does not end there, however; other factors must be considered. First, make certain that you are not denying anyone equal employment opportunity, either inadvertently or because of personal bias. Second, check your employment practices for possible systemic discrimination. Third, make certain that your requirements are job-related and not arbitrarily set. Finally, be aware of your organization's affirmative action goals and take them into consideration when weighing the qualifications of women and minorities versus white males. Full compliance with your affirmative action goals is your objective, and you should make every effort to achieve this end whenever you have an opening to fill.

If after considering all of these factors and assessing both the tangible and intangible qualifications of all your candidates, you determine that the most suitable person for the job is someone who happens to be a white male, you are free to make that person a job offer. However, if the credentials of two candidates—one a white male and the other a minority member or a woman—are essentially the same, and your affirmative action goals are not yet adequately met, you are urged to hire the minority member or the woman.

Bona Fide Occupational Qualifications

Occasionally the requirements of a position seem to be discriminatory in nature. For instance, jobs that stipulate male or female only clearly appear to be discriminatory. However, upon closer investigation it is sometimes evident that the EEO concept of bona fide occupational qualification (BFOQ) prevails. By definition, a BFOQ is a criterion that appears to be discriminatory but can be justified by business necessity. For example, an employer may have an opening for a model to demonstrate a designer's new line of dresses. In this instance being female would be a BFOQ. An example of an unacceptable BFOQ would be a position requiring heavy lifting where only male applicants were considered. The requirement of lifting may be tested; all applicants—male and female—could be asked to lift the amount of weight that would normally be required on the job. Those who were unable to perform this task would not be considered. This would include all men as well as all women who did not meet the requirement. Likewise, women who could lift the weight would have to be given an equal opportunity for the job.

Bona fide occupational qualifications may apply to religion, sex, age, and national origin, but never to race. Furthermore, general company preference does not constitute a legitimate BFOQ. The most valid BFOQ or business-necessity defense is safety.

When there is doubt, the following business-necessity action guidelines should serve to help you:

- Document the business necessity.
- Explore alternative practices.
- Ensure across-the-board administration of the practice.
- Be sure that the business necessity is not based on stereotypical thinking, arbitrary standards, or tradition.

Remember, there are very few instances in which BFOQ applies. If you believe that you have requirements that qualify, it is recommended that you check with your company's EEO officer before proceeding.

Preemployment Inquiries

Most people have a general idea as to what categories to steer clear of during the employment interview. They know that questions relating to race, religion, sex, national origin, and age should be avoided. Some questions, however, have traditionally been considered acceptable during an interview, and the reader may not realize that they are discriminatory in nature.

Before these inquiries are identified, it is important to note that asking these questions is not, in and of itself, illegal. Rather, once you have ascertained the information, you may be charged with illegal use of it. For example, asking a woman applicant if she has children is not an illegal question. However, if you decide not to hire this person because she answers affirmatively and you anticipate excessive absenteeism, then you may be charged with discrimination. This may seem like an insignificant basis for a lawsuit, but not much more is required to get the ball rolling. In fact, all a claimant has to prove is that a given job existed; that he or she is a member of a protected group—certainly easy enough to do, given all the categories of discrimination described earlier; that he or she was qualified for the position, but was rejected in spite of those qualifications; and finally, that the employer continued to look for someone else for the job.

Bear in mind that just because you do not directly ask an

applicant—either via the application form or verbally—for specific information, he or she may offer it. If this occurs, you are equally as liable if a question of illegal use arises. For instance, suppose that you inform an applicant that the position for which she is being considered involves travel. You then ask if she foresees any problem in being able to leave for a business trip with very little advance notice. She responds, "Oh, that will be no problem at all. My mother has been baby-sitting for my three kids ever since my divorce last year." The applicant has just volunteered information regarding two categories that are not job-related: children and marital status. If she is rejected, she might conceivably claim discrimination on the basis of this information, even though you did not solicit it.

Should a candidate provide you with information that you know you should not have, make certain of three things: First, do not, under any circumstances, write the information down; second, do not pursue the subject with the applicant; and third, tell the applicant that the information is not job-related and that you want to return to discussing his or her qualifications in relation to the job opening.

Table 5-1 lists the most common categories and questions to avoid during the employment interview, both verbally and via the application form. Related recommended inquiries are also shown. Many of the recommended inquiries appear on the application form in Appendix F. Certain categories, i.e., security-sensitive jobs, may make BFOQs of some of the inquiries that are not generally recommended.

Remember, a great deal of information that should not be ascertained during the employment interview may be requested for benefits purposes, for example, once an individual is hired.

Education and Experience

At this point it may appear that there is very little that you can ask an applicant. While it is true that there are many categories of information that interviewers must avoid, the categories of education and experience will provide most of the information needed to make an effective hiring decision, without violating any EEO laws. Chapter 6 provides a lengthy list of questions developed from these two areas.

Here are some EEO-related guidelines to keep in mind when setting educational and experiential requirements:

(Text continues on page 136.)

Table 5-1. Preemployment inquiries.

Category of Inquiry	Inquiries Not Recommended	Recommended Inquiries
Name	• What is your maiden name? • Have you ever used any other name? • Have you ever changed your name?	• Have you ever worked for this company under any other name? • Is there any information relative to a change of name that would help us in conducting a reference check?
Address	• Do you rent or own your own home?	• Where do you live? • How long have you lived there?
Age	• How old are you? • What is your date of birth? • Are you between 18 and 24, 25 and 34, etc.? • Proof of age	• Are you above the minimum working age of ____ ?
Physical appearance	• How tall are you? • How much do you weigh?	• No inquiries pertaining to physical appearance
Citizenship and national origin	• Of what country are you a citizen? • Where were you born? • Where were your parents born? • Are you a naturalized or a native-born citizen? • What is your nationality?	• Are you legally permitted to work in this country? If yes, will you be prepared to produce proof at the time of hire, in accordance with the Immigration Reform and Control Act of 1986?

Marital status	What is your marital status? Do you wish to be addressed as Mrs., Miss, or Ms.?	No inquiries pertaining to marital status
Children	Do you have any children? How many children do you have? What child care arrangements have you made?	No inquiries pertaining to children
Police records	Have you ever been arrested?	Have you ever been convicted of a . . . (crime? felony? crime greater than a misdemeanor?)
Religion	What is your religious background? Is there anything in your religious beliefs that would prevent you from working on a Saturday or a Sunday?	No inquiries pertaining to religion. If information regarding, say, weekend availability is needed, ask: Is there any reason you would be unable to work on (Saturday/Sunday) as required of this job?
Disabilities	Do you have any disabilities? Have you ever been treated for any of the following diseases?	Do you have any physical, mental, or medical impairments that would interfere with your ability to perform the job for which you are applying? Are there any positions or duties for which you should not be considered because of medical, physical, or mental disabilities?

(continued)

Table 5-1. (continued)

Category of Inquiry	Inquiries Not Recommended	Recommended Inquiries
Photographs	• Any requirement that a photo be supplied before hiring	• Statement that a photo may be required after hire
Language	• What is your native language? • How did you learn a foreign language?	• As related to the position applied for, what language do you speak, read, and/or write? • What is the degree of fluency?
Relatives	• Who should we notify in the event of an emergency? • Any inquiry calling for the names, addresses, ages, number, or other information regarding the applicant's relatives not employed by the company	• Do you have any relatives already employed by this company?
Military experience	• Have you ever served in the armed forces of any country? • What kind of discharge did you receive from the service?	• Have you ever served in any of the U.S. military services? • Describe your duties while in the U.S. service
Organizations	• What clubs or organizations do you belong to?	• What professional organizations or business activities are you involved with relative to your ability to perform the job for which you are applying?

Category		
References	• A requirement that a reference be supplied by a particular kind of person, for example, a religious leader	• Names of individuals willing to provide character or professional references
Finances	• Do you have any overdue bills?	• No inquiries regarding an applicant's financial status
Education	• Are you a high school/college graduate?	• What is the highest grade that you completed? What academic, vocational, or professional schools have you attended? What was your course of study?
Experience	• Any inquiry regarding non-job-related work experience	• Describe your prior work experience, especially as it relates to the position for which you are applying.

1. Make certain that all educational requirements are job-related. It has been shown that high school diploma requirements have a greater negative impact on minority members than on anyone else. This is true because, historically, minority members have not had the same educational opportunities as others. A high school diploma requirement must be relevant to the job. Do not rely on subjective judgment. Ask yourself whether there is good objective documentation that supports the claim that a high school diploma is necessary in order for an employee to perform the duties and responsibilities of the job. If there is no such documentation, do not require this.

2. With regard to college degrees, the same basic guidelines apply. However, since college degrees are usually required for higher-level positions with less tangible requirements, the guidelines also tend to be somewhat less tangible. For example, degree requirements are permitted when the consequences of employing an unqualified person are grave, especially when public health or safety is involved. Also, positions requiring a great deal of personal judgment often have degree requirements, as well as those requiring knowledge of technical or professional subject matter. Furthermore, when it is difficult to make a reliable assessment of an applicant's absolute qualifications, the degree requirement may provide an adequate substitute mechanism.

3. Although at first glance it appears that it is relatively safe to require a degree, be careful. The burden of proving job-relatedness may easily be yours. The less tangible your reason, the more difficult this will be. It is often wiser to state "degree preferred" or "degree highly desirable." Even better is to clearly spell out exactly what knowledge and skill level you are seeking. This way, individuals who may have additional years of experience or who may have attended college without receiving a degree will not be locked out of consideration. You are helping yourself, as well, by not narrowing the field of choice.

4. Also be certain that educational requirements are relevant to the position for which the applicant is applying. In situations where the degree is not necessary for the immediate job, but *will* be required for future jobs to which the employee will be expected to progress, you may have the requirement, if the job is a true stepping-stone. To be on the safe side, it is even better if your organization offers educational assistance, so that the employee may acquire the necessary educational supplements while working for you.

5. Be careful about changing educational requirements. If you have an opening with specific requirements and find someone you want for the job who does not quite measure up, do not lower the requirements. If you do so, you are leaving yourself wide open to discrimination charges by other applicants. Also, if you have an opening with set educational requirements and an applicant meets them, but you decide in retrospect that the requirements are not stringent enough, you are asking for trouble. If you want to change educational requirements once they are set, you must reevaluate the entire job in relation to the specific duties. Only then can you properly determine whether or not the educational requirements warrant adjustment.

6. As with education, the main criterion for previous work experience requirements should be job relatedness. The standards should never be arbitrary, artificial, or unnecessary.

7. Generally speaking, the more complex the job, the more reasonable it is to have experiential requirements. However, if you have not required specific experience in the past and the job has not changed substantially in terms of its level of responsibility and specific duties, do not initiate such requirements now. If you do so, it is conceivable that women and minorities will suffer more than white males will; in other words, the new requirements may have a greater negative impact on women and minorities. The greater the disparity, the greater the burden will be on you to prove the necessity of the requirements.

8. Also be careful about asking for a specific number of years' experience. It is difficult to prove that four years is not adequate and five years is. How did you determine this? It is not enough to say that the previous incumbent had five years' prior experience and did a fine job. Nor is it sufficient to say that a previous incumbent had only four years' experience and required a great deal of on-the-job training. It is dangerous to use the performance of specific individuals as the basis for your reasoning. It is also difficult to justify a preference for someone with a little more experience, as opposed to just enough. In such a case, say that five years' experience is preferred, not required. Remember, it is not only unwise, from an EEO standpoint, to ask for a specific number of years of experience; you may also be preventing yourself from hiring someone who actually strikes you as the best candidate. If he or she has less experience than required, you cannot safely select this candidate over someone who does meet your stated requirements.

Employment and Termination-at-Will

By definition, "employment and termination-at-will" is the right of an employer to terminate, at any time for any reason, with or without cause, the employment of an individual who does not have a written contract defining the terms of employment. In exercising this employment and termination-at-will right, the employer, under previous case law, incurs no legal liability.

The employment and termination-at-will doctrine has been seriously eroded, however, by legislation such as Title VII of the Civil Rights Act of 1964, The Age Discrimination in Employment Act, as well as other laws described earlier in this chapter. Such legislation prohibits employers from denying equal employment opportunities to all individuals and further prevents them from discharging employees because of non-job-related factors. Employees now have additional rights protecting them from arbitrary acts of termination-at-will. The broadest form of protection, implied covenants of good faith and fair dealing, requires employers to prove "just cause" before terminating an employee. Public policy rights may also protect employees from being fired for exercising rights such as "whistle-blowing"—public disclosure of illegal actions taken by one's company—or for refusal to perform illegal acts on behalf of an employer. Moreover, the issue of implied contract rights may arise when the protection provided by statements on the employment application form, in employee handbooks, or in other company documents is interpreted as binding contracts.

As of October 1987, the following states have recognized public policy exceptions to the employment and termination-at-will doctrine, permitting an employee to recover damages if his or her discharge violates public policy: Arizona, Arkansas, California, Colorado, Connecticut, Delaware, Florida, Hawaii, Idaho, Illinois, Indiana, Kansas, Kentucky, Maine, Maryland, Massachusetts, Michigan, Minnesota, Missouri, Montana, Nevada, New Hampshire, New Jersey, New Mexico, North Carolina, Ohio, Oregon, Pennsylvania, South Carolina, Tennessee, Texas, Virginia, Washington, West Virginia, and Wisconsin. The states of Alabama, Georgia, Mississippi, and New York, and the District of Columbia, have rejected this concept. As of this writing, the remaining states have neither accepted nor rejected the doctrine.

Effective January 1988, courts in thirty-one states and the District of Columbia have ruled that personnel policies and procedures manuals and employee handbooks may be legally binding contracts under their state law. These states are Arizona, California,

Colorado, Connecticut, Idaho, Illinois, Kansas, Maryland, Massachusetts, Michigan, Minnesota, Missouri, Montana, Nebraska, Nevada, New Jersey, New Mexico, New York, North Dakota, Ohio, Oklahoma, Oregon, South Carolina, South Dakota, Texas, Vermont, Virginia, Washington, West Virginia, Wisconsin, and Wyoming, and the city of Washington, D.C. Of the remaining states, courts in five have ruled that manuals and handbooks are not legally binding contracts. These states are Delaware, Florida, Indiana, Iowa, and Louisiana. Lower courts in the remaining states do not consider manuals and handbooks to be legally binding, but such decisions have not been reviewed by higher courts and are not, therefore, binding statewide. These states are Alabama, Alaska, Arkansas, Georgia, Hawaii, Kentucky, Maine, Mississippi, New Hampshire, North Carolina, Pennsylvania, Rhode Island, Tennessee, and Utah. Unless a state court has actually decided a manual or handbook case one way or the other, that state may be assumed to follow the traditional employment and termination-at-will rule—for now.

With regard to the fact that personnel manuals, employee handbooks, and other company documents are increasingly viewed as legally binding contracts, it is advisable for companies to develop at-will policies for inclusion in these documents. The ten guidelines that follow should be applied when developing a company's at-will policy:

1. *State the at-will principle.* It is important to declare that your company's handbook or manual is neither an employment contract nor a guarantee of employment. Consider the following sample from an employee handbook:

> This handbook has been designed to serve as a general summary of our current policies, procedures, and benefits for general information purposes. It provides guidance with regard to what you may expect from us and what we expect from you. We will make every effort to recognize the privileges described herein, unless doing so would impair the operation of business or expose the company to legal liability or financial loss. No provision of this handbook is to be construed as a guarantee of employment.

This simple disclaimer may not be enough, however, since courts have also examined actual practices. Make certain to consult with an attorney knowledgeable in these areas for the most appropriate language to use.

2. *Do not make statements regarding job security.* Avoid phrases such as "as long as your performance is satisfactory, you are guaranteed employment," or "as an employee of (company name), you can look forward to a long and rewarding future," or "we treat employees of (company name) like members of our family and look forward to having you with us for a long time."

3. *Preserve the right to alter policies.* Clearly state that, at the discretion of the employer, certain policies and procedures may be amended, deleted, or replaced as deemed appropriate.

4. *Avoid naming a prospective employee's salary in yearly numbers when extending a written job offer.* A statement of annual salary may imply a one-year employment contract. Instead, weekly, biweekly, or monthly numbers may be used.

5. *Avoid using the word* fair. The term is subject to interpretation. Instead, use the word *consistent.*

6. *Avoid attempting a list that is all-inclusive,* particularly with respect to acts considered cause for disciplinary action.

7. *Avoid using the term* probationary period. It implies that, once a given period of time is over, the employee is there to stay. Likewise, avoid the term *permanent employee*; instead, substitute *regular employee.*

8. *Include employment-at-will statements on tuition reimbursement forms.* This will help safeguard against possible claims that the granting of tuition reimbursement implies a certain degree of job security.

9. *Apply sound, consistent management practices and principles to termination decisions.* Avoid arbitrary, artificial, or non-job-related reasons for termination; apply equal employment opportunity guidelines; document reasons leading up to termination; and terminate for cause only.

10. *Ask employees to acknowledge having read and understood the contents of the company's at-will policy by signing a statement so indicating.* For example, "I understand that the handbook and all other written and oral material provided to me are intended for informational purposes only. Neither it, company practices, nor other communications create an employment contract."

Employers can also minimize the possibility of wrongful discharge allegations and can put the company in a better position to successfully defend against such action by following certain guidelines:

1. Prospective employees should be advised in writing at the beginning of the application process that, if hired, they will be at-will employees. This may best be accomplished by an at-will statement on the application form. A sample at-will statement appears as part of the application form in Appendix F.
2. Application forms should be in full compliance with applicable EEO laws.
3. Managers and supervisors should be trained in effective and legal interviewing skills.
4. Applicants should clearly understand the position they are being considered for prior to being offered the job.
5. All employees should have a clear understanding of what their job entails, in terms of both content and scope of responsibility.
6. Job descriptions should be accurate and job standards consistent with what is actually required.
7. All employees should have an up-to-date copy of the company's employee handbook; it should be made clear that the handbook does not constitute an employment contract.
8. A consistent method of evaluating job performance should be established and followed.
9. Salary increases should be granted according to an individual's skills and knowledge as they relate to a specific job.
10. Managers and supervisors should be skilled at coaching and counseling.
11. Managers and supervisors should be familiar with pertinent EEO and affirmative action laws, rules, and regulations.
12. A progressive disciplinary system should be established and followed.
13. Grievance procedures for employees who are dissatisfied with working terms or conditions should be established and followed.
14. Managers and supervisors should understand and practice effective documentation principles and techniques.
15. All employees should be granted exit interviews.
16. All terminations should be handled such that employees are more likely to feel that they have been treated in a consistent manner and will therefore be less inclined to bring a wrongful dismissal suit against the company.

While employees may now more readily bring claims against employers who terminate employment for capricious or discriminatory reasons, violate public policy rights, or breach implied contracts, there may be restrictions on the damages awarded in such suits. An important example is the 1989 Supreme Court of California ruling in *Foley v. Interactive Data Corporation*. Briefly, the case involved an employee whose performance over his seven years of employment had been deemed, at the least, to be satisfactory. Problems developed when he began reporting to a new supervisor who was under investigation for embezzling from a former employer. The employee reported this information to his former supervisor, adding that he was uncomfortable working for someone who was under investigation for criminal activity. Within approximately two months, the employee was terminated. He sued, claiming three things:

1. The termination violated "public policy" because he had a duty to tell his employer about the criminal investigation of his supervisor.
2. The termination violated the terms of an oral/implied contract in which the employer had promised not to fire him without good cause.
3. The employer had violated its "duty" to act in "good faith" in its dealings with him as an employee.

The first two claims were actions in contract, whereby the object of a decision is to "enforce the intentions of the parties," such as pay them the money they would have earned in salary, benefits, and so on. The last claim was an action in tort, which may result in an award of punitive damages. While contract damages can be substantial, depending on the employee's salary, they are limited; there is no limit to the amount of an award for punitive damages in a tort action.

The court's decision was to limit the employee's damages to lost wages and other "contract" damages. This is a significant precedent, in that employees claiming bad faith in employment and termination-at-will cases are now less likely to be awarded tort damages unless they can prove a tort other than bad faith, such as libel, intentional infliction of emotional distress, or false arrest.

Note that while the court's decision applies to California employers only, legal experts maintain that *Foley* is a landmark case that may well set precedent for similar cases in other states.

Because the legal issues involving employment and termination-at-will are still evolving, including the Uniform Employment Termination Act, employers are advised to have employee handbooks, personnel manuals, application forms, and all other written materials pertaining to the employment process reviewed by counsel annually.

Negligent Hiring and Retention

Negligent hiring and retention, a relatively new form of liability that has been sustained by court decisions since the mid-1980s, occurs when employers fail to exercise reasonable care in hiring or retaining employees. Increasingly, employers are being held liable for the acts of their employees both in the workplace and away from it. Named in such lawsuits are usually the employer, the employee who caused the injury, and the person directly responsible for hiring. Findings of personal liability are not uncommon. Negligent hiring actions have been brought by employees as well as by innocent third parties, such as customers, visitors, and clients who have been injured by the criminal, violent, or negligent acts of an employee.

Plaintiffs must prove that the employee who caused the injury was unfit for hiring or retention, that the employer's hiring or retention of the unfit employee was the cause of the plaintiff's injuries, and that the employer knew or should have known of the employee's unfit condition. The deciding factor is generally whether an employer can establish that he or she exercised reasonable care in ensuring the safety of others. Reasonable care may include conducting preemployment testing, checking references, investigating gaps in an applicant's employment history, verifying academic achievements, conducting a criminal investigation, checking an applicant's credit history, or verifying the individual's driving record. The type of position an employee is hired for often plays a role in how extensive the investigation should be. For example, unsupervised positions in which the employee has a great deal of contact with customers, clients, visitors, or other employees may require more in-depth preemployment investigation than will those jobs that are highly supervised.

Juries may not always be sympathetic to difficulties an employer might encounter in obtaining relevant background information on which to base a hiring decision. Consider, for example, the case involving a teenager hired by a nursing home as a maintenance worker. He had no employment record that could be verified but had been personally recommended by another employee. Within three months of hire, the worker assaulted and raped a woman employee on the premises. He was subsequently convicted of the crime. The victim brought charges of negligent hiring against the employer, maintaining that it should have known that the employee had a record of disciplinary problems in high school and a juvenile criminal record for attacking another woman. While the employer maintained that there was no way it could have ascertained these privileged records, the plantiff was awarded damages by the jury.

Also significant is the court ruling that an employer may be held liable for an employee's behavior, even if the act occurs away from the work site. In *Gaines v. Monsanto,* a mailroom clerk followed a secretary to her home and killed her there. He was later convicted of murder. When the parents of the victim discovered that he had a prior record of rape and conviction, they sued Monsanto. Because part of his duties gave the clerk access to the secretary's address, and since he was known to have harassed other women employees, the court held that it was reasonably foreseeable that an individual with that background could be capable of causing such injury. Consequently, they rejected the employer's motion to dismiss the lawsuit and ruled that the case would be decided by a jury.

Another instance in which employers may be held liable for negligent hiring and retention involves acts that occur outside the scope of an individual's employment. In *DiCosala v. Kay* a boy was injured by a gun belonging to a park ranger who worked for a Boy Scout camp. While use of a gun was not within the scope of the ranger's duties or responsibilities, the court noted that the camp director knew or had reason to know that the ranger had a gun; hence, the issue of negligent retention was properly raised in the lawsuit and the employer was found liable.

Employers are cautioned against being overly concerned with possible charges of negligent hiring by automatically disqualifying a candidate because of some aspect of his or her history. For example, if an investigation reveals that an individual has a conviction record, such information must be relevant to the job in question in order for it to constitute automatic grounds for disqualification.

Employers who end up in court because of negligent hiring or retention charges report that juries, generally, find for the plaintiff. The trial of such actions may involve the examination of a number of issues, including what the employer actually knew about the employee, as opposed to what it tried to learn; whether the potential risk to others could have been reasonably discovered through a reference or background check; and whether the risk to others was greater because of the nature of the job. Consideration of these questions may implicate the employer in an act of negligent hiring or retention. Employers should note that such lawsuits may prove more costly than typical employee litigation because of potentially higher awards of punitive damages. For example, in one negligent hiring case the plaintiff rejected a settlement offer of $500,000; the jury verdict was $5 million.

From all that has been stated, it is apparent that preventive measures are an employer's best defense against charges of negligent hiring or retention. In this regard, employers are advised to:

- Conduct comprehensive employment interviews.
- Check for gaps in employment.
- Determine what kind of background check is needed for each position.
- Conduct preemployment tests as deemed appropriate.
- Conduct thorough professional and, if needed, personal reference checks.
- Keep written notes of information received when checking references.
- Decide whether a criminal investigation, credit check, or other form of investigation is warranted, based on the information received.
- Immediately investigate any allegations of employee misconduct.
- Consult with legal counsel when in doubt as to what course of action to take.

Summary

This chapter has offered an overview of legal issues that affect the hiring process. Specific categories of discrimination have been described, as well as the impact of EEO and affirmative action on the employment process. In addition, the issue of BFOQs with regard to certain job requirements has been discussed. Common preinterview questions have been reviewed, in both recommended and incorrect formats, and the areas of education and prior work experience have been described as the most viable categories for preemployment exploration. Finally, two relatively new areas of employment and the law have been analyzed: employment and termination-at-will, and negligent hiring and retention.

EEO and affirmative action rules are always changing, and employers are reminded to keep abreast of those changes that are likely to affect their business. The importance of familiarity with these aspects of the employment process cannot be stressed enough.

6

Conducting the Interview

Having followed the steps outlined in the preceding chapters, you are now finally prepared to conduct the face-to-face interview! It is a good idea to briefly review the major components of these steps just prior to each meeting. This may be accomplished by asking yourself a series of questions:

1. Am I thoroughly familiar with the specific duties and responsibilities that the employee will be required to perform?
2. Do I know what educational and experiential requirements are needed to successfully perform the essential functions of the job?
3. Am I familiar with the type of individual who will be most compatible with the job?
4. Am I familiar with the reporting relationships that relate to the available position?
5. Can I accurately describe the work environment to the applicant in terms of working conditions, location, required travel, and schedule?
6. Do I know the exemption status of this job?
7. Do I know the salary range for this position?
8. Is this a union position?
9. Can I describe the position's growth opportunities to the applicant?
10. Have I thoroughly reviewed the completed application form and/or résumé, identifying areas requiring discussion?
11. Have I allowed sufficient time for the interview?

12. Is the environment in which the interview will be conducted comfortable and private?
13. Do I clearly understand the departmental and organizational goals as they relate to this position?
14. Am I aware of the role that perception plays in the interview process, in terms of first impressions, information from others, single statements, body language, and ethnocentrism?
15. Have I planned the basic questions to be asked of each applicant?
16. Have I considered how the applicant may be feeling and what I can do to make him or her feel more comfortable?
17. Am I thoroughly familiar with EEO and affirmative action and their impact on the employment process?
18. Are the educational and experiential requirements of this job in compliance with EEO regulations?
19. Are there any BFOQs for this position?
20. Do I know which questions might be considered discriminatory in nature?
21. If there are any tests required as part of the selection process for this job, have they been validated?

Establishing the Format

Now you are ready to consider the format or structure of the interview. It is important to develop a system with which you feel comfortable. It is equally important that the format be practical and that it incorporate all the necessary, concrete components of an interview. These five components are:

1. Asking the applicant questions about his or her education and prior work history as it relates to the requirements of the job
2. Providing information about the job opening
3. Selling the company, in terms of its salary and benefits package, growth opportunities, and the like
4. Allowing the applicant to ask questions
5. Telling the applicant what will happen following the interview

Many interviewers believe that it is best to begin the interview by providing information about the job and the company before asking the applicant any questions. They do this for three primary reasons:

1. By providing this information at the outset, they are less likely to forget something.
2. If they wait to cover these areas until the end of the interview, they may run out of time.
3. The interviewer doing most of the talking at the beginning of the interview will make the applicant feel more at ease.

This procedure has one major drawback: Providing too much information about the job before the applicant describes his or her capabilities often gives away the job. In many cases interviewers inadvertently describe the kind of person they are looking for to such an extent that applicants can simply repeat this information later on in the interview when describing their skills. If the interviewer is unaware of what is happening, he or she may erroneously assume that the ideal candidate has just been found.

Some other approaches might be considered instead. One suggestion is to begin by offering some general information about the organization. This might include a brief description of its overall function and any historical information considered interesting. (Note that some interviewers do not like to do this; they prefer to test the applicant's knowledge of the company later on in the interview.) You might also begin by very briefly describing the job opening. This will ensure that the person is applying for the same position that you are prepared to discuss. Or you can start right in with your first question. However, be aware that this can be unnerving if the applicant has not had a chance to get settled.

Some interviewers like a format that begins with a definitive statement as to what will take place. It might go something like this:

> Good morning, Mr. Turner. My name is Daniel King. I am going to be interviewing you for the position of Marketing Representative with our company. I will begin by giving you an overview of our organization and then ask you some questions about your background and qualifications. I will then describe the responsibilities of the available position. At that point, I will answer any remaining questions you may have about the job or our company. Before we conclude, I will let you know when you may expect to hear from us.

This is a very formal approach. However, if it is accompanied by the appropriate body language and tone of voice, applicants can be made to feel comfortable. Certainly, with this approach there will be no doubt as to the content of the interview.

Other interviewers have a more relaxed style, and therefore their format is far less structured. They might begin by saying: "Hi, Bob. I'm Dan King. I see you're applying for a Marketing Rep opening. Why don't I talk a little bit about our company and then you can tell me some things about yourself. If you think of any questions as we're talking, just jump right in and ask me."

Still others are extremely flexible and capable of conducting both formal and informal interviews. These interviewers like to quickly assess an applicant's general composure and comfort level while they are waiting to be seen, and adjust their approach accordingly. Applicants who appear to be nervous will be met with a casual, relaxed approach. Candidates who seem rather formal will benefit from a more structured format.

It is important that the system you decide on reflects your own personality and style. If you are more comfortable outlining the format of the interview at the outset, that is fine. If you prefer to begin with a brief overview of the company and the job, and then proceed to ask and answer any questions, filling in as you go along, that will work as well. As long as you feel at ease, the applicant is likely to respond well to whatever format you select.

Establishing Rapport

Regardless of the format you use, take a few moments at the beginning of the interview to establish a rapport with the applicant. This is generally accomplished with icebreakers: comments and questions that have no real bearing on the job. Their sole purpose is to put the applicant at ease before beginning the actual interview. Here are some popular icebreakers:

> "Did you have any trouble getting here?"
> "Were you able to find parking nearby?"
> "How was the traffic getting here?"
> "Were the directions my secretary gave you helpful?"
> "Isn't it a beautiful day?"
> "This is some weather we're having!"
> "Do you think it will ever stop raining?"
> "It certainly is hot today!"

Obviously, these are not particularly creative comments or questions; they are not intended to be. In fact, the more neutral they are, the better. At this stage you do not want to discuss any topic that might be considered controversial. This way you will avoid the possibility of forming opinions based on a single, non-job-related statement or being ethnocentric in your interpretation of the applicant's response. Also try to avoid forming first impressions to the extent that they will bias your objectivity. As discussed in Chapter 4, these areas of perception can cloud your ability to judge job suitability. By adhering to subjects such as the weather and commuting, you should accomplish your goal of relaxing the applicant and establishing rapport without drawing premature conclusions.

Just how much time you should spend on icebreakers depends on how comfortable the applicant appears to be. In most instances, fifteen to thirty seconds is sufficient. Sometimes a little longer will be needed. Under no circumstances should this stage of the interview continue for more than a few minutes. Applicants who are still uneasy after this amount of time will probably not respond to additional small talk. The best thing to do in this instance is to ask your first question.

Asking the First Question

Getting started with the core of the interview is often difficult. Some interviewers get caught up in small talk and do not seem to be able to move on. Others want to get started but do not know how to make the transition from the icebreakers to the first important question. Still others simply do not know what to ask first.

For those who get too involved with icebreakers, it is suggested that you consciously limit your time to two minutes. Be certain to select topics that cannot be developed into lengthy discussions. You may also want to limit yourself to two questions. Self-discipline is the key to succeeding at this.

For those who need help in making the transition from small talk to the first question, consider integrating the topic of your icebreaker into a transitional statement. For example:

> "I'm glad you didn't have any trouble getting here. I'm anxious to begin talking with you about your interest in our opening for a Marketing Representative."
> "I'm sorry you had trouble finding parking. I know that those meters where you finally found a space allow only one hour.

Why don't we get started, so that you can be sure to get back to your car before the meter expires?"

"With the weather so beautiful, I'm sure that you're anxious to get back outside, so why don't we get started?"

"Why don't we get started with the interview; it should help take your mind off the fact that you got soaked coming over here."

These statements create a bridge between one stage of the interview and another, thereby eliminating the awkward silence or stammering that can easily occur.

For interviewers who simply do not know where to begin, consider the question suggested in Chapter 4, "Would you please describe your activities during a typical day on the job?" This question accomplishes a great deal:

- It helps to relax a still-nervous applicant by allowing him or her to discuss a familiar subject.
- The open-ended nature of the question encourages the applicant to talk, thereby giving you an opportunity to assess verbal communication skills.
- It allows you time to begin observing the applicant's pattern of body language.
- It provides information upon which you can build additional questions.

Of course, this question is not foolproof. You may find yourself facing an applicant who responds by saying, "Well, that's kind of hard to do. No day is really typical."

When this occurs, be a little more specific in the wording of your question to help the applicant get started. Try adding, "I can appreciate that. Why don't you just pick a day—say yesterday—and describe it for me?"

Once the applicant begins to outline specific tasks, you might interject, "Do you do that every day?" By breaking the question down and encouraging the applicant to talk, you should be able to ascertain the information that you are seeking.

Active Listening

To make sure that you do not miss anything the candidate is saying, it is imperative that you learn and practice active listening skills.

Listening to what the candidate says in response to the icebreaker questions at the beginning of the interview is very different from listening to the answers to questions during the core of the interview. The former is very casual. On the other hand, active listening requires concentration and involves a number of factors. Following are some guidelines to active listening:

1. *Talk less, listen more.* Most interviewers talk entirely too much. No more than 30 percent of your time should be devoted to talking. This 30 percent should be spent asking questions about the applicant's qualifications, clarifying points, providing information about the job and the organization, and answering job-related questions. The remaining 70 percent of time should be spent actively listening.

2. *Listen for connecting themes and ideas.* By not focusing on every word, interviewers are better able to concentrate on key job-related information.

3. *Summarize periodically.* Applicants do not always provide complete answers to questions all at one time. Frequently, you have to bring the pieces together. To make certain that you are doing this accurately, periodically stop and summarize. To illustrate: "Let me make certain that I understand exactly what you have accomplished in this area. You weren't directly responsible for running the department, but your boss was away about 25 percent of the time, and during that time you ran the department. Is this correct?" The applicant may then say, "Well, I didn't exactly run the department; if there were any problems, it was up to me to get in touch with the boss to find out what we should do." This clarification helps you understand the scope and extent of the applicant's responsibility.

4. *Filter out distractions.* As described in Chapter 4, this includes people coming into your office, the phone ringing, and having your thoughts focused elsewhere. The latter can easily occur when applicants are not interesting to listen to. Maybe the work they do strikes you as being dull, or perhaps they speak in a monotone. When this happens, you may find yourself thinking about your last vacation in the Bahamas and how you wish you were there right now. If you find this is happening, remind yourself that not all positions require effective verbal communication skills. The fact that an applicant is not a skilled speaker may not be a job-related factor. It is unfair to judge people on the basis of how well they are able to hold your interest. By not actively listening, you are likely to miss important information that could influence your final hiring decision.

5. *Use free information.* Every time an applicant opens his or her mouth, you get free data. If you do not actively listen, you are going

to miss valuable information. Free information should be the foundation for many of your interview questions.

6. *Screen out ethnocentric thoughts.* Do not allow personal views or opinions to interfere with active listening.

7. *Use thought speed.* This is a wonderful tool available to everyone. Most people think at a rate of approximately 400 words per minute; we speak at a rate of approximately 125 words per minute. Obviously, this means that we think faster than we speak, but there is much more to thought speed than this. While the applicant is talking, you can use thought speed to do the following:

- Prepare your next question.
- Analyze what the applicant is saying.
- Piece together what the applicant is saying now in relation to something said earlier in the interview.
- Glance down at the application and/or résumé to verify information.
- Observe body language.
- Consider how this candidate's background relates to the job requirements.
- Take notes.

Thought speed can also work against you. This can happen if you assume that you know how applicants are going to complete their responses and tune out before they finish, jump to conclusions too soon, compare a candidate's responses with those of a previous applicant, or get too involved in note taking.

Taking Notes

It is important for interviewers to understand that active listening does not preclude note taking. Thought speed allows you to write down key words and ideas during the interview at the same time that you are actively listening to what the applicant is saying. Then, immediately following the interview, you can develop your notes more fully. Doing this right away will ensure that you remember important facts. If you have blocked sufficient time for the interview as discussed in Chapter 4, there should be no problem.

Some interviewers feel that note taking will offend applicants or make them uneasy. If you believe this to be the case, simply tell the applicant at the beginning of the interview that you will be taking some notes to make certain that you have sufficient information with which to make an effective evaluation. Most applicants not only will not mind, but will prefer that you take notes. After all, most jobs have many candidates competing for them. With so many people being considered for each position, how can the interviewer differentiate among candidates without notes? In fact, not taking any notes could convey a lack of interest to the applicant, and consequently he or she may not bother putting his or her best foot forward. Details regarding note taking will be covered in Chapter 7.

Interpreting Nonverbal Communication

As discussed in Chapter 4, perception of nonverbal communication is a vital aspect of the interviewing process. It can be helpful in clarifying confusing verbal messages and often speaks for itself. On the other hand, it can easily be misused and erroneously interpreted. In addition to what was already mentioned in Chapter 4, here are some additional points to keep in mind with regard to nonverbal communication.

To begin with, nonverbal communication encompasses more than facial expressions, body movements, and gestures. The term also refers to pauses in speech, speech rate, vocal tone, pitch, and enunciation. Together, all of these factors "speak" to an interviewer from the very first moment of contact. Often the message can be confusing. For example, body movements such as finger or foot tapping can contradict facial expressions such as smiling. Similarly, an applicant may maintain direct eye contact while answering a question, an indication that he or she has a high degree of self-confidence, but the vocal tone conveys just the opposite. The situation may be further complicated when, coupled with this, the interviewer tries to assess the content of what is being said. The conflict between the verbal and nonverbal message can be confusing, leaving the interviewer wondering which message is the more accurate. Since verbal messages are clearly easier to control than nonverbal ones are, when there is a conflict between the verbal and the nonverbal, the nonverbal is often more persuasive. This may be accurate, however, only to the extent that the person's nonverbal messages are being correctly interpreted.

Nonverbal communication cannot be universally translated. That is, a gesture that you use to express a certain feeling may mean something entirely different when someone else uses it. For example, in the United States it is commonly assumed that nodding the head indicates an affirmative answer or understanding. However, in the Middle East a single nod means no.

This difference in interpretation does not only occur across different cultures. As a result of our individual socialization processes, each of us develops our own pattern of nonverbal messages. That is, we tend to react to a situation in the same nonverbal way each time that it occurs. For example, the applicant who nervously clasps his or her hands while waiting to be interviewed is likely to do the same thing each time that he or she is nervous. Therefore, although there are no universal interpretations to body language cues, each of us has our own nonverbal pattern that may be consistently translated if observed over a period of time.

Even though there are no universal translations of any one gesture, people tend to interpret certain movements in a given way. The following list illustrates this point:

Nonverbal Message	*Typical Interpretation*
Making direct eye contact	Friendly, sincere, self-confident, assertive
Avoiding eye contact	Cold, evasive, indifferent, insecure, passive, frightened, nervous
Shaking head	Disagreeing, shocked, disbelieving
Yawning	Bored
Patting on the back	Encouraging, congratulatory, consoling
Scratching the head	Bewildered, disbelieving
Smiling	Contented, understanding, encouraging
Biting the lip	Nervous, fearful, anxious
Tapping feet	Nervous
Folding arms	Angry, disapproving, disagreeing, defensive, aggressive
Raising eyebrows	Disbelieving, surprised
Narrowing eyes	Disagreeing, resentful, angry, disapproving
Flaring nostrils	Angry, frustrated
Wringing hands	Nervous, anxious, fearful
Leaning forward	Attentive, interested
Slouching in seat	Bored, relaxed
Sitting on edge of seat	Anxious, nervous, apprehensive
Shifting in seat	Restless, bored, nervous, apprehensive
Hunching over	Insecure, passive
Having erect posture	Self-confident, assertive

Paul Ekman, a researcher in nonverbal communication, focuses on facial expressions as a means for interpreting certain emotions. His Facial Affect Scoring Technique (FAST) claims to identify six constants that assess the facial aspect of nonverbal communication. Ekman maintains that disgust is shown in the nose, cheeks, and mouth; fear appears in the eyes; sadness, in the brows, mouth, and eyes; anger is shown in the forehead and brows; and surprise may appear in any facial area.

Interviewers are cautioned against assigning a specific meaning to a given movement or facial expression until they have identified certain nonverbal patterns and can, therefore, be fairly certain that such interpretation is correct. For this reason, applicants should not be sized up within the first few minutes of an interview, and complete interviews should last for at least thirty minutes.

Interviewers should be aware of any sudden changes in nonverbal communication. For example, if an applicant has been sitting quite comfortably for twenty minutes or so, and then suddenly shifts in his or her seat when you ask why he or she left his or her last job, this is a clue that something is amiss. Even if the applicant offers an acceptable response without hesitation, the sudden change in body language should tell you that something is wrong. Additional probing is necessary. The conflict between the verbal and the nonverbal must not be ignored.

Also be careful not to erroneously interpret a person's body language according to his or her reaction to yours. If you are not aware of your own body language, you may incorrectly assume that an applicant is initiating a nonverbal message, instead of reacting to your own. It is critical to be aware of your own body language in terms of how you react to certain emotions or situations.

Your nonverbal responses can be controlled once you are aware of them. It is important to do this during an interview, since your goal is to evaluate the applicant as objectively as possible. It is difficult enough to make a value judgment; adding elements that may not be valid can only serve to make it harder. For example, suppose that you had a fender bender on the way into work and consequently are in a bad mood. If you are not conscious of the body language that you are projecting as a result of this mishap, the applicant may assume that you are reacting negatively to something on his or her résumé or to something that he or she has said in response to one of your questions. This is perfectly understandable. After all, how many of us are so secure or self-confident that we would think, "Oh, I know it couldn't possibly have anything to do with me"?

Also remember that when it comes to perception versus how you really may be feeling, it is perception that counts. To help you understand this point, ask a friend or colleague to observe you during the meeting or throughout a typical workday. Periodically ask for feedback. Ask the person what he or she perceives your mood to be at a given moment based on your nonverbal messages. Remember, the interpretation may differ from what you are actually feeling. This simple exercise can help you understand your patterns and thus help you control your body language during an interview.

By being aware of your own nonverbal communication, you can consciously choose to project certain nonverbal messages to applicants. For example, by knowing that nodding one's head is generally interpreted as a sign of understanding, you can use this gesture to encourage an applicant to continue talking. Likewise, if you are aware that leaning forward in one's chair implies interest or attentiveness, you can assume this position when interviewing in order to indicate interest in whatever the applicant may be saying.

Encouraging the Applicant to Talk

One of the greatest challenges for an interviewer is encouraging an applicant to talk. Of course, some applicants are well-prepared, self-confident, and more than willing to converse with you. Indeed, it is difficult to prevent some of them from talking too much and for too long. With others, however, talking to an interviewer can be intimidating and unnerving; regardless of how much they may want the job, selling themselves may be very difficult for them. Therefore, you must help them. Here are six ways in which you can encourage an applicant to speak freely:

1. One technique is *repetition*. This encourages the applicant to continue talking and also helps to clarify certain points. Repeating the last few words of an applicant's statement and letting your voice trail off as a question mark will encourage the person to elaborate. For example, suppose that the last point an applicant made was "The most difficult part of being a manager was that I was in charge of twenty-five people." You could follow up by saying, "You supervised twenty-five people . . . ?" The applicant might then reply, "Well, not directly. I was in charge of three supervisors, each of whom monitored the work of about seven workers." To further clarify, you might then say: "So, you were directly responsible for supervising three people. Is this correct?" The applicant would then

state, "Yes, that is correct, although my supervisors always came to me when they were having trouble with their workers."

This dialogue presents a far more accurate picture of the applicant's supervisory responsibilities than did the original statements that were made. Using repetition encouraged the applicant to provide valuable additional information.

2. A second technique that may encourage the applicant to talk is *summarization*. Like repetition, this allows the candidate to clarify the points made thus far in the interview, and to elaborate as is necessary. It further ensures an accurate understanding on your part. Summarization may be used at specific time intervals in the interview (e.g., every ten to fifteen minutes or after a certain topic has been discussed). For instance, you and the candidate may have just devoted approximately ten minutes to reviewing his or her prior work experience as it relates to the available position. At that point, you might say: "Let me make certain that I understand what you have said thus far. All of your employment since graduating high school has been as a mechanic. This includes the time that you spent in the Marine Corps. You enjoy this line of work and want to continue doing it. However, you feel that you were underpaid at your last job and that's why you left. Is this correct?"

The applicant can now confirm all or part of what you have just summarized. Be careful not to include more than four or five statements in your summary. This way, if part of it is inaccurate or requires clarification, it will not be difficult to isolate. Also, in order to ensure accuracy, make certain to employ the active listening guidelines outlined earlier in this chapter.

3. While asking open-ended questions will yield the most information, some applicants have difficulty talking and may respond better to a series of *direct, close-ended questions* (both forms of questions will be discussed in more detail in this chapter). Interviewers are cautioned, however, against using close-ended questions as a substitute for the more probing open-ended variety. Nevertheless, the former may be used for the limited purpose of allowing the applicant to achieve a certain comfort level before you move on to more information-producing forms of inquiry.

4. Employing *certain phrases* can also encourage an applicant to continue talking. These phrases include "I see." "How interesting." "Is that right?" "Really?" and "I didn't know that." It is important to note that none of these phrases express an opinion or show agreement or disagreement; they merely show interest and understanding.

5. In order for these phrases of understanding to be effective, they must be accompanied by *encouraging body language*. Examples of body language that usually shows interest are nodding, smiling, direct eye contact, and leaning forward.

Conveying these nonverbal messages consistently throughout the interview will establish your interest in what the applicant is saying, thereby helping the person to provide additional information.

6. One final tool that may be utilized in encouraging applicants to talk is *silence*. Most people find silence to be awkward and uncomfortable. Consequently, interviewers often feel compelled to talk whenever the applicant stops talking. However, unless you are ready to ask another question, talking when you need additional information from the applicant is not going to help you to make a hiring decision. When the applicant stops talking and you want him or her to continue, try silently and slowly counting to five before speaking. This pause often compels a candidate to go on. Of course, you must be careful not to carry silence too far. The interview can easily become a stressful situation if you simply continue to stare at an applicant who has nothing more to say or needs your help. However, if you combine silence with positive body language, the applicant should continue talking within a few seconds. Silence very clearly conveys the message that more information is wanted.

Providing Information

Ascertaining information about the applicant is only part of the interview; providing information to the applicant is also important. Just as interviewers must decide if candidates are appropriate for a given job opening, the candidates must decide whether the job and company are right for them. This is particularly true when unemployment is low and applicants can afford to be selective about job opportunities.

Many interviewers erroneously assume that applicants come to the interview armed with information about both the company and the job opening. Perhaps there was a detailed description in the newspaper advertisement to which the applicant responded; maybe the applicant has been referred by a long-term employee who has extensive knowledge of the company and the available job; or perhaps, while waiting in the reception area, the applicant was seen perusing the company's annual report or newsletter. It is also possible that the candidate is a former employee or one who has been away on a leave of absence. Regardless of how much the applicant may presumably or actually know, interviewers are responsible for informing all job candidates about certain aspects of the company and the available position. In this way, applicants will be certain to understand key elements of their prospective employment.

Information about the job and company may be provided at the beginning of the interview or may be "sprinkled" throughout the interview, in between asking and answering questions. As mentioned in Chapter 4 with regard to telephone screening, and earlier in this chapter, care must be exercised not to give away too much regarding the characteristics of an ideal candidate in the early stages of the interview. Of course, the specific information offered will depend on the level of the available position and scope of its responsibility.

Generally speaking, applicants should be informed about the organization in terms of what it does and how long it has been in business, as well as offered brief statements about its origins, growth to date, and projected growth. Additional company-related descriptions, such as the number of exempt and nonexempt employees, divisions, and departments, may also be given. A brief summary of company benefits should also be provided. More specific information concerning the department that has the available opening may then be offered, including its function, the different tasks performed, how it interrelates with other departments, a description of who is in charge, the chain of command, and the work setting.

This naturally leads to a description of the specific job opening, details of which may best be offered by providing the applicant with a copy of the job description. Allow him or her a few moments to read it and then encourage questions based on its contents. If the job description is comprehensive and well written, this process will ensure a clear understanding of what the job entails and requires. Be certain to cover the work schedule and other factors discussed in Chapter 2 and in Appendix A. In addition, discuss growth opportunities available via job posting, career planning, training programs, tuition reimbursement, or other in-house and outside means for career development. Be certain to cover any negative features. Let the applicant react now, during the interview, rather than later as a disgruntled employee.

Whether or not salary is discussed depends on each particular company policy. It is advisable for interviewers to provide at least general information about the range for a given job. If the salary is fixed and nonnegotiable, the applicant should be so informed. This can facilitate a determination of whether continued discussion of that particular job is warranted.

A brief description of the neighborhood surrounding the office building should also be offered. This might include a discussion of transportation options, restaurants, stores, and, since Americans have become increasingly health-conscious, any health/exercise facilities in the area.

Finally, be certain to tell the applicant what happens after the interview is over. Describe approximately how long it will be before he or she may expect to hear from you, whether it is likely that there will be additional interviews, and what he or she should do if there are additional questions. Be certain you have a current telephone number and/or address so there will be no problem with any future communication.

Asking Different Types of Interview Questions

Although all of the factors discussed thus far are critical for effective interviewing, success often depends on the specific type of question asked. There are six main categories of questions that are commonly used by interviewers. Generally speaking, any thought can be expressed in each of the six ways. The wording you choose for each question will essentially determine how much valid information you receive:

1. *Close-ended questions.* These are questions that may be answered with a single word—generally yes or no. They may also offer multiple choice answers. With regard to the latter, care must be exercised not to offer too many choices; two or three are the most effective number. For example, "Would you describe yourself as a team player or an independent worker?" is more effective than "Which one of the following terms best describes you? (a) Team player, (b) Lone ranger, (c) Leader of the pack, (d) An idea person, or (e) Follow the leader." In general, however, even limited multiple choice questions should be avoided, since they force applicants to choose, as opposed to allowing them to offer information.

As mentioned earlier in this chapter, close-ended questions may be of limited use. For instance, asking a series of close-ended questions at the beginning of an interview can help certain applicants feel more at ease and thus more likely to volunteer pertinent information. Close-ended questions may also be helpful to an interviewer seeking certain information at the outset, such as when the starting salary for a given opening is rather low and the interviewer is aware that many applicants have expressed a lack of interest in the job as a result. In such a situation, it may make sense to mention this fact at the beginning of the interview by asking, "Are you aware that the salary for this job is $425 per week?" This close-ended question will elicit a straightforward yes or no response. The answer will determine whether or not it is worthwhile to continue discussing the job (this does not necessarily mean that the interview should end, however; sometimes interviewers have other, more appropriate positions that may be discussed).

2. *Probing questions*. These are questions that allow the interviewer to delve more deeply for needed information. They are usually short and simply worded. Following are some effective probing questions:

"Why?"
"What caused that to happen?"
"Under what circumstances did that occur?"
"Who else was involved in that decision?"
"What happened next?"

Interviewers are cautioned against asking too many probing questions in a row, as they tend to make applicants feel defensive. In addition, accompanying body language should express interest and not seem accusing. Gestures such as narrowing eyes and raising eyebrows should be avoided when asking probing questions.

3. *Hypothetical questions*. These questions can become valuable interviewing tools. Hypothetical situations based on specific job-related facts are presented to the applicant for solutions. The questions are generally introduced with words and phrases such as "What would you do if . . ."; "How would you handle . . ."; "How would you solve . . ."; "In the event that. . . ."

Although the answers to hypothetical questions can yield information about an applicant's reasoning ability and thought process, care must be taken not to expect "right" answers. Without being familiar with the organization, the applicant can only offer responses based on his or her previous experiences.

4. *Loaded questions*. These are questions that force an applicant to choose between two often undesirable alternatives. For instance, the question "Are you the union-organizing type or are you anti-union?" puts the applicant on the spot. Perhaps he or she is neither.

However, since the interviewer has only offered these two choices, the candidate may not want to appear contrary and is therefore likely to select the one that most closely reflects his or her views. Loaded questions do not provide any valid information about an applicant and should be avoided.

5. *Leading questions*. Leading questions imply that there is a single correct answer. The interviewer sets up the question so that the applicant provides the desired response. Here are some examples:

"You do intend to finish college, don't you?"

"Don't you agree that most workers need to be watched very closely?"

"When you were in school, how much time did you waste taking art and music classes?"

It is obvious from the wording of these questions that the interviewer is seeking a particular reply. When leading questions are asked, the interviewer cannot hope to learn anything about the applicant.

6. *Open-ended questions*. These may be described as questions that cannot be answered by a yes or no, and they are clearly the most effective questions that an interviewer can ask. They yield the greatest amount of information and allow the applicant latitude in responding. They also permit the interviewer to assess verbal communication skills and to observe the applicant's pattern of nonverbal communication. Most importantly, open-ended questions provide information upon which interviewers can build additional questions.

There are, however, two possible problems with open-ended questions. The first is that the applicant's response may include information that is irrelevant or that violates EEO laws. As soon as this occurs, the interviewer must bring the applicant back to the focus of the question. One way to do this is to say: "Excuse me, but we seem to have strayed from the original question of why you left your last job. I would like to get back to that." Another effective response might be "Excuse me, but that information is not job-related. Let us get back to your description of a typical day at the office." This is especially appropriate if information being volunteered has the potential for illegal use.

The second possible concern with open-ended questions is that they can be too broad in scope. The classic request "Tell me about yourself" illustrates this point. Questions that require applicants to summarize many years in a single response are also not effective. An example of this might be "Describe your work history" when you are addressing an applicant who has worked for over thirty years. Instead, say, "Please describe your work experience over the past two years." This is still open-ended, but it provides some helpful boundaries.

It is important to note that any question that can be answered by a yes or no can be converted into an open-ended question. For example, "Did you like your last job?" can easily be changed to "What did you like about your last job?" The open-ended version will yield more valuable information.

Asking Specific Employment Interview Questions

In Chapter 5, it was noted that interview inquiries relating to education and experience will generally provide most of the information needed to make an effective hiring decision without violating any EEO laws, if properly phrased. Although each specific position in terms of its level, requirements, and responsibilities will dictate the most appropriate questions to ask, the following list of inquiries regarding work and education will provide interviewers with a good source of effective, legal, open-ended questions from which to choose. The list is by no means complete, and interviewers are cautioned against merely selecting questions from the list without supplementing with questions of their own. In addition, interviewers are reminded that applicants constantly provide unsolicited or free information in response to open-ended questions; this information usually provides the basis for additional areas of inquiry.

Many of the questions that follow relate to past performance that is likely to reflect the candidate's ability to execute the duties, requirements, and responsibilities of the available position. Moreover, many of the questions probe for negative information, so that the interviewer can obtain a balanced picture of the candidate. Finally, it is not always necessary to ask questions in the interrogative form; statements can often be just as effective.

Questions Regarding Education

1. What were your favorite and least favorite subjects in high school/college? Why?
2. How were your grades in your favorite and least favorite subjects?

3. What subjects did you do best in? Poorest in?
4. Why did you decide to go to college?
5. Why did you major in _____ ?
6. Why did you decide to attend _____ ?
7. What type of extracurricular activities did you participate in? Why did you select those?
8. What career plans did you have at the beginning of college?
9. What career plans did you have when you graduated high school/college?
10. What did you gain by attending high school/college?
11. If you had the opportunity to attend school all over again, what, if anything, would you do differently? Why?
12. What elective courses did you take? Why?
13. How did high school/college prepare you for the "real world"?
14. Describe your studies in the area of _____ (whatever field the job opening is in).
15. How do you feel your studies in the area of _____ have prepared you for this job opening?
16. When did you decide that you wanted to major in _____ ?
17. Who were your favorite and least favorite teachers in high school/college? Why?
18. Describe your study habits in high school/college.
19. Describe any part-time jobs you had while attending high school/college.
20. Which of your part-time jobs did you find most/least interesting?
21. How did you spend your summers while attending high school/college?
22. Why did you work while attending high school/college?
23. What plans do you have, if any, to continue with school?
24. What did you find to be most difficult about working and attending school at the same time?
25. What advice would you give to someone who wanted to work and attend school simultaneously?
26. Describe a conflict you had with a particular teacher and how it was resolved.
27. Describe a time when you received a lower grade than you felt you deserved; how did you handle it?
28. Describe the one course that you felt was the most valuable and explain why.
29. Describe the teacher who influenced you the most.

30. Describe a time when you were tempted to quit school; how did you turn yourself around?
31. What advice would you give to someone who wanted to pursue the same course of study that you did?
32. What could the department head of the course you majored in have done to make the curriculum more interesting?
33. How did you handle required courses that were not of particular interest to you?
34. Describe a time when you signed up for a course that did not turn out the way you expected.
35. Describe what you consider to be characteristics of the ideal teacher.

Questions Relating to Previous Experience and Other Work-Related Categories

1. Please describe your activities during a typical day on the job.
2. What is your description of the ideal manager? Employee? Co-worker?
3. What kind of people do you find it difficult/easy to work with? Why?
4. What did you like most/least about your last job?
5. What is your description of the ideal work environment?
6. What motivates you? Why?
7. What makes you an effective supervisor?
8. What is the greatest accomplishment of your career to date? Why?
9. Describe a situation at your last job involving pressure. How did you handle it?
10. What do you feel an employer owes an employee?
11. How do you feel about work-related travel?
12. Describe your past experience with work-related travel in terms of duration and frequency.
13. How do you feel about relocation? Are there any places where you would not be willing to relocate?
14. What were some of the duties of your last job that you found to be difficult?
15. How do you feel about the progress that you have made in your career to date?
16. What are some of the problems you encountered in your last job? How did you resolve them?

17. How does your present job differ from the one you had before it?
18. Of all the jobs you have had, which did you find the most/least rewarding?
19. In what ways do you feel your present job has prepared you to assume additional responsibilities?
20. What has been the most frustrating situation you have encountered in your career to date?
21. Why do you want to leave your present job?
22. How did you feel about the way in which your department/division was managed at your last job?
23. If I were to ask your supervisor to describe your work, what do you think he or she would say?
24. What would you do if . . . ?
25. How would you handle . . . ?
26. What does the prospect of this job offer you that your last job did not?
27. What are you looking for in a company?
28. How does your experience in the military relate to your chosen field?
29. Please describe the work you performed while in the military.
30. What immediate and long-term career goals have you set for yourself?
31. What would you like to avoid in future jobs?
32. What are your salary requirements?
33. Who or what has influenced you with regard to your career goals? In what way?
34. To what do you attribute your career success thus far?
35. What do you consider to be your greatest strength?
36. What are the areas in which you require improvement? How would you go about making these improvements?
37. How would you describe yourself as a manager? Employee? Co-worker?
38. What aspects of your work give you the greatest satisfaction?
39. How do you approach tasks that you dislike?
40. How do you manage your time?
41. What is your management style?
42. What did you learn from each of your previous jobs?
43. Please give me some examples of decisions you have made on the job. What were the ramifications of these decisions?
44. How do you go about making a decision?

45. How would you describe your delegation skills?
46. How would you describe your standards of performance, both for yourself and for those reporting to you?
47. How would you describe your relationship with your last supervisor?
48. Please give me an example of a project that did not turn out the way you planned. What happened?
49. Why are you applying for a position with our company?
50. Why did you go to work for your last employer?
51. What is your greatest responsibility at your present job?
52. Describe your progression at your last job.
53. What have past employers complimented/criticized you for?
54. What can you offer our organization?
55. How does this opening fit in with your career objectives?
56. What types of work-related situations make you feel most comfortable/uneasy?
57. Why are you willing to take a reduction in pay?
58. Why did you decide to become a _____ ?
59. Why do you want to change fields?
60. What is a manager's/employee's greatest responsibility?
61. How do you feel about repetitious tasks?
62. How do you feel about having your work closely supervised?
63. How do you feel about working overtime?
64. How do you feel about being on call?
65. What would motivate you to stay with this company until you are ready to retire?
66. What would make you resign from a position with this company?
67. Under what circumstances, if any, do you feel a supervisor or manager should perform the duties of those reporting to him or her?
68. How would you handle an employee who was consistently tardy?
69. This job calls for the ability to _____ . What experience have you had in doing this?
70. What is the most difficult/rewarding aspect of being a _____ ?
71. If you were asked to perform a task that was not in your job description, how would you respond?
72. What is your definition of company loyalty? How far does it extend?

73. How would you go about discussing job dissatisfaction with your boss?

74. What could your previous employer(s) have done to convince you not to leave?

75. If you have ever fired someone, please describe what it was like and how you went about doing it.

76. Describe a time when you were asked to work overtime but you had other commitments. How did you handle it?

77. Describe a former employer whose management style differed from your own; how did you reconcile your differences?

78. Describe a time when you feel you exercised poor judgment; what would you do differently now?

79. How would you handle a long-term employee whose performance has always been outstanding, but who recently has started to make a number of mistakes in his or her work?

80. Why do you work?

81. Describe the ideal work schedule.

82. How would you handle an employee who challenged your authority?

83. What does the term *progressive discipline* mean to you? What role do you believe it plays in an organization?

84. Describe a time when you were asked to complete work submitted by three different supervisors who all said their projects were urgent. How did you prioritize the assignments?

85. Describe the first time you were left in charge of your department while your boss was out of town.

86. Describe a time when you were asked, at the last minute, to go out of town on an assignment for which you were not prepared.

87. What do you feel an employee owes an employer?

88. Under what circumstances, if any, would you find acceptable an employee going over your head to your supervisor?

89. Describe the chain of command in your present department and where you fit in.

90. Describe a time when you were asked to complete an assignment for which you were not trained; what did you do?

91. How do you prepare for a verbal presentation?

92. During or after a verbal presentation, how do you respond to questions to which you do not know the answer?

93. Select a work-related goal you have set for yourself in the past and describe the steps you took in order to accomplish it.

94. Describe an instance in which you approached a rather routine task in a creative way.

95. Describe a situation in which you were a member of a team but disagreed with the way the others wanted to approach a project.

96. Tell me about a time when you were able to convince your colleagues to see things your way.

97. Explain how you are able to balance working and going to school at the same time.

98. What would you do if you "inherited" an employee whose work record was excellent, but who made it perfectly clear that he or she did not like working for you?

99. How would you handle working for someone you did not like?

100. What else should I know about you that would help me make a hiring decision in your favor?

Interviewing Problem Applicants

Most applicants are eager to make a good impression on the interviewer. They try to answer all inquiries as fully as possible, project positive body language, and ask appropriate questions. Occasionally, however, you will find yourself faced with a problem applicant, someone who falls into one of the following categories: (1) shy or nervous; (2) overly talkative; (3) overly aggressive; (4) highly emotional or distraught; or (5) dominant (tries to take over the interview).

At the first indication that you are dealing with a problem applicant, you must make certain adjustments in your handling of the interview:

1. *Shy or nervous applicants.* Within the first few seconds of the icebreaker portion of the interview, it will become apparent if an applicant is especially shy or nervous. This type of person needs to be drawn out slowly; a broad, open-ended question might be too intimidating if used right off the bat. Instead, try a few close-ended inquiries to put the candidate more at ease. Make them simple,

relating to areas with which the applicant is likely to feel comfortable. Also make certain that your first open-ended question pertains to a topic with which the individual has experience, thereby ensuring a certain degree of ease. In addition, try using a softer tone of voice, positive body language, and words of encouragement. Let the applicant know, in every way possible, that you are interested in what he or she has to say.

2. *Overly talkative applicants.* Some candidates seem to be capable of talking nonstop. They not only answer your questions, but volunteer a great deal more information, much of which is irrelevant, unnecessary, and sometimes illegal. These people are often very personable and really quite delightful to talk with. However, you must remind yourself that you are not there to engage in a social conversation. Your goal is to ascertain sufficient information upon which to base a hiring decision.

The key to effectively dealing with applicants who talk too much is control. You must remember that you are in charge of the interview and that you control the amount of time devoted to questions and answers. When you feel that enough data have been gathered, say to the applicant: "Everything you have told me is very interesting. I now have enough information upon which to base my decision. Thank you very much for your time. You will be hearing from us by the end of this week."

Sometimes applicants do not respond to this cue to leave. They remain seated and resume talking. If this occurs, escalate your efforts somewhat. Tell the applicant, "I am afraid that is all the time we have. I do have other applicants waiting." If even this does not work, as a last resort you can add, "I am sure that if you were waiting to see me, you would appreciate my meeting you on time." At this point, if the applicant is still seated, stand up and extend your hand. As you shake hands, gently guide the applicant to the door.

3. *Overly aggressive applicants.* Some applicants present themselves in an overly aggressive or hostile way. Perhaps they have been out of work for a long time, or perhaps they have applied for a job with your company before and were rejected. When confronted with an angry applicant, you must stay calm and maintain your objectivity. Try to find out why the applicant is so upset. Explain that you cannot continue the interview as long as he or she remains agitated. Try to complete the interview and judge the applicant as fairly as possible, taking into account any extenuating circumstances.

4. *Highly emotional or distraught applicants.* An applicant who begins to weep in your office can be quite unnerving. If this should occur, extending empathy rather than sympathy will enable you to remain objective, in charge of the situation, and better able to help the individual regain his or her composure. Explain that you understand what the applicant is experiencing and offer him or her a few moments of privacy. Most applicants will be able to continue with the interview at this point. In some rare instances, however, it may be preferable to reschedule the interview.

Occasionally, applicants become emotional or distraught when you question their answer "personal" in response to the question why they left their last job. When this occurs, you should stop and come back to this question later in the interview, perhaps after a better rapport has been established. It is important to emphasize to the applicant that this information is vital for continued consideration. Often this message will be sufficient to encourage even the most reluctant applicant to provide a fuller explanation. You may also find it necessary to pose very specific questions instead of simply asking the applicant to elaborate. For instance, you might ask if the departure had anything to do with the immediate supervisor, the working conditions, fellow employees, or benefits. Another way to encourage the applicant is to indicate that a reference check will be made, including an inquiry as to why he or she left.

5. *Dominant applicants.* At times an applicant will try to gain control of the interview, usually when trying to cover up for a lack of sufficient job experience. The attempted takeover may manifest itself in a variety of ways, i.e., steering the conversation to a discussion of the interviewer's career or interests, or discussing books or photos in the room. If this takes place during the interview, all is not lost. Remind yourself that you are in charge and say to the applicant: "Excuse me, but we seem to have strayed. Let's get back to. . . ."

One-on-One Versus Team Interviewing

Most interviews involve two people: the interviewer and the applicant. Occasionally, however, the team approach may be employed. This involves more than one interviewer—usually two or three. The team may consist of a human resources representative, the department supervisor, and possibly a division head. This is commonly done for one of two reasons: (1) to save the time it would take to schedule two or three separate interviews and (2) to be able to compare impressions of the applicant.

If carefully planned, team interviews can be very effective. The role that each person is going to play should be agreed upon ahead of time. Perhaps the human resources representative will begin by asking some broad questions to determine overall job suitability; then the department supervisor will ask more detailed, technical questions; finally, the division head will pursue the candidate's potential, and other intangible factors.

Applicants should always be advised ahead of time that the team approach is going to be used. Otherwise, it can be very unnerving to see more than one interviewer in the room. Seating should also be carefully arranged. Unlike a one-on-one interview, where the proximity of the interviewer's chair to the applicant's chair is inconsequential, seating in a team interview situation can create an uncomfortable environment. Do not, for example, surround the candidate's chair. As Figure 6-1 illustrates, this involves one seat on either side and one seat directly in front of the applicant. This can result in a "tennis match" sort of interview, with the candidate continually turning his or her head from one side to the other, trying to address everyone in the room.

Figure 6-1. Surrounding the candidate.

Applicant

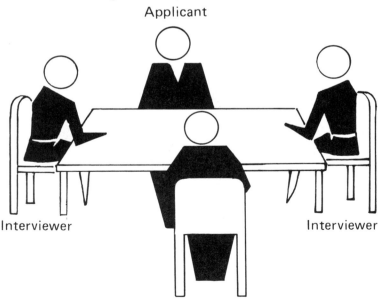

Interviewer

Interviewer

Interviewer

Instead, offer the applicant a seat and form a soft arc in front of him or her. As Figure 6-2 illustrates, this setting is less structured and more conducive to a productive exchange.

Avoiding Stress Interviews

In a stress interview the applicant is deliberately put on guard, made to feel ill at ease, or "tested" for some purpose known only to the interviewer. This technique is not recommended under any circumstance. Proponents of stress interviewing claim that they ferret out some significant job-related traits, i.e., how applicants will handle uncomfortable situations, that cannot be discovered through questioning, assessing nonverbal communication skills, weighing intangible factors, and so forth. In truth, stress interviews are often nothing more than a smoke screen for ineffective interviewing skills.

Since stress interviews are occasionally utilized, however, some actual examples are cited in this book. *Readers are urged to view these as illustrations of what to avoid!*

Stress Interviews in the Office

1. The interviewer slowly eyes the applicant from head to toe, staring for some time at the candidate's feet. Finally he or

Figure 6-2. Suggested seating arrangement for a team interview.

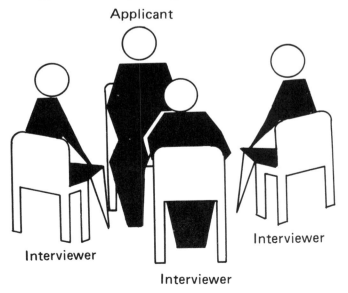

she says, "I never would have worn those socks with those shoes."

2. The interviewer makes certain that his or her chair is considerably higher than that of the applicant.

3. The interviewer invites the applicant to sit in an oversized chair, making it difficult for the applicant to rise up out of it.

4. The interviewer invites the applicant to sit in a chair with one leg slightly shorter than the others, causing it to wobble.

5. The applicant is offered a chair that looks like one used by a five-year-old.

6. The applicant is offered a chair that faces the window. On a sunny day, with the drapes open, the sun will then shine directly in the applicant's eyes.

7. The interviewer seats himself or herself in front of a window on a sunny day with the drapes open, thereby causing a "halo" effect around his or her head.

8. The interviewer begins firing questions at the applicant as soon as he or she enters the room.

9. The interviewer does not ask the applicant any questions; rather, he or she simply stares at the applicant, waiting to see what the person will say or do.

10. The interviewer asks questions while looking down at his or her desk or while doing other work.

11. The interviewer answers the phone during the course of the interview, puts the person on hold, turns to the applicant and says, "Go ahead; I can keep him on hold for a minute."

12. The interviewer makes a series of phone calls during the interview.

13. The interviewer leaves the room for several minutes.

14. The interviewer begins the interview by saying, "Is there anything you'd like to tell me?"

15. The interviewer begins the interview by saying, "Go ahead—impress me."

16. The interviewer asks the applicant during the course of the interview, "Do you always wear your hair that way?"

17. The interviewer takes off his or her watch, places it on the desk, and says, "We have exactly forty-five minutes."

18. After responding to a question, the applicant is asked, "Are you sure that's the answer you want to give?"

19. The interviewer stares at the applicant for some time and finally says, "You're rather young, aren't you?"
20. The interview is conducted in an open area, where other interviews are taking place simultaneously. The interviewer begins listening to a conversation between another interviewer and applicant and soon begins asking questions of the other applicant.

Mealtime Stress Interviews

Mealtime interviews are generally reserved for professional-level applicants. They can be appropriate and, indeed, quite comfortable for both the interviewer and the applicant if the same guidelines that govern office interviews are adhered to. Unfortunately, meals also provide an ideal arena for proponents of stress interviews, based on the justification that eating and drinking habits may be a valid reflection of decision making on the job. Consider these actual examples:

1. The interviewer waits until the applicant has a mouthful of soup before asking a question.

2. The applicant is rejected because he or she orders a cheeseburger; that is to say, food that requires direct handling with one's hands. The premise here is that an applicant should assume that he or she will be asked to review papers during the course of a mealtime interview; this cannot be done with greasy fingers.

3. The applicant is rejected because he or she orders shrimp scampi when the interviewer orders a chef's salad. The point here is that the scampi takes approximately eight bites to complete while the salad requires more than one hundred bites to consume; therefore, the applicant will be finished eating long before the interviewer will, leaving the latter feeling rushed.

4. The applicant accepts an offer of an alcoholic drink and is rejected on the basis that he or she might have a tendency to drink too much.

5. The applicant refuses an offer of an alcoholic drink and is rejected on the basis that he or she might formerly have had a drinking problem.

6. The applicant is rejected for refusing to check his or her coat upon entering the restaurant, the assumption being that this person is insecure about parting with possessions.

7. The applicant is evaluated on his or her knowledge of the correct utensils to use during various points in the meal.

8. The applicant is found acceptable because he or she orders something from the menu that costs the same or less than what the interviewer orders.

9. The interviewer fires a steady stream of open-ended questions at the applicant as soon as his or her food arrives, to see whether or not the applicant can eat and talk at the same time.

10. The interviewer tries to slip in some non-job-related questions during the course of the meal.

11. The interviewer assesses the applicant's level of assertiveness in dealing with a disagreeable waiter or waitress.

12. The interviewer identifies several other diners who work at the same organization; later in the meal, the applicant is asked about them to see how closely he or she was paying attention.

Interviewing Guidelines and Pitfalls

With all that has been said thus far about the face-to-face interview, it is a good idea to pause at this point and review some important guidelines:

1. *Establish the format.* Make certain that you develop a system that encompasses all of the important ingredients of an interview. Be sure that it reflects your own style and personality.

2. *Establish rapport.* Taking a few moments out at the beginning of an interview to put the applicant at ease will result in a greater exchange of information.

3. *Carefully select your first question.* A well-worded, open-ended question can provide several additional categories for the interviewer to explore.

4. *Practice active listening skills.* Concentrating closely on what the applicant says and talking no more than 30 percent of the time will enable you to make more effective hiring decisions.

5. *Take notes.* Jot down key words and phrases during the interview and embellish these immediately after the applicant leaves.

6. *Practice positive nonverbal communication skills.* Employ those gestures and movements that are likely to be interpreted in an encouraging way. Strive for consistency between verbal statements and nonverbal expressions.

7. *Encourage the applicant to talk.* Repetition, summarization, direct close-ended questions, encouraging phrases, positive body language, and silence may all be used to encourage applicants to talk.

8. *Provide information.* Make certain the applicant has a clear and complete understanding of both the organization and the available job.

9. *Consider different types of interview questions.* Virtually every thought can be expressed in six different question forms: close-ended, open-ended, probing, hypothetical, leading, and loaded. Almost without exception, the open-ended question is the most effective, yielding the most information. Hypothetical questions can also be very productive.

10. *Consider specific employment interview questions.* Be prepared to ask effective, relevant, information-producing questions about education and prior work experience.

11. *Adjust your approach when dealing with problem applicants.* Shy, nervous, overly aggressive, highly emotional, very talkative, or dominant applicants each require some variation from your regular interviewing approach. Be careful not to become too emotionally involved in these instances—practice empathy, not sympathy. Also be careful not to lose control of the interview.

12. *Plan team interviews carefully.* If carefully planned, the team approach can be very effective. This planning includes the seating arrangement as well as the role played by each team member.

In addition to these guidelines, there are some pitfalls that interviewers should try to avoid:

1. Avoid interrupting the applicant, as long as he or she is saying something relevant.
2. Avoid agreement or disagreement; instead, express interest and understanding.
3. Avoid using terminology that the applicant is unlikely to be familiar with.
4. Avoid reading the application or résumé back to the applicant.
5. Avoid comparisons with the incumbent, previous employees, yourself, or other candidates.
6. Avoid asking unrelated questions.
7. Avoid talking down to an applicant.
8. Avoid talking about yourself.

9. Avoid hiring an unqualified applicant simply because you are desperate to fill an opening.
10. Avoid trying to duplicate someone else's interviewing style.
11. Avoid allowing applicants to interview you or to control the interview.
12. Avoid hasty decisions based solely upon first impressions, information from others, a single response, nonverbal communication, or your biases.
13. Avoid asking questions, even in a roundabout way, that might be considered violations of EEO laws.
14. Avoid judging applicants on the basis of cultural or educational differences.
15. Avoid conducting stress interviews of any sort.

Closing the Interview

Just as some interviewers have trouble knowing how to begin interviews, others are uncertain about how to close them. To help you decide if it is time to end an interview, ask yourself the following questions:

- Have I asked the applicant enough questions about his or her education and previous experience to determine job suitability?
- Have I adequately described the available position and provided sufficient information about this organization?
- Have I discussed salary, benefits, growth opportunities, and other related topics to the extent that the policy of this company permits?
- Have I allowed the applicant to ask questions?

If your answers to all four questions are yes, then you are ready to make your closing remarks. These should entail telling the applicant what happens next. For example:

Interviewer: Well, Ms. Ryan, I believe that I have all the information I need. If I have answered all your questions, I would like to close by telling you what will happen now. We still have a dozen or so more candidates to interview throughout the remainder of this week. After this, we will check references and make our final selection. Everyone will be notified by mail regarding our decision. In the interim, if you have any additional questions, please do not hesitate to call me. I want to thank you for coming in. I have enjoyed talking with you.

Summary

This chapter has described the essential components of an effective face-to-face employment interview, beginning with an outline of various interview formats. The importance of establishing rapport was then discussed, followed by suggestions for getting to the heart of the interview with the very first question. Active listening guidelines were offered, in addition to suggestions for note taking. The role of nonverbal communication was described, as were methods for encouraging applicants to talk. Specific information that interviewers should provide to applicants was discussed next. Different types of interview questions were assessed, and 135 examples of open-ended questions relating to education and experience were offered. Techniques for dealing with problem applicants were also provided. The merits and drawbacks of team interviewing were dealt with, followed by some examples of stress interviews. Finally, a list of interviewing guidelines and pitfalls preceded suggestions for effectively closing the interview.

Having concluded the interview, you are now ready to review your impressions of the candidate and elaborate on the notes taken during the interview.

7

Writing Up the Interview

In the previous chapter it was suggested that key words and phrases be jotted down throughout the face-to-face interview. Further, it was recommended that the interviewer elaborate on these notes immediately after the interview. This documentation is a permanent record of your interview and should be written with care. Whether you use a separate preprinted form, a section of the employment application form, or a blank piece of paper, the same guidelines relating to your notes or documentation will apply.

In addition to serving as a permanent record of an interview, documentation enables the interviewer to assess a particular applicant's job suitability. After the interview process is completed and all candidates have been seen, the interview notes for each should be placed side by side with the job description. The interviewer may then compare the applicant's relevant experience, skills, and accomplishments, as documented, with the requirements, duties, and responsibilities of the available position as outlined in the job description.

Postinterview documentation may also be used to compare the notes pertaining to those applicants "in the final running." Each set of notes should be closely measured against the others and all examples of outstanding achievements and shortcomings should be identified.

Moreover, these notes will prove useful to the original interviewer and others considering rejected applicants for future job openings. In addition, postinterview documentation is frequently scrutinized as potential evidence in employment discrimination suits.

For these reasons, it is important for interviewers to carefully document all interviews. The following guidelines should enable even those who are wary of committing their observations to paper to confidently write up an interview.

Avoiding Subjective Language

Avoiding subjective language, even if complimentary, is one of the most important requirements for effective postinterview documentation. Stated another way, all language that is written down should be objective. For example, saying that an applicant is attractive is a subjective statement. On the other hand, writing that "the applicant's appearance is consistent with the employee image desired by the organization for this position" would be objective.

As you can see from this example, objective language generally takes longer to write and requires greater effort. It is clearly much easier to say that someone is attractive than it is to write the objective version of the very same thought. However, the term *attractive* may not mean the same thing to everyone as it does to you; hence, it would not be very helpful to future interviewers reviewing your notes, or even to you if your opinion as to what constitutes attractiveness changes over time! In addition, it certainly could create an issue in an EEO investigation.

Following are some additional examples of subjective language that should be avoided:

Abrasive	Energetic
Acted high	Erratic
Acts like a real know-it-all	Fake smile
Appears to be rich	Fidgety
A real sales job	Full of hot air
A real workaholic	Good sense of humor
Arrogant	Greedy
Bad dresser	Has a bad attitude
Boring	Ideal candidate
Calculating	Ingenious
Careless	Interesting
Chip on his/her shoulder	Jovial
Cocky	Lacks luster
Cultured	Looks like a model
Curt	Looks too old
Diligent	Looks too young
Easily distracted	Makes lots of mistakes
Eccentric	Manipulative

Money-hungry	Sarcastic
Narrow-minded	Sharp
Needs polish	Shrewd
No roots	Sloppy
No sense of humor	Sluggish
Not serious about working	Smart
Perfect	Snappy dresser
Personable	Somber
Polished	Tactful
Pompous	Too hyper
Pontificates	Too much makeup
Pretentious	Too pushy
Refined	Tried too hard
Reserved	Uptight
Restless	Vain
Rude	Very nervous

Avoiding Recording Opinions

In addition to avoiding subjective language, interviewers are cautioned against recording their opinions. These are statements that generally begin with phrases such as the following:

> "I feel . . ."
> "In my opinion . . ."
> "I believe . . ."
> "It is apparent to me that . . ."
> "In my judgment . . ."
> "I am of the opinion that . . ."
> "I think . . ."
> "It is my view that . . ."
> "To my way of thinking . . ."

These phrases imply that the interviewer has drawn some conclusions, but they fail to identify what information these conclusions were gleaned from. Such broad, summarizing statements do not refer to concrete or factual qualifications. Reading interview notes containing statements such as these would not be useful in determining the applicant's job suitability.

Following are some expressions that illustrate the ineffectiveness of recording opinions:

"I feel Ms. Jenkins would make an excellent supervisor."

"In my opinion, Mr. Martin does not have what it takes to be a sales representative."

"I believe Ms. Salamander is just what we're looking for!"

"It is apparent to me that Mr. Brock can't do this job."

"In my judgment, Ms. Princeton will make an excellent project coordinator."

"I am of the opinion that Mr. Valentine will make a good addition to our staff."

"I think Mr. Turner will make a good mechanic."

"It is my view that we would be making a mistake if we hired this applicant."

"To my way of thinking, Ms. Davis appears to be perfect for the office assistant position."

"I believe Mr. Curtis is the perfect candidate for this job."

"I consider Ms. Hastings to be excellent secretarial material."

"It is my view that Ms. Heller will do quite well as a data processing operator."

"As I see it, Mr. Murphy is just right for this job."

"To my way of thinking, Mr. Windsor will make a great switchboard operator."

"If you ask me, we've found our next assistant vice-president of marketing."

"Mr. Casper seems to be the best administrative applicant we've seen so far."

"I think Ms. Richards will do just fine."

"I believe, with a little training, this candidate will work out."

"I feel we'd be lucky if Mr. Jenkins accepted our offer."

"I think we've got ourselves a winner!"

None of these statements tells us anything about the candidate's qualifications for a given job and all should, therefore, be avoided.

Referring to Job-Related Facts

Thus far, the focus has been on what should be avoided in writing up interview notes: Neither subjective language nor opinions should be recorded. Next considered will be the two documentation techniques that best enable the interviewer to assess job suitability, compare the qualifications of several candidates, measure the applicant for future job matches, and preclude the possibility of referencing any information that might violate EEO laws.

The more effective of these two techniques requires that only job-related facts be referred to. This is a rather simple process, if the relevant job descriptions are well-written and if active listening techniques were practiced during the interview. As soon after the interview as possible, refer directly to each duty and requirement of the position and then indicate whether or not the applicant has the necessary skills and experience. In addition, you may want to record direct quotes of the applicant.

The latter is of particular significance when a candidate possesses all of the concrete requirements of the job but is lacking in some intangible, nonrecordable quality. For example, you are about three-quarters of the way through an interview; even though the candidate can clearly handle the duties of the job, you have an uneasy feeling about her "attitude" toward a number of factors. Since recording that the applicant has "a bad attitude" would be subjective, you need to continue to probe until you come across some job-related reason for rejecting her. Among other things, you explore with her the fact that this job requires extensive overtime with little advance notice. Your question to her in this regard might be "Describe a time in your last job when you were asked to work overtime at the last minute; how did you react?" She replies, "I told my boss I didn't like the idea of being asked at the last minute! I mean, obviously I stayed, but I didn't like it." You might then say, "Are you then saying that you have a problem with working overtime, especially on short notice?" She might then reply, "I'll do it— but only when I absolutely have to."

When it is time to write up this interview, you might write: "This job requires extensive overtime with little advance notice. When asked how she felt about working overtime on short notice, applicant replied, 'I'll do it—but only when I absolutely have to.' "

By writing up your notes in this manner, you have clearly indicated that the applicant has effectively eliminated herself because she finds objectionable one of the requirements of the job— working overtime with little advance notice.

Following is another, more comprehensive illustration of the usefulness of referring directly to the position's duties/requirements and recording direct quotes of the applicant:

You are trying to fill the position of secretary to the president of your organization. Here are the primary duties and responsibilities of the job, taken from the job description:

1. Takes, transcribes, and edits dictation. Dictation may be taken directly, over the phone, or from a machine. Editing

    of dictation includes research for the completion of correspondence and/or reports involved.

2. Schedules all appointments and meetings for the president. Arranges the president's travel itinerary, including commutation, reservations, and accommodations.
3. Screens all calls and visitors to the president's office.
4. Opens, reroutes, and disposes of all correspondence directed to the president.
5. Replies to routine inquiries.
6. Supervises record and filing system of all correspondence and reports in the president's office, including confidential information.
7. Delegates routine typing and filing to clerk-typists and supervises work of same.
8. Prepares and writes formal minutes of all board of directors meetings, as well as shareholders and executive committee meetings.
9. Prepares various reports required for meetings of the board of directors, shareholders, and executive committee.
10. Performs other related secretarial duties as required.

As you interview each candidate applying for this position, refer to the specific job requirements. A partial sample interview might go something like this:

Interviewer: Please describe the extent of your experience taking dictation over the past three years in your present position as senior secretary.

Applicant: Well, my boss, who is a vice-president, dictates by machine about three times a week. Sometimes she dictates directly to me and I take down everything in shorthand and then transcribe it.

Interviewer: How much research does this involve?

Applicant: None. I just type what she says.

Interviewer: What are your responsibilities with regard to scheduling appointments and meetings?

Applicant: Oh, I do all of that. I even arrange international trips, because my boss travels to Europe about a half-dozen times a year. It's up to me to book her hotel reservations and everything like that.

Interviewer: What do you do when someone calls or stops by your office and wants to speak with or see your boss?

Applicant: By now, I pretty much know who she wants to see and who I should turn away. I use my judgment and may tell someone she's in a meeting and cannot be disturbed. I will also offer my help. Sometimes the person has a question that I can answer.

Interviewer: What happens if someone insists, saying it is urgent?

Applicant: I repeat myself, saying she is in a meeting, and again offer to help. I try to be polite and professional at all times, even though some people can get pretty nasty.

Interviewer: What are your responsibilities with regard to the mail?

Applicant: I open all the mail, except envelopes marked "confidential." Then I stamp everything and put the pile on my boss's desk. She likes to go through everything herself.

Interviewer: Then what happens?

Applicant: Then, about midmorning, she returns those letters, memos, and reports requiring action. She attaches little notes to everything, telling me who to call or what to type.

Interviewer: What is the extent of any supervisory responsibility you may have?

Applicant: I don't have any. I do everything myself.

Interviewer: Am I correct in understanding, then, that you do not delegate any typing or filing to anyone else?

Applicant: That's correct. I do it all myself. My boss gives some typing and filing to a clerk-typist in the office, but I don't get involved with that.

Interviewer: What about taking minutes at meetings?

Applicant: No, I don't do that. The president's secretary does it.

Interviewer: What kind of things do you type on a regular basis?

Applicant: The usual: letters, memos, that kind of thing.

Interviewer: What about things you type less frequently?

Applicant: I type a monthly project status report and then a quarterly report.

Interviewer: What is the quarterly report about?

Applicant: It includes quarterly accomplishments and the goals for the next quarter.

Interviewer: What other secretarial duties do you perform?

Applicant: I also type our department's budget.

Interviewer: How frequently does that occur?

Applicant: Only twice a year, but it takes a long time to do.

This partial interview illustrates the importance of writing down job-related facts as they relate to the duties and requirements of a job. The interviewer related each question to one of the responsibilities listed in the job description. As the applicant responded, the interviewer might have jotted down the following key words and phrases.

> V.P.
> Dictate: three times per week (mach/direct)
> No research
> Appt's, meetgs, travel (internat)
> See/call: judgment; offer help; polite and profess at all times
> All mail—not confid; stamp only
> No super/delegat
> No minutes
> Types memos, letters, reports—reg. basis
> Types quarterly proj. status report + biannual dept. budget

After the applicant has gone, the interviewer can review these thoughts and elaborate on his or her notes. By once again referring to the position's requirements, he or she can determine overall job suitability. The final set of notes, based on this portion of the interview, might read like this:

> Applicant has worked as secretary to V.P. for three years. Regular responsibilities include dictation (by machine and shorthand); scheduling appointments, meetings, and making travel arrangements (domestic and international); opening and stamping mail; typing memos, letters, and reports; and screening calls and visitors. When asked how she would handle persistent callers, she responded, "I try to be polite and professional at all times." Also types departmental biannual budget. Lacks experience with research, supervision, delegation, and taking minutes.

Everything written is a job-related fact, including the quote, which reflects an intangible quality that is important in this position.

Being Descriptive

The second technique that is effective in postinterview documentation entails recording a description of the applicant's behavior, speech, attire, or appearance. This technique may be utilized by interviewers conducting interviews for entry-level jobs as well as volume interviews; that is, they schedule perhaps forty or more interviews a week. After seeing so many people, the interviewer has difficulty referring back to each person's application or résumé and differentiating one from another. Even notes that are objective, factual, and job-related may not succeed in jogging your recollection of a specific candidate. To help you with this, consider the occasional use of descriptive phrases. Their purpose is limited to identifying the person and helping you recall the specific interview. Care must be taken in the use of such phrases for two primary reasons: First, they can easily become subjective; and second, even though factual, they are not job-related. To illustrate, "Applicant was dressed entirely in yellow" is an objective descriptive phrase. The addition of just one word, however, could make it subjective: "Applicant was garishly dressed entirely in yellow."

Here are some additional examples of objective descriptions:

Smiled during the entire thirty minutes of the interview
Hair extended below waist
Wore blue nail polish
Wore pearl cuff links
Chain-smoked throughout entire ninety minutes of the interview
Twirled hair
Played with paper clips
Tapped fingers
Taller than 6′6″ (doorway to office is 6′6″)
Laughed frequently
Chewed gum
Rocked in chair

Interviewers are cautioned against using any of these descriptive terms in the selection process. They are only intended to help you remember the applicant, not to determine job suitability.

Tape-Recording Interviews

Some interviewers feel that there are too many problems relating to note taking, including the amount of time it takes and the possibility of writing something down that violates EEO regulations. Instead of following the simple rules just cited, they reason that it is easier to tape-record the entire interview. Of course, it is difficult to refute the fact that it's easier to record than to write. However, there are two very good reasons for not doing this:

1. If the applicant knows that you are recording the interview, this is almost guaranteed to make him or her feel nervous and reluctant to speak freely. It also causes some candidates to become angry and defensive.
2. If the applicant does not know that you are recording the interview, you are violating his or her right to privacy.

The only time that a tape recorder can reasonably be used as part of the employment process is after an interview is completed; the interviewer may then choose to record his or her observations before the next scheduled candidate arrives. Even if this is done, however, the interviewer should transfer the dictated thoughts to paper; written notes should accompany every application or résumé.

Assigning Numerical Values

Some organizations incorporate a point system in the note-taking stage of the interview. When using this method, the interviewer assigns a numerical value to each factor evaluated. Factors appear on a preprinted form with a key that briefly explains the point value of each rating. For example, the overall rating for a five-point value system might look like this:

1 Superior overall skills and qualifications
2 Above-average skills and qualifications
3 Meets the requirements of the job
4 Fails to meet all of the requirements of the job
5 Not qualified

Then, each individual factor might be evaluated according to the following scale:

1 Outstanding.
2 Very good
3 Good
4 Fair
5 Poor

There are a number of problems with this kind of system:

- The accompanying point value form may contain factors that are subjective and are not job-related. These may include appearance, personality, awareness, maturity, tact, and self-confidence.

- As explained earlier, using subjective terms such as *outstanding* or *poor* to judge someone is meaningless.
- Busy interviewers who rely on forms with several preprinted categories tend to quickly check off boxes without giving enough thought to each person's actual skill level.
- Without specific written details regarding each applicant, it will be extremely difficult to distinguish one person from another at a later date.

If forms are used, they should include only job-related factors (i.e., various aspects of education and experience). In addition, ample space should be allowed for the interviewer's notes. Overall evaluation categories of "meets job requirements" and "fails to meet job requirements" may be included as well. A sample interview evaluation form appears in Appendix H.

Of course, a form does not have to be used at all; a blank space left at the bottom of the application, or a blank piece of paper attached to the application or résumé, will suffice. Just remember to restrict your comments to objective, factual, and job-related information, with occasional descriptive comments as needed.

Interviewing for Jobs With No Requirements

You may find yourself recruiting for jobs that do not carry any experiential or educational requirements. These are usually entry-level positions or jobs requiring very simple, repetitive tasks. Naturally, when this occurs you cannot evaluate someone's demonstrated skill level. In these instances, consider posing hypothetical questions relative to the specific tasks of the job and recording the applicant's reply. For instance, suppose that the opening for a messenger calls for picking up presorted mail from the mail room and distributing it to each employee. During the course of the interview, you might ask an applicant, "What would you do if an employee told you that he or she was expecting a very important letter, but it wasn't included in the mail you had just brought to him or her?" The applicant might reply, "I would give that person the name and extension of my supervisor to check on it." Your notes for this interview might then include the following reference to the job-related activity: "When asked how would handle missing mail, said, 'Tell employee to check with supervisor.' "

Therefore, even with applicants who lack prior work experience, postinterview documentation can be objective, factual, and job-related.

Taking Effective Notes

At this time it will be helpful to illustrate both effective and ineffective note taking. An abridged job description for the position of human resources assistant, and excerpts from an interview for this position, will be presented. It should be noted that the interview excerpts only include questions asked by the interviewer and responses by the applicant. They do not include detailed information provided about the job and the company, nor do they include questions asked by the applicant. Following the interview excerpts are examples of effective and ineffective note taking.

Job Description for Human Resources Assistant

Duties and Responsibilities

Primary Duties and Responsibilities include:

1. Recruits applicants for nonexempt-level positions via various recruitment sources.
2. Interviews and screens all applicants for nonexempt positions; refers qualified candidates to appropriate department manager/supervisor.
3. Assists department manager/supervisor with hiring decisions.
4. Performs reference checks on potential employees, by telephone and in writing.
5. Processes new employees in terms of payroll and benefits; informs new employees of all pertinent information.
6. Is responsible for conveying all necessary insurance information to employees and assisting them with questions, processing of claims, etc.
7. Assists in the implementation of policies and procedures; may explain or interpret certain policies as required.
8. Assists in the maintenance and administration of company's wage and salary administration program; monitors salary increase recommendations as they are received to ensure compliance with merit increase guidelines.
9. Advises managers/supervisors of employee performance

review schedule; follows up on delinquent or inconsistent reviews.

10. Is responsible for the orderly and systematic maintenance of all employee records and files.

11. Assists EEO officer with advising managers/supervisors on matters of equal employment opportunity and affirmative action as they pertain to the interviewing and hiring process and employer-employee relations.

12. Assists in the maintenance of up-to-date job descriptions of positions throughout the company.

13. Maintains all necessary personnel records and reports; this includes unemployment insurance reports, flow-log recording, EEO reports, change notices, and identification card records.

14. Conducts exit interviews for terminating nonexempt employees.

15. Assists human resources manager and human resources director with the planning and conducting of each month's organizational orientation program.

16. Performs other related duties and assignments as required.

Prior Experience and/or Education

1. Thorough general knowledge and understanding of the human resources function

2. Prior experience as a nonexempt interviewer, preferably in a manufacturing environment

3. Ability to work effectively with all levels of management and large numbers of employees

4. Ability to deal effectively with applicants and referral sources

Partial Interview for Human Resources Assistant

Interviewer: Good morning, Ms. Oliver. Thank you for coming in. Please be seated.

Applicant: Thank you. I'm glad to be here and, by the way, it's *Mrs.* Oliver, but you can call me Sandra.

Interviewer: Did you have any difficulty getting here, Sandra?

Applicant: No, my daughter attends nursery school about one mile from here, so I'm very familiar with the area.

Interviewer: Well, I'm glad that you didn't have any trouble. I'm anxious to begin talking with you about your interest in our opening for a human resources assistant.

Applicant: Oh, I'm ready! I've been looking forward to this all week. I really want this job!

Interviewer: Fine. Then why don't we begin to discuss your qualifications as they relate to the responsibilities of this job.

Applicant: Great!

Interviewer: To begin with, the job requires recruiting, interviewing, and screening applicants for all of our nonexempt positions. Please describe your experience in this regard.

Applicant: Well, that's exactly what I've been doing for the past year at Circuits, Inc.

Interviewer: Please explain what you mean.

Applicant: Well, whenever I receive an approved job requisition, it's up to me to start recruiting. The first thing I do is talk with department heads to make sure that I understand the requirements and duties of the job. I also try to visit the department in order to get a feel for the work environment and to see firsthand what the person will be doing. It also helps beef up my rapport with the department head. Let's see; where was I? Oh, yes; then I start to explore different recruitment sources.

Interviewer: Such as?

Applicant: The usual: agencies, want ads, walk-ins, employee referrals.

Interviewer: Any others?

Applicant: That's usually all it takes. We don't have any trouble attracting applicants. We have a fine reputation in the manufacturing industry, as I'm sure you know.

Interviewer: Please, continue.

Applicant: Well, I interview and screen all the applicants and then refer those qualified to the department head.

Interviewer: Where did you learn to interview?

Applicant: I have a degree in personnel administration, as you can see on my résumé, and then I received on-the-job training when I first joined Circuits, Inc.

Interviewer: How much time was devoted to on-the-job training?

Applicant: About three months; then I was left on my own.

Interviewer: I see. Please go on.

Applicant: Okay. As I said, I refer qualified candidates to the department head. Then, we get together and decide on who to hire.

Interviewer: Who finally makes the actual hiring decision?

Applicant: The department heads and I usually agree, but if we disagree, they decide. After all, they're the ones who have to work with the person.

Interviewer: What are your responsibilities with regard to reference checks?

Applicant: I run both written and telephone references on only those applicants we're interested in.

Interviewer: Once the applicant is selected, what do you do?

Applicant: I arrange the starting date and schedule them for orientation. It's also my job to put them on payroll and take care of their benefits.

Interviewer: So then, it is your responsibility to explain all of the company benefits?

Applicant: No, not exactly. I just process the paperwork. Someone from the benefits department explains all of that during orientation.

Interviewer: I understand. Tell me, Sandra, does Circuits, Inc. have a policies and procedures manual?

Applicant: Yes, it does.

Interviewer: What are your responsibilities with regard to this manual?

Applicant: Sometimes if my boss, the human resources manager, is not around, I try to answer questions from department heads, but I don't usually get involved with that.

Interviewer: In addition to recruiting, interviewing, screening, and processing payroll and benefits paperwork, what other areas of human resources are you involved with?

Applicant: Well, let's see. Let me think for a minute. Oh yes, I'm in charge of performance reviews.

Interviewer: In what way are you in charge of performance reviews?

Applicant: I keep a log of when each nonexempt employee's review is due and notify the department head if they don't get them in on time.

Interviewer: I see. Is there anything else, say with regard to salary administration?

Applicant: We have a wage and salary manager who takes care of that.

Interviewer: What about EEO and affirmative action?

Applicant: No. Our EEO officer handles that. I know a lot about those areas though.

Interviewer: You know a lot about EEO and affirmative action?

Applicant: Yes. I studied it in school and attended a three-day seminar on it about six months ago. I'd like to specialize in EEO some day.

Interviewer: What other human resources responsibilities do you have as a human resources assistant at Circuits, Inc.?

Applicant: Well, I help with job descriptions.

Interviewer: In what way?

Applicant: Whenever there's a nonexempt job opening, I check with the department head to make sure that the job has not changed significantly and that the existing job description is still valid. If it needs revamping, I tell my boss and she takes over from there.

Interviewer: What are your responsibilities with regard to personnel files and records?

Applicant: I keep an applicant flow-log and process employment change notices.

Interviewer: Any other forms?

Applicant: None that I can think of.

Interviewer: What about any involvement with exit interviews?

Applicant: Oh, yes, I forgot about that! I do all exit interviews for nonexempt employees. I enjoy that!

Interviewer: What is it that you enjoy about it?

Applicant: I like finding out why a person is leaving and what the company might do in the future to prevent good people from leaving.

Interviewer: I see. That's very interesting.

Applicant: Yes. I really like that part of my job.

Interviewer: What other aspects of your work do you enjoy?

Applicant: I like the interviewing: you know, talking to so many different people.

Interviewer: What don't you like about your job, Sandra?

Applicant: If I had to pick one thing, I guess it would be the paperwork: mostly the employment change notices.

Interviewer: What aspect of your job do you find to be the most difficult?

Applicant: I guess that would be my part in the monthly orientation program.

Interviewer: You participate in the orientation program?

Applicant: Yes, didn't I mention that? I have to give an opening talk of about twenty minutes about the history of Circuits, Inc., why it's such a great place to work, that sort of thing.

Interviewer: What is it about doing this that you find difficult?

Applicant: I get nervous talking in front of people.

Interviewer: I see. Sandra, I'd like to get back for a moment to your educational training in personnel administration. What made you decide to pursue this field?

Applicant: It seemed challenging and varied. It also seemed to offer a lot in the way of growth opportunities.

Interviewer: What level do you ultimately want to achieve?

Applicant: I think I'd like to be an EEO officer.

Interviewer: What were your grades like in college, both in personnel courses and in other courses?

Applicant: I graduated with a 3.0 average. I did pretty well in everything except math. I failed statistics.

Interviewer: What did your personnel courses consist of?

Applicant: Everything: The degree prepared us to be generalists.

Interviewer: I know you said that you particularly like EEO. What aspects of human resources do you enjoy the least?

Applicant: That would have to be benefits. I really find it kind of dry and boring.

Interviewer: I understand. Sandra, I have just a few more questions to ask you. Tell me, what would you do if an applicant acted up? By that I mean, became aggressive or cried.

Applicant: I'd try to calm them down. That's happened a few times to me and after a few minutes they usually settled down.

Interviewer: What did you say to make the applicant settle down?

Applicant: I told them that I wanted to learn about their qualifications, but that I couldn't do so if they didn't stop shouting or whatever it was they were doing. It worked.

Interviewer: How did that make you feel?

Applicant: I felt bad for them. I could see how much they wanted the job. But I also knew I had to remain objective if I was going to evaluate them fairly.

Interviewer: What does the prospect of this job offer you that your present job does not?

Applicant: It's time for a change.

Interviewer: A change?

Applicant: Yes. One year in Circuits, Inc. is long enough. It's not the most exciting place in the world to work.

Interviewer: What is your idea of an ideal work environment?

Applicant: One where employees who prove themselves can grow; also, where managers don't look over your shoulder all the time. Of course, I would like to be paid more, too!

Interviewer: What type of employee are you?

Applicant: I like to work independently. I don't need close supervision.

Interviewer: What do you feel you could offer our company?

Applicant: I'm a hard worker and I love the field of human resources.

Interviewer: Is there anything else I should know about your qualifications that would help me to make a hiring decision in your favor?

Applicant: I can't think of anything else.

Interviewer: Fine, Sandra, I'd like to thank you again for coming in. We will be interviewing for the next five days or so, and will make our decision at the end of that time. All applicants will be notified by mail. If you have any questions in the interim, please do not hesitate to call me. I've enjoyed talking with you.

Applicant: Thank you. I've enjoyed talking with you, too. I really want this job!

Interviewer: I understand. Good-bye, Sandra.

Applicant: Good-bye.

Examples of Ineffective Notes

Here are the ineffective notes taken as a result of the interview:

Married; young daughter
Too anxious
Tends to ramble
Only nine months' real experience; degree okay
Likes P&P involvement
Had trouble remembering what else she does
Interested in EEO; I smell trouble
No real J.D. experience
Light record keeping
Sounds like a troublemaker; loves to find out why people leave
    the company, then tries to get company to make changes
Dislikes doing orientation
Dislikes benefits
Light experience with problem applicants
Bored with present job
Wants more money and to move up
Doesn't like supervision

Summarizing Statement

I don't feel Mrs. Oliver would make a very good h.r. assistant. She just doesn't seem reliable. Also, she hasn't demonstrated a thorough knowledge of h.r.

As you can see, these statements are highly subjective. In addition, many of the comments are not job-related.

Examples of Effective Notes

Now, let us review the effective notes:

Circuits, Inc., manufacturing
Nonexempt interviewing experience—9 mos.; 3 mos. O.J.T.
Degree in personnel admin.
Recruits, interviews (enjoys), screens, and recommends for hire
Telephone and written references
Processes payroll and benefits paperwork
P&P manual; most questions handled by h.r. mgr. (boss)
No sal. admin. respon.
Expressed interest in pursuing field of EEO
Checks on accuracy of existing j.d.s
Flow-log and employee change notices (enjoys least)
Exit interviews for all nonexempt employees (enjoys)
Participates in monthly orientation prog.: "nervous talking in
    front of people"
Least favorite: benefits
Reason for leaving: "time for a change"
Has dealt with applicants who have acted up; knew it was
    important to remain objective
"Like to work independently"
"I'm a hard worker; I love the field of human resources."

Summarizing Statement

This job calls for a thorough general knowledge and understanding of human resources and prior experience as a nonexempt interviewer. Ms. Oliver has had three months' on-the-job training and nine months' actual experience in the following areas of h.r. at Circuits, Inc.: nonexempt recruitment, interviewing, screening, references, processing payroll and benefits paperwork, checking accuracy of job descriptions, flow-logs and employee change notices, exit interviews, monthly orientation. Also has a degree in personnel administration. Recommends hiring; interested in EEO; enjoys exit interviews; least favorite—benefits. "Wants a change"; "Likes to work independently"; "hard worker"; "loves h.r."

These statements are all objective, factual, and job-related. Anyone reading them would have an immediate understanding of the applicant's skill level as it relates to the requirements of the job.

Summary

This chapter examined the four main ingredients of effective post-interview note taking. In summary, they are as follows:

1. Avoid subjective language.
2. Avoid recording opinions.
3. Refer to job-related facts.
4. Be descriptive.

In addition, the problems of tape-recording interviews and of using a numerical value or point system were examined. Suggestions were also offered regarding documentation for jobs without educational or experiential requirements. Finally, examples of effective and ineffective interview notes were provided.

8

Preemployment and Employment Testing

We live in a society that relies on testing. Children and young adults may be subjected to twenty or more years of testing, beginning in preschool and continuing through graduate school and beyond. The process continues at work, as tests are given to screen out, evaluate, classify, predict, and promote. We may also be asked to take tests to determine if we are strong enough, smart enough, or healthy enough. Then there are honesty tests, drug tests, and personality tests. It is doubtful that many of us have ever stopped to think about how many tests we have taken so far in our lives, but if we did, the resulting number would undoubtedly be startling.

What is this fixation we have with tests? More significantly, why do so many people believe in a test's reliability to predict suitability, i.e., for employment? Are tests, in fact, valid indicators of job success?

Some employers believe so strongly in tests being virtually infallible and reliable predictors of job suitability that they will not even conduct the face-to-face interview without first administering a series of tests and assessing the results. Others, however, feel that tests are basically worthless, perhaps even dangerous, in that they may result in inaccurate, inappropriate, or incomplete conclusions. These individuals usually place a great deal of emphasis on the employment interview to determine job suitability.

In addition to the controversy over the benefits of preemployment and employment testing, there are also the legal issues of test validation and the relationship between tests and discrimination. In this regard, many questions need to be addressed, including what constitutes a valid test, when tests should be given, who is qualified to administer various types of tests, how to interpret test results, the issue of adverse impact, and the possible ramifications of using unvalidated tests.

If tests are to be considered as part of the recruitment and selection process, a careful and objective analysis of testing in terms of its characteristics, guidelines for validation, scoring, and relationship to discrimination should first take place. Various types of tests should then be reviewed for applicability to specific jobs. Numerous classifications exist, including intelligence, personality, physical ability, honesty, and drug use; knowing which tests are most suitable for a given job can be a challenge in and of itself.

Testing Characteristics

In simplest terms, preemployment and employment tests may be defined as procedures for determining job suitability. This is accomplished by examining the skills, knowledge, and/or physical capabilities of employees or employment candidates according to a predetermined set of objective guidelines. The results are assessed in relation to the requirements and responsibilities of a given position and conclusions are drawn as to the appropriateness of the applicant's qualifications.

While many tests evaluate a job candidate's achievements and, hence, measure current skill level, others focus on aptitude, or a person's potential ability. Tests may also help determine how motivated a person is likely to be in a certain type of job and/or work environment. In addition, they may be used to screen out individuals with certain undesirable traits, such as job-related physical shortcomings or drug use.

Based on this description, tests certainly seem to be useful recruitment and selection tools. They can help employers select employees who are more capable, better motivated, and less likely to bring certain unacceptable qualities to the job. Also, tests can help distinguish between otherwise similarly qualified candidates. In addition, the objective nature of testing can help employers make unbiased, job-related employment decisions. This lends itself to another benefit of testing; that is, when tests are fair representations of the skills and knowledge needed to perform a given job, employers are likely to be portrayed as impartial; this, in turn, may serve to enhance the overall image of the organization.

Not surprisingly, there are some disadvantages to testing. A tendency to overrely on tests for screening or hiring purposes is one of the greatest concerns expressed by opponents. Even if a test is well designed and properly used, the results can only indicate which individuals are most *likely* to do well. No test can point with certainty to those people who *will* do well. Hence, employers are cautioned against using test scores exclusively to make employment decisions; tests should, instead, be viewed as one of many factors contributing to selection.

While there are several multipurpose tests, many tests are designed to emphasize—and, therefore, seek out individuals who possess—specific skills or knowledge. This can screen out candidates who might otherwise make good employees. In some instances, the qualities being sought via testing may be acquired through a minimal amount of on-the-job training or education.

Opponents to testing also point out that many people react negatively to the mere idea of a test; others, who may, in fact, be qualified, simply do not do well on tests. This can result in a distorted or incomplete picture of a candidate if too much emphasis is placed on test scores.

Weighing the pros and cons of testing can make difficult a decision as to when testing is appropriate, how much weight to place on test results, and whether or not to use tests at all. To help resolve these issues, begin by ascertaining the specific skills, knowledge, and abilities needed to perform the duties and responsibilities of a given job. This usually calls for a written job description. Ask yourself whether an applicant could acquire the required skills on the job in a relatively short period of time or should come to the job already possessing certain abilities. Also, anticipate any possible consequences of hiring (or promoting, transferring, etc.) someone into the available position without the required knowledge. Next, determine the importance of excellence in relation to the requirements of the job. If the job opening can readily be filled by any one of a number of candidates with comparable abilities, then testing to distinguish superiority may not be necessary. Also, decide if there might be other, equally effective means for determining job suitability. Certain verifiable credentials and certifications might adequately indicate acceptable skill/knowledge level. Information obtained via the face-to-face interview and through employment or educational reference checks may also provide sufficient data, precluding any need for formal testing.

Uniform Guidelines on Employee Selection

Even proponents of testing admit that there are a myriad of stipulations and conditions that must be contended with before the administration of legitimate preemployment and employment tests. Fortunately, the Equal Employment Opportunity Commission (EEOC), the Department of Labor's Office of Federal Contract Compliance Programs (OFCCP), the Civil Service Commission (renamed the Office of Personnel Management), the Department of Justice, and the Department of the Treasury together set forth, in 1978, a comprehensive set of *Uniform Guidelines on Employee Selection Procedures* that help guide employers through the testing process. The primary purpose of these guidelines is to provide a framework for determining the proper use of preemployment tests relative to referral or hiring decisions; and employment tests pertaining to promotions, demotions, transfers, training, retention, and any other employment decisions. Selection procedures other than tests, including interviews, application forms, references, and performance evaluations, are also covered by the guidelines. Hence, the more encompassing expression *selection procedure* is preferred over the term *test*.

These guidelines apply to private employers with fifteen or more employees, state and local governments, most employment agencies, labor organizations, and contractors/subcontractors of the federal government.

The guidelines are designed to make certain that tests and other selection procedures do not have an adverse impact on the employment opportunities of individuals of a particular race, sex, religion, or national origin. Employers are, therefore, required to conduct validity studies of tests where adverse impact has occurred, and, in general, are advised to only use valid tests, even if adverse impact has not been shown. Validation refers to the demonstration of the job relatedness of any test or other selection procedure. Adverse impact is defined by the guidelines as "a substantially different rate of selection in hiring, promotion or other employment decision which works to the disadvantage of members of a race, sex or ethnic group." A selection rate for any race, sex, religion, or national origin that is less than four-fifths, or 80 percent, of the selection rate for the group with the highest selection rate is considered a substantially different rate of selection. This is referred to as the "four-fifths" or "80 percent" rule of thumb. The four-fifths rule of thumb does not mean that up to 20 percent discrimination is tolerable; rather, it establishes a basis for requiring additional information.

The process of validation can be unnerving if one does not clearly understand how it works. In broad terms, validation begins with a thorough job analysis to identify the requirements of the job. The next step entails identifying selection devices and standards that will isolate those applicants or employees meeting the job requirements. Testing current employees and applicants without using the test scores to influence any employment-related decisions can help measure the effectiveness of the selection device being tested. This process should take place over a long period of time and be applied to a large sample population to make more credible the validity of the results. The last phase involves preparing a detailed validation report that outlines and documents the steps taken.

The *Uniform Guidelines* recognize three specific methods of determining validity:

1. *Criterion-related validity* is a statistical demonstration of a relationship between scores on a selection procedure and job performance of a sample of workers.
2. *Content validity* is a demonstration that the content of a selection procedure is representative of important aspects of performance on the job.
3. *Construct validity* is a demonstration that a selection procedure measures something believed to be an underlying human trait or characteristic, i.e., honesty, and that this trait or characteristic is important for successful job performance.

While the *Uniform Guidelines* do not state a preference of one validity method over the others, it is generally agreed that the criterion-related process, while effective, can be a long and expensive procedure to administer. Construct validity has been the source of much debate, in that the soundness of any trait claimed to support successful job performance is difficult to establish. Consequently, most employers rely on content validation, believing that it most accurately predicts job success.

Employers who choose to continue using a test with an adverse impact may be found to be engaged in discriminatory practices and hence be held liable for various penalties, including back pay awards, plaintiffs' attorney fees, and the loss of government contracts. If, however, an employer has substantial evidence of validity or has a study under way that is designed to document the evidence required by the guidelines within a reasonable time, an employer may continue to use a test that is not yet fully supported by the required evidence of validity. In such an instance, employers are discouraged from making hiring decisions based on unvalidated test results. In addition, alternative selection procedures should be explored.

Many employers turn to industrial and personnel psychologists with expertise in the conduct of validation research for help with the validation of their selection procedures. These trained psychologists may be faculty members in colleges and universities, independent consultants, or members of a consulting organization. Additional information regarding individuals qualified to conduct validation studies may be obtained from the American Psychological Association, 1200 17th Street, NW, Washington, D.C. 20036.

In addition to test validation, other areas for which trained professionals should be consulted are creating employment tests or tailoring existing tests to better meet the needs of a specific employer's business. "Homemade" tests developed by nonprofessionals place employers at greater risk of liability since such tests are harder to validate than are professionally developed and researched tests. Tests developed by professionals are also considered more likely to be good predictors of job performance than are homemade tests.

Caution should be exercised, however, in purchasing a prepackaged test from any vendor, including expert psychologists. The credentials and reputation of any vendor should be checked carefully. In addition, the vendor's publication record should be reviewed. Most importantly, a test's relevance to your objectives should be determined. This may be accomplished by examining the test's underlying research, then bypassing those tests for which little or no validation research exists, or which claim validity for use with occupational groups unlike those in your organization. Also, beware of vendors who use terms like *valid, reliable,* and *court defensible* without substantial supporting documentation.

Purchasing or using a test that does not have a sound base can only increase your potential liability; furthermore, it will do little to assure that you have hired those candidates with the best chance for success on the job.

Testing and Discrimination

Title VII of the Civil Rights Act of 1964 made illegal the discrimination against any individual with respect to any term or condition of employment, on the basis of race, color, religion, sex, or national origin. Two years later, we saw one of the first cases to focus on specific employment testing discrimination in Illinois with *Myart v.*

Motorola. Leon Myart, a black applicant for a job at a Motorola factory, alleged that the hiring practices at Motorola were racially discriminatory in that he had been asked to take a qualifying test containing questions requiring familiarity with a predominantly white, middle-class culture. A hearing examiner for the Illinois Fair Employment Practices Commission agreed that this was discriminatory, but the Illinois Supreme Court overturned the examiner's ruling. Nevertheless, news of this case alerted the public to the issue of testing and discrimination.

Griggs v. Duke Power Co. drew even greater attention to the issue of testing and discrimination with its landmark ruling in 1971. Up until the passage of Title VII, Duke Power Co. openly practiced racial discrimination by employing black workers only in the labor department where they were paid less than workers in other, all-white departments. Once Title VII rendered such practice illegal, the company opened up job opportunities to blacks in all departments but established a new set of hiring requirements, including a high school diploma and satisfactory scores on two aptitude tests: the Wonderlic Personnel Test and the Bennett Mechanical Aptitude Test. Blacks argued that the tests and diploma requirements had an adverse effect, were arbitrary, and were not job-related. The trial court ruled that the tests did not violate Title VII, because Duke Power did not have a discriminatory intent. The U.S. Supreme Court disagreed. It stated that Title VII was concerned with consequences of employment practices, not motivation, drawing an important distinction between intent and effect. The Court further criticized employment testing in general, and while *Griggs v. Duke Power Co.* left companies free to use tests, it limited the use of tests having an adverse impact on minorities by its holding that "Congress has forbidden giving [testing or measuring procedures] controlling force unless they are demonstrably a reasonable measure of job performance."

In addition to *Griggs*, another landmark case with regard to testing and discrimination is *Albemarle Paper Co. v. Moody*, decided by the U.S. Supreme Court in 1975. While this case also involved employment requirements of a high school diploma and two tests, what made it particularly significant was that Albemarle had hired a psychologist who found a significant correlation between the test scores for current employees and their performance evaluations. The Supreme Court was not impressed and stipulated that having a psychologist claim that the test was a valid indicator of job success was not sufficient.

Connecticut v. Teal, decided in 1982, focused on yet another aspect of testing and discrimination. This case concerned an employer who required employees to pass a written test in order to qualify for promotion. The written test had not been validated and the proportion of blacks passing the test was only 68 percent of the proportion of whites. However, not everyone who passed the test was promoted, and the percentage of blacks who were promoted was actually higher than that of whites. This, however, did not influence the U.S. Supreme Court's ruling that tests still had to be validated. The high percentage of blacks who were promoted did not compensate for the possibility that the test had discriminated against those blacks who failed it.

In 1988 Clara Watson, a black woman, was denied a promotion on the basis of the evaluation of her work by white supervisors. She sued in *Watson v. Fort Worth Bank & Trust* and offered evidence that, on the average, black workers received lower performance ratings and fewer promotions than did whites. The U.S. Supreme Court agreed with Watson, ruling that subjective employment practices are subject to the same standards as are the objective criteria, such as tests, used to make hiring decisions.

Employers should note that employment tests are governed not only by federal laws, but also by state laws covering fair employment practices. This is significant, in that many state laws allow discrimination claims to be tried by juries that may award punitive damages in addition to back pay. On the other hand, it takes much longer—often years—to go to trial in state court.

Testing Policies

Companies administering tests should have a written policy that clearly states that the primary objective of their preemployment and employment testing program is to select qualified candidates, regardless of race, creed, religion, national origin, sex, age, or disability. The policy should then describe how various tests are administered, evaluated, and interpreted. Details of this policy should be made available to all those directly involved in the testing process. In addition, a testing policy statement should be distributed to all managers involved in employee hiring decisions.

Those involved in the testing process should be trained in proper administration procedures. Following are some general guidelines for test administration:

- Tests should be given only when job-related criteria indicate a direct correlation between test results and job performance.

- Tests should never be given exclusively to members of selected groups, i.e., women, minorities, or the disabled.
- The testing environment should be the same each time a test is given. This includes factors such as lighting, ventilation, seating, space, and noise.
- The same tools or materials should be distributed in exactly the same order and manner each time a test is given.
- The purpose of the test should be explained to test takers at the outset. The language used to describe the purpose of the test should be identical each time the test is administered.
- Oral instructions should be recited at the same rate of speech using the same tone of voice and at the same pitch and volume. In addition, the exact identical words should be used. Since even the same person's voice can vary from time to time, prerecorded instructions may be used.
- The same amount of time should be allotted for the test each time it is administered.
- Care should be taken not to project expectations about the test results.
- Every effort should be made to eliminate known anxiety-producing factors, such as an excessively long waiting period before the test is administered, uncomfortable seating, noise, faulty equipment, flickering lights, or inadequate heating or air conditioning.
- The number of people who have access to copies of the test and any answer or scoring sheets should be limited.
- Care must be exercised when scoring objective tests, i.e., those in a multiple choice format or those resulting in numerical scores, to use the correct answer key. Computers may be used to score these types of tests. Subjective tests, such as personality and intelligence tests, should only be scored by experts with the appropriate training.
- The opportunity for retesting and reconsideration must be afforded across the board.

To help ensure the uniformity of test administration, some test publishers have started developing computer-administered versions of standard employment tests. These tests allow test takers to read the instructions and questions from a computer monitor and then respond by using either a light pen, which allows "writing" directly on the screen; a "mouse," a desktop device that is moved in one of several directions as the test taker selects an item on the screen; or a keyboard, which allows for typing out answers. The answers to test questions posed by all of these methods are then keyed directly into the computer.

Proponents of computer-administered tests maintain that these procedures eliminate any possibility of administrator bias, thereby ensuring standardized testing procedures. On the other hand, test scores may be adversely affected if users are not comfortable or familiar with computers. In addition, supplying a sufficient number of computer terminals for all test takers can be costly.

A modified version of computer-administered tests gaining in popularity is computerized adaptive testing or tailored testing. In this method, the computer selects questions of appropriate difficulty for the test taker based on that person's demonstrated ability to answer earlier questions during a preliminary evaluative test. This technique is favored by many who are concerned with test security, since different candidates receive different questions. It is also favored because it saves time and reduces frustration for test takers who are asked questions that are too easy or too hard.

Opponents, however, argue that uniformity, one of the principal requirements of testing, is adversely affected when different questions are asked of different applicants for the same job. They also worry about premature decisions being made based on the preliminary evaluative test results.

All variations of computer-based testing are subject to the standards and requirements for selection procedures as outlined in the *Uniform Guidelines on Employee Selection Procedures.*

The uniformity rule of testing is, generally, put aside for disabled test takers who require special accommodations. For example, visually impaired applicants may need to have tests presented via cassette tapes, with the assistance of a reader, or written in large print or Braille. In addition, visually impaired applicants will probably require additional time to complete a test. According to at least one 1984 study, "Employment Testing for Handicapped Persons," Braille readers need from 2.1 to 3.3 times longer than average to complete a test, and readers of large print need from 1.7 to 2.4 times as long.

Local agencies that provide vocational rehabilitation for the visually impaired can suggest sources that will prepare adapted tests for applicants with special needs.

Hearing-impaired test takers will also require special accommodations. Spoken instructions will have to be replaced with written information and possibly sign language. Allowances may also have to be made for the fact that people born with hearing impairments may suffer significant language deprivation and, consequently, score consistently poorly on word-oriented tests.

Test takers with motor disabilities may require a variety of accommodations to compensate for their inability to walk, write, or work with specific tools. Special access to test sites should be provided for wheelchair-bound applicants. Computer-administered tests may help some motor-disabled test takers who find it easier to work a keyboard than to hold a pencil or turn pages. In addition, specially adapted equipment or personal help may also be required. In certain instances, it may be deemed appropriate to waive the test altogether and permit some alternative demonstration of job ability instead.

Test scores and results should be disclosed only to test administrators, human resources representatives, and any managers directly involved in the testing and hiring process. Disclosing test results to the test takers themselves may be dictated by state law. Some states, including California, Connecticut, Delaware, Illinois, Maine, Massachusetts, Michigan, Nevada, New Hampshire, Oregon, Pennsylvania, Rhode Island, Utah (public employees only), Washington, and Wisconsin, allow employees and former employees (but not applicants) access to their personnel files and all the information contained therein that was used to make an employment decision. Unless specific exceptions are cited, as is the case in Connecticut and Illinois, test information is also accessible. State and local government civil service laws generally require government employers to notify test takers of their total scores and of the cutoff score for qualification.

Many employers disclose test results to test takers as a matter of fairness. Those reluctant to reveal the results generally base their decision on the belief that disclosure without explanation may result in a misinterpretation of scores. In addition, there is concern over compromising test security.

Employers with fifteen or more employees are required by Title VII of the Civil Rights Act of 1964 to keep copies of tests, test results, and any related validation studies for a minimum of six months. If a charge of discrimination is filed, these records must be retained until the matter is resolved. State and local civil rights laws may require longer retention.

Types of Tests

In an attempt to diminish any confusion over the vast array of tests available, two primary test classifications, with additional subclassifications, are offered:

Achievement and Aptitude Tests

- Tests of job knowledge
- Work samples
- Physical ability and psychomotor tests
- Intelligence tests
- Personality tests

Physical and Security-Related Tests

- Preemployment physical exams
- Drug tests
- AIDS testing
- Polygraph tests
- Written honesty tests

Achievement tests are designed to measure current skills and indicate a person's existing abilities. *Aptitude tests* are intended to measure a person's potential ability to perform a given task. Professional testers recognize the distinction in terms, but prefer to categorize achievement and ability tests together, maintaining that both measure developed ability and, therefore, yield related results.

Job Knowledge Tests

Tests of job knowledge, also known as trade tests, require applicants to demonstrate the degree of existing knowledge they have regarding how a given job is performed. Hence, job knowledge tests screen prospective employees to ensure they have the experience claimed. These tests are based on the belief that the more closely a test resembles a job and the more it measures performance against actual samples of tasks performed, the better it will be able to predict actual job performance. The majority of companies that conduct job knowledge tests require them for clerical and other office positions, production and service jobs, and technical work. Tests may include office math, office procedures, general clerical ability, stenographic skills, secretarial procedures, mechanical familiarity and knowledge, accounting procedures, typing, and word processing.

Job knowledge tests may be oral or written. Oral tests may consist of a series of questions asked by a test administrator or may be more structured, with a panel asking job applicants a preselected set of questions. A structured scoring system determines the results. Oral tests generally take less time to administer than do written tests, but they are not easily standardized, making a challenge more probable. Written tests of job knowledge are more common and are usually scored on a pass/fail basis. They are more easily administered and standardized, and more comprehensive than are most oral exams. They may, however, be costly to develop and, by virtue of the fact that they are written, tend to emphasize literacy. This last point could pose problems if literacy skills are not relevant to the job.

Most job knowledge tests are developed according to the content-validation approach and, overall, are considered to have fairly high validity. Many companies develop and validate their own tests internally; others choose to purchase commercially developed job knowledge tests. Anyone purchasing a test should first conduct a thorough job analysis to determine the absolute appropriateness of the purchased test. Additional information regarding commercially developed job knowledge tests may be obtained from Employers' Tests and Services Associates in Chambersburg, Pennsylvania (717-264-9509), the National Business Education Association in Reston, Virginia (703-860-8300), the Psychological Corporation in San Antonio, Texas (512-299-1061), or Purdue University in West Lafayette, Indiana (317-743-9618).

Work Samples

Work samples differ from job knowledge tests in that they require applicants to demonstrate the level of skill they possess, as opposed to degree of knowledge. Work samples may be used with actual job-related equipment, such as a typing test, or performed on simulated equipment, such as a repair simulation test. Since work samples test an existing level of achievement, they are best used to select experienced workers who already have a degree of proficiency in a given area. For this reason, they are often considered useful in making promotion decisions.

There are two basic types of work samples: motor and verbal. Motor work samples might include programming tests for computer operators and stenographic tests for secretaries. Common verbal work samples include in-basket tests for managers and tests of ability to write business letters. Both motor and verbal work samples are considered to be highly valid predictors of job proficiency. Because of this and the fact that they are generally well accepted by job applicants and employees, work sample tests are growing in popularity. They are, however, time-consuming to administer.

In developing work samples, the most critical factor is that a complete and thorough job analysis be conducted. Furthermore, in order to adequately protect themselves from challenges to a work sample's validity, employers should fully document all the steps in its development.

Large companies generally contact qualified outside professionals for assistance in preparing work samples. The Educational Testing Service in Princeton, New Jersey (609-921-9000); National Computer Systems Professional Assessment Services in Minneapolis, Minnesota (800-328-6759); and QUIZ, Inc. in Atlanta, Georgia (404-843-1124) are but a few of the suppliers who will either help an organization custom-develop work samples or provide prepared samples for selected fields and skills.

Physical Ability and Psychomotor Tests

Many on-the-job injuries occur because the tasks require more strength and endurance than the employee can exert without excessive stress. These injuries can lead to increased absenteeism and turnover, not to mention workers compensation and health insurance claims. Since it is extremely difficult, if not impossible, to judge a person's strength and level of endurance on the basis of body size and appearance, physical ability tests, also known as strength and endurance tests, can be helpful preemployment selection devices for positions requiring physical performance.

Several strength and endurance factors have been identified as being relevant to employee selection, including dynamic strength, involving the power of arm and leg muscles to continuously support or move the body's own weight; trunk strength, which is dynamic strength specific to trunk muscles; explosive strength, which involves a burst of muscular effort; static strength, the muscular force needed to lift, push, or pull heavy objects; dynamic flexibility, the ability to make repeated trunk or limb flexing movements; gross body equilibrium, which measures the body's ability to maintain or regain balance; and stamina, the ability to sustain physical activity over long periods of time.

The preferred validation method for physical ability tests is content validity. Simply stated, this means that a thorough job analysis has determined that a given test accurately reflects the primary duties and responsibilities of a specific job. Many employers contact private agencies or clinics for assistance with physical ability testing. The cost per person is generally in the range of twenty to thirty dollars.

Psychomotor tests measure such abilities as manual dexterity, motor ability, and hand-eye coordination. They are used primarily for semiskilled, repetitive work, such as packing and certain forms of inspection. Most psychomotor tests are simulation tests, although some written tests may be considered useful. The most valid psychomotor test should call for the use of the same muscle groups as the job requires. Custom-made tests that reproduce the combination of motor abilities required have been shown to have fair validity. Several prepared psychomotor tests are available, including the Purdue Pegboard, the Hand-Tool Dexterity Test, The Crawford Small Parts Dexterity Test, and the O'Connor Finger Dexterity Test. Although these tests may be based on validity studies, local validation is still recommended.

Intelligence Tests

Experts do not seem to be able to agree as to just what intelligence is. Some experts maintain that there is an intelligence quotient (IQ) that measures a person's ability to perform all cognitive or thinking tasks. Others believe that intelligence is multidimensional, that is, it consists of separate mental abilities that cannot be "averaged out" to equal one level. Others contend that intelligence consists of many cognitive abilities that together result in an overall mental ability.

The controversy over the definition of intelligence leads, not surprisingly, to disagreement over its measurement. Some believe in using general intelligence tests that concentrate on abstract functions involving the use of verbal or numerical reasoning. Tests such as the Personnel Tests for Industry (The Psychological Corporation, San Antonio, Texas, 800-233-5682), which include a five-minute verbal test and a twenty-minute numerical test, and the Thurstone Test of Mental Alertness (Science Research Associates, Inc., Chicago, Illinois, 312-984-7016), a twenty-minute test of 126 questions relating to word meaning, definitions, and arithmetic reasoning, are available for use in business.

The effectiveness of such tests for specific jobs is questioned, however, by many employers who choose, instead, to use aptitude tests that evaluate more practical abilities. A number of such aptitude tests are available for measuring clerical, mechanical, and computer-related abilities. Examples include the Minnesota Clerical Test, the Bennett Mechanical Comprehension Test (both distributed by The Psychological Corporation), and the Computer Programmer Aptitude Battery (distributed by Science Research Associates, Inc.).

There are also several multiple-aptitude tests that measure a variety of job-related aptitudes. The General Aptitude Test Battery (GATB), developed by the U.S. Employment Service, for example, consists of twelve tests and includes measurements of verbal, numerical, and spatial abilities. Widely used by private employers and state job services across the country since 1947, the GATB is, as of this writing, facing discontinuance for a period of two years by the federal government. During this time the Department of Labor (DOL) will conduct an investigation of the test's "within-group" scoring method, whereby separate scoring scales for different racial groups are permitted in order to avoid adverse impact on minority groups. The result according to the DOL may be reverse discrimination. If the reevaluation of this test results in its permanent discontinuance, other tests are likely to be challenged as well.

The Flanagan Aptitude Classification Test is another multiple-aptitude test measuring aptitude for sixteen different job skills, including basic arithmetic, knowledge of correct English grammar, sentence structure, problem-solving, and the ability to use good judgment in practical situations.

Published intelligence tests cost an average of three to five dollars per person; multiple-aptitude tests cost more. Volume discounts are usually available. Employers who want to purchase intelligence tests should ask for proven evidence that the test is valid relative to the type of job for which it will be used. In general, multiple-aptitude tests have a higher validity rate than do single tests. Additional information regarding an intelligence test's validity may also be found in such test directories as the *Mental Measurements Yearbook*.

Personality Tests

Personality tests may focus on a variety of psychological characteristics. For example, there are tests for measuring a person's emotional stability; ability to work under pressure; and susceptibility to depression, paranoia, hysteria, or schizophrenia. Even drug abuse and eating disorders may be identified via such tests as the Minnesota Multiphasic Personality Inventory, which was recently updated to more accurately reflect today's language, concerns, and culture. Such tests are usually designed by psychologists with expertise in human behavior and statistical analysis. Test publishers generally sell personality tests only to those trained in psychological testing. For example, the *1990 Personnel and Career Assessment Catalog*, published by The Psychological Corporation, provides a lengthy description of rules and qualifications governing the sale of testing materials. In addition, it maintains the right to require evidence of the purchaser's qualifications. Likewise, the *1989 CPP Catalog of Tests and Materials for Business* (Consulting Psychologists Press, Inc.) clearly states, "Psychological tests have potential to benefit humankind when they are properly used. Improperly used, they are at best of little value, at worst dangerous. For this reason, the Committee on Ethical Standards of the American Psychological Association requires that distributors of certain restricted tests limit their sale to persons whose education and experience should enable them to use tests appropriately." The message goes on to define the qualifications for various levels of testing.

Information regarding the services of industrial psychologists who might assist your organization with the development and/or implementation of validated psychological tests may be obtained from the American Psychological Association (202-955-7600).

There is a great deal of controversy surrounding personality tests. Proponents of this preemployment and employment assessment tool maintain that an objective personality test, coupled with other traditional selection devices, can provide a clear picture of a person's abilities, interests, and potential. This, it is argued, can result in lower turnover rates and greater productivity. Proponents also maintain that personality tests gather information in such a way that the people taking these tests are unaware of exactly what they are revealing. Hence, there is little chance of charges of discrimination and resulting lawsuits.

Opponents of personality tests argue, however, that personality is extremely difficult to measure. Even if tests could perfectly measure an individual's personality, there is no reason to assume that this would result in more productive work. There is also concern over the apparent inherent assumption that personalities do not change, thereby implying that matches deemed appropriate or inappropriate via testing will remain so. Furthermore, there is doubt as to the validity of personality tests that fail to take into account the role of motivation: An unmotivated employee is not apt to perform well on the job, even with the desired personality traits.

One form of personality test gaining in popularity claims to offer broad character assessment: *graphology,* or handwriting analysis. Supporters of this method claim that a person's handwriting reveals information about emotional stability, impulsiveness, vulnerability to stress, assertiveness, social skills, integrity, and a host of other characteristics. It is further maintained that handwriting cannot be faked; therefore, it is concluded, graphology is likely to provide a clear picture of a person's strengths and shortcomings.

Not everyone agrees that the size, slant, loops, space between letters, pressure, and rhythm of someone's handwriting can reveal job-related personality traits. Indeed, there is little empirical evidence supporting the validity of graphology as a preemployment or employment selection device. On the contrary, Wayne Camara, a testing expert with the American Psychological Association, has been quoted as saying, "Handwriting analysis tends to have low reliability."

Employers who decide to use graphology as a selection device are cautioned against relying on it as the primary or exclusive means for determining job suitability. Other, more reliable measures of past experience, ability, and predictors of potential should be focused on, with graphology used only as a possible means of acquiring additional information.

Another type of personality test that is just beginning to capture the attention of employers is based on *color psychology*. It is called the Lüscher personality test, named after its originator, Dr. Max Lüscher, a Swiss psychologist. Originally used in 1947 by psychologists and physicians as an aid for diagnosing conditions of strain or psychosomatic illness, it also revealed personality characteristics. The Lüscher Color Test has since been modified for use in business. Assessments are based on the test taker's preference for various shades of color and combinations of colors. The underlying premise of the test is that people will choose colors that reflect their physical and psychological needs. These needs, in turn, reflect a person's psychological and physical condition. The test takes approximately five minutes to complete. No questions are asked.

Proponents assert that the test is appropriate for all individuals, regardless of education, cultural background, or intellect. It is further claimed that normal types of color blindness have no bearing on the validity of the test.

The soundness and validity of this test as an employment selection device is questionable and not yet adequately proven. Potential administrators of the Lüscher Color Test should be questioned about their formal training, credentials, and experience. Samples of their work and references from other employers who have used the test should be ascertained. In addition, employers who use this, or any relatively new and undocumented personality test, for that matter, should collect their own validity data, regardless of evidence of adverse impact. The simplicity of the process should not lull employers into attempting self-administration.

Physical and security-related tests are intended to ensure a work force of individuals who are physically able to perform the essential functions of their jobs, do not threaten the health or safety of others, have been honest in the representation of their skills and background, and may be trusted in their daily dealings on the job.

Preemployment Physical Exams

Preemployment physical examinations can help identify individuals who are physically unable to perform the essential functions of a given job in a safe and effective manner. More specifically, they may disclose a person's past and present state of health, prior exposure to harmful substances or an injurious environment, family health history, and genetic composition. (It should be noted that proponents of genetic testing maintain that such tests can identify certain job applicants or employees predisposed to specific types of occupational illnesses. Opponents, however, argue that genetic testing is not routinely warranted for employment purposes and could unfairly exclude qualified workers.) Predictive screening can also assess an applicant's susceptibility to future injury.

Employers are subject to the prevailing preemployment physical restrictions and guidelines of their respective states. These generally include requiring the employer to pay for the entire cost of the examination, providing the employee with a copy of the test results, and maintaining the confidentiality of the results. State regulations may also control the timing of tests and who may or may not be tested. Some states restrict preemployment physicals to only those applicants who have been extended an offer of employment. In these instances, employment is generally conditioned on the successful completion of the medical exam. Other jurisdictions stipulate that preemployment medical exams must be given to all applicants. This includes applicants with prevailing disabilities. Depending on the test results, accommodation for those with physical or other impairments may be required, barring undue hardship to the employer. Note also the stipulation in the ADA (see Chapter 5) that disabled individuals cannot be singled out for physical exams.

Employers are advised to ascertain their state's specific requirements before beginning or continuing with preemployment physical tests. This can usually be accomplished by examining state fair employment acts or civil rights acts, or by consulting with an attorney knowledgeable in this area.

In these litigious times, ever-increasing numbers of employers are requiring applicants and employees to sign a waiver acknowledging that the company does not guarantee the accuracy of its physician's conclusions. This sort of waiver is an attempt to limit the employer's liability for negligence if the employee later suffers an on-the-job injury as a result of a condition that was not detected during the preemployment physical. The Occupational Safety and Health Act (OSHA) requires employer retention of employee medical records for the duration of employment plus thirty years.

Preemployment physical exams can be significant in their detective and evaluative abilities, assuming the physician administering the exam is familiar with those tasks that are essential to the performance of each job applied for and evaluation is limited to the candidate's ability to perform those tasks. Test results are not always accurate, however, and offer limited predictive qualities. Consequently, physicals are best used as one of several selection devices.

Drug Tests

Drug testing is clearly one of the most anxiety-producing issues confronting human resources specialists and managers today. On the basis of a recent dramatic rise in use, it appears that drug testing will remain a controversial matter with which more and more employers will have to contend.

According to a recent *Business & Legal Reports (BLR)* survey of over twenty-three hundred employers from many areas and industries in the United States as described in the January 1990 issue of the *Personnel Manager's Legal Reporter*, 33 percent of the respondents reported testing all applicants for drug use. An additional 14 percent tested some applicants. In 1988 a similar *BLR* study showed that only 21 percent of the surveyed employers were testing all applicants. Specific industries reported even higher percentages. For example, 61 percent of the manufacturing companies surveyed test all applicants. The more recent survey also showed an increase from 15 percent in 1988 to 31 percent in 1989 in testing of employees "for cause" by all employers surveyed. Twelve percent test employees on a random basis, the most controversial form of drug testing—an increase from one percent just one year earlier.

Random testing programs are slowly gaining support from the courts. For example, in May 1990, New York state's highest court upheld random drug testing for prison guards in New York City. This decision, say legal experts, is likely to prompt an increase in the random testing of whole classes of workers throughout the state, as well as influence the decisions of other state courts in upcoming cases. Lower courts in other states have also upheld random drug testing. For example, prison guards in Iowa are subject to random testing, as are police officers and firefighters in Annapolis, Maryland.

Other surveys indicate that most employers favor some form of drug testing. This is exemplified by a survey released on December 13, 1989, conducted by the Gallup Organization for the U.S. Chamber of Commerce. It revealed that of the more than one thousand employers surveyed nationwide, 97 percent feel that drug testing in the workplace is appropriate, at least under some circumstances, and 55 percent believe periodic drug testing is warranted.

The first employer to regularly practice drug testing was the Department of Defense, beginning in the early 1970s, to screen returning Vietnam War veterans for drug use. By 1982 every branch of the U.S. armed forces was conducting mandatory urine testing for drugs. In September of 1986, President Reagan issued Executive Order 12564, calling for drug testing of federal employees. In December 1989 the Department of Transportation began enforcing its antidrug regulations, affecting nearly 4 million workers whose jobs have safety or security implications in the transportation industry. In addition, the U.S. Department of Health and Human Services adopted guidelines for drug testing programs impacting 1.1 million federal employees.

Drug testing is on the rise for a very simple reason: Drug use in the workplace has escalated, resulting in numerous problems, including increased absenteeism, more on-the-job accidents, a higher incidence of theft, and greater medical costs. In addition, the passage of the Drug-free Workplace Act of 1988, which requires all grant recipients and private sector businesses with federal contracts in excess of $25,000 to certify that they will maintain a drug-free workplace, has prompted many employers to implement drug testing programs—even though this is not mandated by the Act.

In spite of this, objections have been raised to drug testing in the workplace. For instance, across-the-board drug testing as part of a "zero tolerance" policy designed to deter drug use off the job as well as on the job has been criticized by some courts as an unwarranted invasion of privacy. In addition, opponents object to drug testing because of potential legal liability, the excessive costs for properly conducted drug testing programs, an adverse effect on employee morale, and the possibility of erroneous results.

Concern over the possibility of erroneous results is grounded in the technique most commonly used for drug detection: *urine testing*. The two categories of urine tests, screening and confirmatory, can both result in false positives, with screening tests being less accurate than confirmatory tests. Screening tests cost less to conduct—from six to eleven dollars each as opposed to between sixty and one hundred dollars per sample for confirmatory tests—and are easier to administer; they are, therefore, often the tests of choice for many employers. Accordingly, there is a great deal of concern over "clean" applicants and employees being falsely accused of drug use. When positive screening test results occur, employers are advised to conduct a second, confirmatory test. If the second test reveals illegal drug use, employers may deny applicants employment or may terminate an employee after ample opportunity is provided for treatment or cessation of drug abuse.

This course of action has legal ramifications in the form of suits filed by applicants/employees claiming they have been falsely accused of drug use. One common reason for such lawsuits is the allegation that positive test results may not prove any act of wrongdoing. Urine can retain traces of drugs for anywhere from a few days, e.g., in the case of cocaine and amphetamines, to a month, as with the drug classification cannabinoids. Consequently, while a urine test may indicate use of an illegal drug, it cannot establish any of the following with certainty: that the drug was used during working hours, impaired the employee's ability to perform his or her work, interfered with the work of others, or endangered the safety of others.

Other lawsuits stem from false positive test results caused by the use of legitimate, over-the-counter drugs. This is most likely to occur when screening tests are used, since they frequently report "drug detected" without distinguishing which drug is involved. To reduce this possibility, it is advisable to ask test takers to identify all drug products used in the weeks prior to the test.

Because positive urine tests do not tie in directly with any allegations of wrongdoing and since these tests often detect common drugstore items, some employers are seeking alternatives to urine tests. One option is a *blood test,* which is, according to Dr. Lawrence Miike of the Congressional Office of Technology Assessment, ". . . a surer indication than detectable urine levels that the person has used the drug very recently, usually within a matter of hours." Alternative nonmedical tests, such as *balance and reflex performance checks,* may also be considered as substitutes for urine tests. As with blood tests, the results of nonmedical tests can indicate on-the-job impairment.

Another nonmedical drug test that has recently been introduced to the workplace is the *critical tracking test.* This test is intended to assess on-the-spot employee fitness by measuring fine hand-eye coordination and quick reaction time. In addition to detecting drug impairment, it is also designed to detect alcohol use, lack of sleep, emotional stress, and illness. It is considered most appropriate for workers in jobs where safety is a critical factor.

The test takes approximately one minute to administer. Workers are asked to keep an electronic pointer centered on a computer screen; since the point continuously moves, test takers must manipulate a knob to return it to the center of the screen. The longer employees are able to control the pointer, the higher their psychomotor performance rating. Performance on any given day is measured by the computer against the worker's previously established normal performance.

Some employers who administer the test to groups of workers, e.g., drivers, do so each day before they begin their shift. Anyone who fails the test is temporarily assigned to other duties.

Supporters of the critical tracking test applaud the fact that it focuses on job-related impairment and provides immediate results. Opponents express concern over possible inappropriate reactions by employers toward employees who fail the test. They also question the applicability of the test to positions requiring the performance of complex tasks and decision making.

In addition to blood tests and various nonmedical drug tests, other alternatives to urine tests are being utilized. One such test, which is highly controversial, is *hair analysis*. In this process, hair samples are examined using radioimmunoassay, then confirmed by gas chromatography or mass spectrometry. This is the same technique used to test urine samples. The premise of the hair analysis test is that chemicals in the bloodstream, both legal and illegal, are left in hair follicles and subsequently trapped as the hair grows, thereby providing a record of past drug use. Types of drugs and frequency and duration of use can all be determined. Supporters of hair analysis maintain that it is a valid drug test accepted by courts in criminal trials; however, there have been no court cases involving hair analysis in the employment context as of March 1990, according to the annual report of the American Bar Association's Subcommittee on Drug and Alcohol Abuse in the Workplace. Proponents also contend that the test provides a detailed record of drug use, and is less embarrassing than urinalysis. Opponents claim that the process is highly invasive in that it provides information about an individual's drug-use history, instead of determining whether or not he or she is able to function safely on the job.

Another alternative to urine testing is the *pupillary-reaction test*. Here, an individual's eyes are examined by a trained professional who determines how the pupils react when shined on with a flashlight. The premise is that the pupils of subjects under the influence of drugs or alcohol will react differently to light. Urine tests are usually required to confirm the results of the pupillary-reaction test. Supporters maintain that the test is noninvasive. Opponents argue that certain medical conditions may give a false positive reading and that follow-up tests are necessary. In addition, a trained professional is needed to administer the test.

Employers who plan to utilize any form of drug testing should develop and implement a set of well-defined, written guidelines, available to all employees. These guidelines should include a description of the purpose of drug testing, who is to be tested, what method of testing will be used, where and when testing will take place, who will administer the test, and how the test will be administered. If urine tests are to be conducted, the guidelines should include a description of the manner in which specimens will be collected (privacy and dignity should be preserved without compromising test security or hampering test results). In addition, all applicants and employees being tested should be asked to sign a consent form, agreeing to the drug test and to the release of the results to the employer.

State laws on drug testing vary and should be checked carefully by employers and their legal counsel. In addition, employers should consult with an attorney before implementing a drug testing program of any kind.

AIDS Testing

Acquired immune deficiency syndrome (AIDS) is an area of increasing concern for all employers. A survey conducted by the American Society for Personnel Administration (now the Society for Human Resource Management) in 1987 stated that 33 percent of employers reported AIDS cases in their workplace; and a survey by Alexander & Alexander Consulting Group reported in 1988 that approximately one in ten companies has had one or more employees with AIDS. Consequently, many companies have developed AIDS policy statements affirming that terms of employment, benefits, training, and termination relating to employees with AIDS do not discriminate. Since such special policy statements imply that basing employment decisions on AIDS-related factors would be discriminatory, there is little justification for employers to implement an AIDS testing program. In addition, there is no direct test for AIDS itself. Current tests can show only whether a person has developed antibodies in response to the AIDS virus. The presence of antibodies, or of the AIDS virus itself, does not mean for certain that the person will develop AIDS, or, perhaps more significantly, is infectious. According to the Surgeon General's report on AIDS, "Everyday living does not present any risk of infection. You cannot get AIDS from casual social contact. . . . Nor has AIDS been contracted from . . . eating in restaurants (even if a restaurant worker has AIDS or carries the AIDS virus). You cannot get AIDS from toilets, doorknobs, telephones . . . [or] office machinery."

The Surgeon General's conclusions regarding AIDS have led many courts to declare that there is no risk to co-workers from AIDS virus carriers or AIDS-infected individuals.

In addition to statements by the Surgeon General and the courts, the Centers for Disease Control (CDC) has taken a stand with regard to this disease. It has issued recommendations for preventing the transmission of AIDS in the workplace. These recommendations pertain, in particular, to health care workers, persons providing personal services, and those preparing and serving food and beverages. According to the CDC, AIDS is not proved to be spread by casual contact; nor is it known to be transmitted through the preparation or serving of food. Hence, routine AIDS antibody screening for these and other groups is not recommended. The CDC does, however, recommend that testing be made available to health care workers and others who wish to know their AIDS status.

Copies of the CDC guidelines on AIDS may be obtained from the Office of Public Affairs, Centers for Disease Control, 1600 Clifton Road, N.E., Atlanta, Georgia 30333.

Outside of the U.S. Defense Department, the Job Corps, and the Foreign Service, all of which have AIDS testing programs, few private employers test for AIDS. In those few instances where an employer may determine that there is a legitimate basis for testing an applicant or employee for AIDS or, more accurately, for AIDS antibodies, prior consent should be obtained from the individual. A reliable test, such as the Enzyme-Linked Immunosorbent Assay (ELISA) test, should be used. If the results are positive, a confirmation test, such as the HIVAGEN Test, should be given. The applicant or employee should also be informed of test results, which must be kept in the utmost confidence.

Additional information regarding AIDS and AIDS testing may be obtained by calling the AIDS hot line (1-800-342-AIDS) or by writing to the U.S. Public Health Service, Public Affairs Office, Hubert H. Humphrey Building, 200 Independence Avenue, S.W., Washington, DC 20201.

Polygraph Tests

Like drug testing, polygraphs, which are mechanical lie detector tests, have been the subject of much controversy. However, unlike drug tests, whose future is yet to be told, polygraphs have been all but banned from use by private sector employers, effective December 1988, according to the Employee Polygraph Protection Act, a federal statute. The greatest implication of this Act is that lie detectors are no longer permitted for use as screening devices for job applicants.

There are certain exceptions where polygraph testing is permitted, among them when employers hire workers for security-sensitive jobs and pharmaceutical work. Employers involved in manufacturing, distributing, or dispensing controlled substances are also exempt from this legislation. In addition, the Employee Polygraph Protection Act does not apply to the federal government, state or local governments, or industries with national defense or national security contracts. Moreover, businesses with access to highly classified information may continue to use polygraph tests. However, although these employers are exempt, they may not use the results of the polygraphs as the sole basis for making an employment-related decision.

Use of polygraph tests to investigate employees reasonably suspected of stealing or committing other infractions is also permitted. Access to stolen property alone, however, is not considered a reasonable basis for suspicion. An employee believed to have committed an infraction must first receive a written notice that identifies the loss being investigated and the employer's basis for suspicion and explains the employee's statutory rights under the Act. Employees must also be advised of their right to consult with counsel before and during the examination.

Employees and applicants may refuse to take the polygraph test or may terminate it at any time. No test is allowed to last longer than ninety minutes. In addition, upon learning of the test results, they may request a second test and/or hire an independent examiner for a second opinion. Test takers must not be asked degrading or intrusive questions, or questions about sexual behavior, union activities, or religious, racial, or political beliefs. They must be given advance notice relative to testing conditions, and, before the test begins, they must be permitted to review all questions. Afterward, they must receive a written copy of the test questions, their responses, and any opinions based on the test results.

Employers may test according to these exceptions and guidelines only if they utilize the services of licensed, bonded examiners.

Violators of the Employee Polygraph Protection Act may be fined up to $10,000 per test; may be required to hire, reinstate, or promote the employee or applicant; and/or may have to pay lost wages and benefits, as well as attorneys' fees. Employers are required to conspicuously post a notice of this law where all applicants and employees may see it.

Some states have polygraph laws that are even more restrictive than the federal statute. These state laws will not be preempted by federal law unless the state provisions conflict with the federal Act. Employers who use polygraph tests unlawfully risk not only violation of federal and state statutes, but also legal liability on the basis of defamation and invasion of privacy.

Written Honesty Tests

Not surprisingly, since the Employee Polygraph Protection Act virtually banned the use of the most popular form of lie detector test, there has been an increase in the use of written honesty or integrity tests. With employee theft estimated at $40 billion a year nationwide, according to the U.S. Chamber of Commerce, employers are legitimately concerned over finding a means for ferreting out applicants who are likely to steal. Many believe written honesty tests are the answer. Most of these tests pose a series of direct and indirect questions related to thievery and deceit, while others also seek out the potential for unsafe work habits, drug abuse, and counterproductivity. These tests generally take about twenty minutes to complete and are scored by computer in approximately six seconds. The cost ranges from seven to fifteen dollars per exam.

While most people agree that written honesty tests are less intimidating than polygraphs, there is a great deal of concern expressed over the validity of these tests. Indeed, there are reports of companies who are simply transferring polygraph questions onto paper.

Test publishers argue that their written honesty tests are highly accurate and based on extensive research. However, many experts express concern over relying on such test results to determine job suitability. Robin Inwald, founder of Hilson Research Inc., recently stated, "Each test carries a probability of accuracy. You can't tell if a person will be honest or not just by looking at the score."

As of this writing, the Office of Technology Assessment is studying the accuracy of many integrity tests. The American Psychological Association is working on a similar study. In addition, the Association of Personnel Test Publishers is expected to issue voluntary guidelines for the testing industry and client companies. Several of these guidelines for clients were published in *The New York Times* on February 11, 1990:

1. Do not automatically assume low test scorers are dishonest.
2. Do not assume that tests can always accurately predict human behavior.
3. Do not accept any publishers' claims that their tests are absolutely accurate.
4. Do not make tests the sole basis for hiring decisions.

The guidelines also warn employers that most incidents of employee theft remain undetected.

Alternative Selection Procedures

Even proponents of testing agree that tests should not be the sole determining factor in making an employment decision. Other selection procedures, such as the face-to-face interview, the employment application form, and references, should also be used for making hiring decisions. These selection procedures are all covered by the EEOC's *Uniform Guidelines on Employee Selection Procedures* and are treated in detail in other chapters of this book.

Finally, although they are not discussed in this book, performance appraisals are also considered an alternative selection procedure in matters of promotion, transfer, demotion, changes in salary, job posting, and career pathing. An evaluation program should consist of criteria that are directly related to the primary duties and responsibilities of a particular job. The criteria should be specific, observable, and measurable. Factors to be considered might include the amount of time spent performing various duties, their level of difficulty, their frequency of performance, and the consequence of errors. The nature of each position, as well as its level of responsibility, should determine the amount of weight assigned to each of these factors. In addition, to be considered valid, an appraisal system should yield consistent data and show a direct correlation between the factors being measured and those that are critical elements of a particular job. Also, a performance appraisal system should be standardized in its design and consistent in its administration. Any employer using the system should be given written guidelines and be trained in their implementation.

Summary

The number and variety of tests utilized in relation to employment are on the increase. As some are deemed inappropriate, i.e., the polygraph test, others, such as written honesty tests, are available to replace them. The interpretive and evaluative potential of employment testing is, overall, controversial; and many specific test categories, like drug testing and AIDS testing, are the subject of much debate.

Employers who are interested in exploring the use of tests today must contend with numerous questions. For example:

- What constitutes a test?
- What are the benefits and disadvantages of testing?
- What is validation and how are certain tests validated?
- Is it advisable to buy a prepackaged validated test?
- What is the relationship between testing and discrimination?
- What kind of testing policy is best?
- What are the differences between certain types of tests?
- How costly is testing?
- How reliable are the results in terms of making an employment decision?

The purpose of discussing these and other test-related issues in this chapter has been to offer clear guidelines for effective decision making relevant to the use of employment testing.

9

Making the Selection

Finally, after all your prerecruitment preparation, exploration of various recruitment sources, preinterview planning, familiarization with EEO laws, interviewing, and documentation, it is time to make your final selection. For many interviewers, this is the most difficult step in the employment process. Often there are several candidates possessing the required qualifications, making the choice difficult; or the interviewer may feel uneasy when there is only one viable candidate, wondering if the recruitment effort has been thorough enough or the screening process too critical. Doubts may also arise because of the heavy responsibility in making a hiring decision, including the possible consequences of a poor selection.

How does an interviewer gauge who will make the best employee? What are the factors to consider? Who should make the final decision? These are some of the issues that will be covered in this chapter. The answers provided should enable interviewers to feel more comfortable with the selection process.

Conducting Reference Checks

Most interviewers will not make a hiring decision without first checking a candidate's references. In spite of well-honed recruiting, screening, and interviewing skills, interviewers do not feel comfortable in extending a job offer, for any level of employment, without more closely examining the background of the candidate of choice. This usually means talking with, or ascertaining written information from, former employers and verifying educational credentials. Most professionals agree that personal references rarely have any merit, since the candidate will obviously list only those references likely to

230

rave about him or her. Occasionally, however, these may be useful to supplement other character or professional references. In addition, receiving feedback from those who know the candidate on a personal basis may serve to ferret out potential negligent hiring and retention situations (see Chapter 5). All of these efforts, it is anticipated, will further the selection process by confirming the interviewer's own impressions of the candidate.

Invasion of Privacy and Defamation of Character

While most employers agree that references can be a valuable employment selection tool, few readily provide information to other employers. In fact, it is becoming increasingly common for companies to refuse to give references for former workers. This trend is founded on fear of being sued by a former employee for giving a less than flattering reference. Accordingly, many employers only verify dates of employment in an effort to reduce or eliminate any exposure to legal action on the basis of invasion of privacy or defamation of character.

Although it is difficult to blame employers for being careful in this regard, employers may be overly cautious, failing to realize that a great deal of information can be legitimately and legally imparted without fear of retaliation from the former employee. Although apprehension of being sued for defamation motivates many employers, understanding the meaning of the term should alleviate this concern somewhat. Defamation occurs when one person makes a statement about another that is false or harms the person's reputation. The statement may be either oral or written. In employment situations, allegations of defamation frequently arise when a former employer tells a prospective employer why an individual was terminated. The key to whether defamation has actually occurred is truth or falsity of the information. To be actionable, a statement must be a personal attack, lacking in veracity. Thus, if a former employer gives a prospective employer a false and damaging reason for an employee's termination or gives the discharged person a false basis for the discharge and the applicant repeats this to a prospective employer, then the candidate may have been defamed.

Employers fearing charges of defamation should also be aware that, based on case law, truth is an absolute defense, even if the statements made about a former employee are negative. However, the truth, too, may be actionable if it is communicated with malicious intent to do harm. Opinions or statements that are disputable are also protected by a limited privilege; that is, such communications must be malicious to be actionable.

Common-Law Doctrine of Qualified Privilege

Employers are further protected by the common-law principle of qualified privilege. This doctrine is premised on the public policy that an exchange of information relative to the job suitability of employees is in the best interest of both employers and the general public. Consequently, if such information is defamatory but without malice, it is deemed privileged.

This privilege is not without certain limitations, however. The information must be provided in good faith and in accordance with the questions asked. For example, if a prospective employer asks about a former employee's ability to work unsupervised, the voluntary statement that he or she had a problem getting in on time is not protected. Also, information about an individual's private life should not be offered unless relevant to work performance. Moreover, it should be ascertained that the information is being provided to the appropriate party and is relevant to the requirements of the job. Failure to comply with any of these conditions could eliminate the protection provided by the qualified privilege.

References and Negligent Hiring

In spite of the degree of protection afforded former employers by case law and the common-law doctrine of qualified privilege, many still fear liability and hesitate to provide references. The result has been a proliferation of lawsuits based on negligent hiring and retention (see Chapter 5). The only effective defense against charges of negligent hiring would be based on a complete investigation of all job-related facets of a candidate's background prior to employment. This may include reference checks of previous convictions and driving record violations, where deemed appropriate. Workers compensation records for positions requiring physical labor may also be checked to alert future employers to potential problems. Educational records, to be discussed shortly, should also be reviewed, if relevant.

This situation presents quite a dilemma for employers: Former employers can be sued for defamation or invasion of privacy for providing improper references; prospective employers can also be sued for negligent hiring and retention if references are not properly checked. Employment experts have suggested that a possible solution is to require job applicants to sign waivers relieving former employers from liability if they are not hired because of unflattering references. However, such waivers would be of questionable legal enforceability.

Guidelines for Releasing Information

A more workable solution would involve establishing guidelines governing both the release and ascertainment of reference information. With regard to releasing such information, consider the following ten guidelines:

1. One person, or a limited number of persons, should be in charge of releasing information about former employees. These individuals should be trained in matters relating to laws of defamation and qualified privilege.

2. Supervisors should be discouraged from releasing information over the telephone even though, as will be discussed shortly, telephone references are the preferred method for acquiring information. Releasing information by telephone may result in loss of the protection afforded by principles of qualified privilege.

3. Verification of dates of employment may be made by telephone; requests for all other information should be made in writing.

4. During exit interviews, tell terminating employees what information will be provided during a reference check. If the employee is being asked to leave, make certain he or she knows the reason.

5. If possible, obtain a signed consent form from a terminating employee, authorizing you to provide relevant reference information to prospective employers.

6. Always tell the truth and make certain you have documentation to back it up. Provide examples to support your statements.

7. Make certain that the person to whom you are providing reference information has a legitimate and legal right to it.

8. Be certain all information provided is job related.

9. Do not volunteer unsolicited information.

10. Try to say something good about a former employee to demonstrate that you are acting in good faith.

Guidelines for Obtaining Information

With regard to obtaining information on applicants under consideration for hire, consider the following twelve guidelines:

1. Conduct all reference checks in a uniform manner. That is to say, never single out only women or minorities for reference checks or follow up on only those candidates who strike you as "suspect." Inconsistency may be viewed as discriminatory.

2. If an applicant is ultimately rejected because of a negative recommendation, be prepared to document the job-related reason.

3. If, while conducting a reference check, it is discovered that an applicant has filed an EEO charge against his or her former employer, keep in mind that it is illegal to refuse to employ someone for this reason.

4. Obtain permission from applicants on the application form to contact former employers.

5. Carefully question the validity of comments made by former employers. In spite of possible legal ramifications, it is not uncommon for employers to express negative feelings toward a good employee who resigned for a better position. Likewise, employees terminated for poor performance sometimes work out a deal with their former employers that ensures them of positive reference checks. Therefore, probe for objective statements regarding job performance.

6. Exercise caution when interpreting a respondent's tone of voice, use of silence, or implication. Be aware, too, of phrases that may be interpreted in more than one way. For example, if a former employer were to say, "She gave every impression of being a conscientious worker," it would behoove you to probe and ask for examples.

7. Since reference checks are generally reserved for applicants making it to the final stage of consideration, these individuals should be given the opportunity to refute any information resulting from the reference check that contradicts impressions or information obtained during the interview.

8. If possible, check with a minimum of two previous employers to rule out the possibility of either positive or negative bias. This may also disclose patterns in an individual's work habits.

9. Reference checks should be conducted by the person who interviewed the applicant. If the interview was conducted by representatives from both human resources and the department in which the opening exists, the human resources specialist usually does the checking.

10. Do not automatically assume that a reported personality clash is the applicant's fault.

11. Having been fired does not necessarily mean that an applicant is a bad risk. Employees are terminated for many reasons; get an explanation before jumping to conclusions.

12. Since it is unlikely that an applicant will give permission to contact his or her present employer, it is wise to tell the applicant that any job offer that may be extended will be contingent upon a satisfactory reference from his or her present employer.

Telephone References

The most effective means for gathering information on an applicant under consideration for hire is via the telephone. Even though many employers hesitate to verify much more than dates of employment, it is worth a try. Telephone reference checks will enable you to listen to the former employer's tone of voice and voice inflections. It also allows for clarification of comments that may have a double meaning, such as "You'll be lucky to get him to work for you." Not only is a telephone reference likely to produce more valuable information; it takes less time to conduct.

Conducting telephone reference checks is much like conducting an interview. Virtually all the same skills (e.g., active listening and encouraging the other person to talk) are employed. In fact, just about the only facet of an employment interview that cannot be incorporated into a telephone reference check is nonverbal communication. Because of this similarity to an interview, preparation for a telephone reference check plays a key role. Begin by deciding who to call. Ask the applicant for the names of his or her former immediate supervisors and anyone else who is qualified to comment on the quality of his or her work. Also ascertain the name of someone you may contact in the human resources department. It may be necessary to speak with more than one person: The supervisor and others with whom the applicant directly worked will be able to discuss work performance; human resources will provide information regarding such matters as job title, dates of employment, absenteeism, tardiness, and salary history.

It is also important to prepare a phone-reference form in advance. As with a written reference form, you may want to have one for exempt positions and one for nonexempt positions. The same form can actually be used for both written and phone references. However, in designing the forms, keep in mind that phone references will yield more information and therefore will require more space for your notes. It is also likely that you will ask some questions in addition to those on the form. Therefore, allow ample room between questions to take notes. A sample reference form for exempt positions is provided in Appendix I and a sample form for nonexempt positions is found in Appendix J.

When conducting a telephone reference check, first identify yourself, your organization, and the reason for your call. To illustrate:

Interviewer: Good morning, Mr. White. My name is Peter Fisher. I am the human resources representative for Valdart, Ltd., and I am conducting a reference check on your former employee, Ms. Susan Downey.

If there is any reluctance on the part of the previous employer, offer your phone number and suggest that he or she call you to verify your identity. If it is a long-distance call, offer to receive the call collect.

Always begin by verifying the information provided by the applicant. This will help the former employer recall specific information about the individual. For example:

Interviewer: Ms. Downey has informed me that she worked for you in the payroll department as a clerk-typist, from June 1982 through April 1984. She indicated that she typed various letters, memos, and reports and was also in charge of the department's filing. Is this correct?

While listening to your opening statement, the respondent's thought speed will enable him or her to think about other facts regarding this person's work. At this point you will be able to proceed with the other categories on your reference form. As soon as you feel that the former employer is willing to volunteer information, shift from close-ended questions to open-ended questions.

Written References

Written references usually employ form letters that are designed to verify facts provided by the applicant. Unless directed to the attention of a specific supervisor or department head, these forms are often completed by human resources clerks who rely on the former employee's file for information. Even when addressed to the applicant's former manager, these inquiries may be routinely turned over to the company's human resources department for response because of the increased number of lawsuits resulting from reference-related matters. Indeed, many employers hesitate to provide any unfavorable information and many will only confirm the person's job title and dates of employment and the company's policy regarding eligibility for rehire. Therefore, a true picture of the candidate's skill level is generally not ascertained.

Another drawback to a written reference is the amount of time it takes to receive a response. Even if the request is marked "Rush," it generally takes a minimum of one to two weeks for a reply. This is valuable time lost if you are waiting for the reference to be returned before making a hiring decision. In fact, the person you finally select may have accepted another job offer in the interim.

Make certain that your written request is comprehensive, but not too time-consuming. Each question should be straightforward, easy to understand, and work-related. It is also advisable to have two separate form letters: one for exempt employees and another for nonexempt employees. In addition, try to direct your request to the applicant's former supervisor. You may also want to call this person prior to sending the letter. This way, you can make certain that he or she is still employed with the company and in addition you can stress the importance of a speedy reply. A follow-up phone call approximately three to four days after your request has been mailed may also help to expedite a reply.

Educational References

Applicants must provide written consent before a school may release educational records to a prospective employer. The Family Education Rights and Privacy Act (Buckley Amendment) allows students to inspect their scholastic records and to deny schools permission to release certain information. In an employment setting, a space for this permission should appear on the application form or a separate release form. Once the proper release has been obtained, academic information may be ascertained by the prospective employer, usually for a small fee.

Be certain to include the following inquiries when you check educational credentials: dates attended, major and minor courses of study, specific courses relevant to the position applied for, degree and honors received, attendance record, work-study program participation, and grade averages.

In considering this last point, remember that the value of scholastic achievement varies from school to school. An overall index of 3.5 in one college might be equivalent to an index of 2.8 in another. Therefore, it is important to know something about the standing and reputation of a particular school.

Also be careful about drawing conclusions based on grades. Not everyone does well on tests or in a classroom setting. This does not mean, however, that the applicant has not gained the knowledge needed to perform a particular job. Likewise, outstanding grades do not, in and of themselves, mean that someone will excel in a position.

Educational references are generally most useful in confirming the validity of information provided by an applicant. This can be important, since applicants have been known to falsely claim to possess degrees. Educational references may also prove to be valuable when an applicant has had little or no previous work experience. Remember, however, that these references should only be conducted when a job description clearly calls for specific educational achievements.

Personal References

Most application forms ask candidates to provide names of personal references. Usually, three names are called for, along with their relationship to the applicant, titles, phone numbers, and addresses. Although asking someone to provide references guaranteed to offer only praise seems like a waste of time, many interviewers check personal references and maintain that the information gleaned is valid and useful. Specifically, it is felt that personal references may reveal significant data relevant to the issue of negligent hiring and retention. Some go so far as to ask the references to refer still others who can describe certain qualities and behavior characteristics. By talking with people not directly referred to by the applicant, they feel they are more likely to get a complete and accurate picture. Still others believe that the type of person used as a reference is significant; that is, whether the person is a doctor, lawyer, teacher, or whatever.

As with employment references, personal reference checks may result in charges of discrimination if potential employers do not abide by the guidelines described earlier in this chapter. Incorrectly, some employers believe that these guidelines do not apply when talking with someone not connected with the applicant's former employment and therefore ask non-job-related and sometimes even illegal questions, believing that an acquaintance is more likely to reveal information relevant to the intangible qualities being sought.

Generally speaking, personal references should be avoided unless interviewers have absolutely no other source of employment or educational information and in instances when the issue of negligent hiring is a factor. When personal references are checked, the information ascertained should be sifted carefully, and any data that appear to be biased and not based on fact should be filtered out.

Evaluating References

While obtaining reference information is important, it will be of no real value if not properly evaluated. By and large, reference checks should be viewed the same as an interview, that is, the person conducting the check must listen to or read the information carefully in relation to the requirements and responsibilities of the available job. In some ways, references are more difficult to assess than are interviews, in that they tend to be more subjective. Regardless of how well worded your questions may be, references will offer biased responses, both positive and negative. This may cloud the picture of a candidate and justifies more than one reference check for any given person. Also, loss of one job does not necessarily mean failure in another, nor does it indicate employee deficiencies. It is conceivable that termination could have been avoided if there had been a more appropriate job match or if the employee's personality had been more compatible with that of his or her supervisor.

The safest way to approach and evaluate reference checks is to view them as just one of the factors to consider in making a final selection. This does not deemphasize their value; it merely puts them in proper perspective. In addition, while each individual's impression is subjective, an overall consensus may be more readily treated as an objective fact.

Considering Other Factors

In addition to checking references, there are additional factors to consider before making the final selection:

1. *Review your objectives.* Remind yourself of the company purpose to be served in filling the job and how it fits in with other positions in the department, division, and organization. Consider its projected impact on both departmental and organizational goals.

2. *Review the job description to ensure thorough familiarity with the concrete requirements, duties, and responsibilities of the position.* Identify

the critical and secondary aspects of the job. In addition, review the approximate amount of time to be devoted to each task.

3. *Review the work history and relevant educational credentials of each candidate.* Identify all experiences and training that would prepare the candidate for the available job.

4. *Consider the intangible requirements of the job.* Remember that certain intangible qualities, although subjective by definition, can still be job related. Therefore, identify and evaluate only those intangibles that have a bearing on the job performance.

5. *Evaluate applicants' reactions to various questions and statements.* For example, if the job requires extensive overtime and standing for long periods of time, cite each applicant's reaction to this information.

6. *Document and correlate each applicant's nonverbal communication with his or her verbal communication.* Recollect patterns of body language and carefully interpret what was being said with certain gestures or movements.

7. *Take each applicant's salary requirements into consideration and compare them to the salary range for the available position.* The salary offered should be comfortable for both the prospective employee and the company.

8. *Assess the reasons offered for leaving previous employers.* If you see a pattern emerging every two years or so, i.e., "no room for growth," it is possible that within a short time your company's name will be on this candidate's résumé.

9. *Consider the applicant's potential, especially if the opening is a stepping-stone to other positions.* Look for a future employee whose strengths are most likely to further the company's goals.

10. *Determine whether your organization and the available job are appropriate for the applicant.* Since it takes more than words to motivate another person, you can assess what your company offers in the way of career growth and other opportunities, and correlate this information to your understanding of what the candidate is seeking in the way of a position and a work environment.

It is recommended that the job description reflecting the position's primary duties, responsibilities, and requirements be reviewed side by side with a chart describing how each promising candidate measures up against the determining factors. This will enable you to fill in the chart and more effectively compare the qualifications of each applicant. A sample chart appears in Appendix K, "Selection Checklist."

These steps will often reveal qualities that tip the scales in favor of one applicant over the others under final consideration. Also, keep in mind the role of your organization's affirmative action goals in the selection process, as described in Chapter 5.

Determining Who Should Choose

Reviewing the results of reference checks, going through the steps just outlined, and considering your affirmative action goals should ideally be done by everyone who participated in the interviewing process. This usually means a member of the human resources department and one or more representatives from the unit where the opening exists. These individuals should meet, sharing their views regarding the candidates under consideration. The selection checklist identifying the concrete and intangible requirements of the job may then be reviewed. In most instances, an assessment of all the data collected will point in the direction of one candidate and everyone concerned will agree as to who will make the best employee. Occasionally, however, the departmental representative will favor one person and the human resources specialist will prefer another. If after listening to each other's reasons, both parties still disagree, then the departmental representative should make the final selection. After all, he or she is the one who will be working directly with the employee on a day-to-day basis.

Notifying the Chosen Candidate

Upon making a hiring decision, many interviewers immediately send letters to those candidates who were not chosen. This is a mistake. Letters of rejection should not go out until the chosen applicant has been offered the job and accepted the offer. This is important. You may have decided to hire someone who has already accepted another position. Or perhaps the exact starting salary offered may not be deemed acceptable. Therefore, you may have to select someone else. It is extremely awkward to approach your second choice after having just sent him or her a letter of rejection.

Offers for all jobs should be in writing. This can be done after a verbal offer has been made and accepted. Details regarding such matters as starting date and preemployment physicals are also worked out by phone. With most exempt-level positions, both the offer and the acceptance are confirmed in writing. Letters are usually sent by the human resources specialist with copies to all department representatives concerned. It is extremely important that the content be concise and accurate, with no room for misunderstanding. The following elements should be included:

- Official job title
- Department and division in which the position exists
- Starting salary
- Starting date
- Time to report to work
- Location
- Person to see
- Arrangements made regarding a preemployment physical, if relevant
- Agreement regarding a reference check with the present employer
- Identification of any literature enclosed
- Who to contact with questions

The sample letter shown in Figure 9-1 incorporates these elements.

Note that the language in this job offer avoids any commitment for a specific term of employment. Since this letter could be interpreted as representing an employment contract, it would be imprudent to give any indication that the position offered is permanent. In this regard, it may be desirable to go a step further by inserting an employment- and termination-at-will clause, similar to the one in the application that the applicant previously completed. This step is not essential, and many employers believe it detracts from the welcome being extended to the new employee. Accordingly, reference to the employment-at-will doctrine on the application form as well as in the employee handbook distributed and explained to every new hire, preferably during orientation, is considered sufficient by many employers.

Writing Rejection Letters

Once a candidate has been selected and your job offer has been accepted, it is time to notify the other applicants. Rejection letters should refer to the specific position for which an individual applied.

Figure 9-1. Sample letter confirming a job offer.

August 8, 1991

Ms. Elizabeth Downey
55 Poplar Street
Plainfield, New Jersey 07060

Dear Ms. Downey:

We are pleased to confirm our offer for the position of clerk-typist in the payroll department of Valdart, Ltd. at a starting salary of $450.00 per week. As discussed, you will begin work at 9:00 A.M. on Monday, August 26, 1991. At that time, please report to Ms. Taylor, the payroll supervisor, in room 219 on the second floor of our building, located at the address noted above.

The nursing office has been apprised of your starting date and will be expecting you for your preemployment physical anytime before that date, Monday through Friday, between 9:00 A.M. and 12:00 noon.

As agreed, you will resign from your present position upon receipt of this job offer. Upon doing so, please notify this office so that we may conduct a reference check. It is understood that this job offer is contingent upon receiving a satisfactory reference from your present employer.

Enclosed is a benefits package describing your health and life insurance options, as well as other company benefits. Also enclosed is our employee handbook for your review. Please bring both items with you when you begin work on August 26. There will be an orientation program scheduled for later that morning, during which time these and other matters will be discussed.

If you have any questions, please do not hesitate to call me at (212) 555-2200, extension 442.

We look forward to having you join our organization.

Sincerely,

Peter Fisher

Peter Fisher
Human Resources Representative

PF/ed

In other words, do not reject the person overall; you may want to consider him or her for another position in the future.

The tone of your letter should be professional and sincere. Without going into detail, a statement as to why another candidate has been accepted should be included. This is far more desirable than saying that the person was found unacceptable.

Rejection letters should also be fairly brief in length and are usually sent by the human resources representative who interviewed the candidate. In addition, the sender should personalize the letter by signing it, and not leave this up to a clerk or secretary to do. Finally, rejection letters should begin and end on a positive note. The sample letter shown in Figure 9-2 encompasses these points.

Figure 9-2. Sample rejection letter.

August 19, 1991

Ms. Mary Parker
128 Field Avenue
Union, New Jersey 07083

Dear Ms. Parker:

Thank you for meeting with us to discuss the position of project coordinator in the Management Information Services department of Valdart, Ltd.

We found your background and skills to be impressive. However, after a careful evaluation of all factors, we have selected another candidate whose qualifications are more suitable to our requirements.

Your résumé will be kept on file and we will contact you if a position that more nearly matches your abilities becomes available.

We wish you the best of luck in your future endeavors.

Sincerely,

Peter Fisher

Peter Fisher
Human Resources Representative

PF/ed

While some employers may attempt to make applicants feel better by disclosing that the person selected had, say, ten years' experience as opposed to their three, it is not considered wise to offer specific information about the successful candidate. To include such information in a rejection letter without permission of the new hire could be an invasion of privacy. In addition, a rejected applicant could utilize the disclosures as the basis for a claim of discrimination.

Summary

In this chapter, the components of the final selection process were discussed, including the essentials of conducting effective employment reference checks; the potential for charges of defamation of character when references are checked; the qualified privilege attached to reference inquiries; references and negligent hiring; guidelines for both releasing reference information and obtaining it; telephone and written reference checks; educational and personal references; and guidelines for evaluating references.

Also covered in this chapter was an assessment of the different factors to be considered in making a final selection, a discussion of responsibility for the actual hiring decision, and suggestions for how to notify the chosen candidate as well as those not selected.

10

Orientation

Well, you have finally done it! After all your preparation, planning, analyses, and comparisons, the job opening has been filled. If you have followed the guidelines mapped out in previous chapters, the new hire should have a fairly clear idea as to not only what his or her job will entail, but what it will be like to work for the company. Regardless of how much may be known ahead of time, however, starting any new job can be unnerving. Even former employees returning after a lengthy leave of absence report feeling somewhat uneasy during the first few days or weeks back on the job. Until such time as the new employee becomes familiar with the surroundings, feels comfortable with the details and routine of a typical day, and develops an understanding of company and departmental expectations, it will be difficult to focus fully on job performance.

It is for this reason that all organizations, regardless of size, should conduct orientation programs for new hires. To many employers, the term *orientation* means sending new employees to a brief meeting, usually no more than two hours in duration, during which the company's history, rules, and benefits are described. Often there is no opportunity for interaction among attendees and little time, if any, for questions. Literature is distributed, placing the onus on the employees to read, understand, and apply the contents, and then to immediately start work in their departments, only to discover that department heads or managers are often unavailable or unable to answer any questions that may develop subsequently.

While this is an accurate description of how orientation is handled by many organizations, it does not represent an effective program. The company's history, rules, and benefits are certainly important elements of an individual's introduction to the new work environment; however, this cannot be accomplished effectively in a couple of hours. It is also impractical to assume that a new hire will come away knowing all he or she requires. Each employee's supervisor, manager, or department head, or a knowledgeable designee, should be available to provide the guidance needed for proper acclimation during the start of any new job.

In this connection, a comprehensive orientation program for new employees consists of three main components: the first day of work; a multitiered formal organizational orientation program; and a less formal, but still structured, departmental orientation. Careful preparation for these segments will ensure more effective employer/employee relations.

The First Day of Work

As soon as a prospective employee's starting date is confirmed, his or her supervisor or manager should make a notation to keep that day as free of appointments as possible. This way, full attention may be given to meeting the needs of the new worker. If a clear calendar cannot be arranged, then at least some time during the day—preferably first thing in the morning—should be set aside to spend with the new employee. Arrangements should also be made for someone else (e.g., another supervisor or manager from within the department) to assist the new employee in getting settled.

Introductory Remarks

When the new employee reports to work for the first time, devote several minutes to putting him or her at ease and establishing rapport. To accomplish this, employ the same techniques used during the interview process, including icebreaker questions and statements. Consider the following examples:

> I'm sorry we couldn't arrange better weather for your first day of work; the weather report predicts that the rain should stop early this afternoon, however.

> We at Valdart, Ltd. try to think of everything. We even arranged a beautiful sunny day for your first day of work!

> I'll bet the construction on the expressway cost you about fifteen minutes this morning. Before you leave today, I'll have someone give you directions for an alternate route.

You're lucky you didn't start here two weeks ago when the transit workers were on strike; commuting then was a nightmare.

Were you able to locate your assigned parking space without much difficulty?

Be careful that your initial icebreaker statements do not make the new employee feel unduly pressured. For instance, a greeting such as "Thank goodness you're finally here! The work on your desk is already a mile high!" could make the employee wonder if he or she made a mistake in accepting your job offer. All you want to do at this stage is to calm first-day jitters and make the individual feel comfortable.

Following your icebreaker remarks, take a few moments to describe the scheduled activities of the day. If a great deal has been planned, then a typed agenda might be appropriate. Otherwise, briefly describe what is to occur. To illustrate:

Manager: Janet, after we finish talking, I'll take you around the department to meet everyone. Then, I'm going to turn you over to Bruce Jenkins, our production manager. He'll show you your office, tell you where everything is, and essentially explain how to get around. I'll meet you back here at 11:45 so we can go to lunch. I've made reservations for us at the officers' dining room. The food there is quite good. Then, at 1:30, Bruce will take you over to the Human Resources Department for the first part of the organizational orientation program. When that ends at 4:30, come back to my office so we can talk. I'll answer any questions you may have formed throughout the day, and we can discuss what's been scheduled for tomorrow.

Before moving on from this step in the employee's first day of work, be sure to tell the person how you wish to be addressed. This may not seem terribly important to you, but to a nervous employee who wants to make a good impression, it can result in some awkward moments. Simply say:

Manager: By the way, we're very casual around here, so please call me Phyllis. Everyone is on a first-name basis except when you get to the executive vice-presidents' level and above: They like things a bit more formal; in fact, they'll address you as Ms. Bower. The only time they relax on this is at the annual picnic. I guess when they're playing softball and eating hot dogs, they feel it's okay to use first names!

The introductory remarks described thus far take only a few minutes to accomplish, yet they contribute a great deal to a new employee's perception about the company. These perceptions will affect the employee's attitudes toward his or her job, which, in turn, will affect productivity. Therefore, care should be taken to be as encouraging, supportive, and sincere as possible.

Introductions

Now it is time to introduce the new worker to others with whom he or she will be working. Generally, these individuals will all be in the same department. Sometimes, however, introductions extend to employees in other units. This may occur when the new person will be working on a regular basis with other departments. If there are to be more than a half a dozen introductions, it is a good idea to have a sheet typed up in advance with everyone's name, title, office location or number, and telephone extension. This can help make the experience less overwhelming, since the new employee will have it to refer to after the introductions have been completed.

As you take the new employee around, be careful not to express your opinions about the other people. For example, "Janet, the next person you're going to meet is Bob Johnson. Watch out for him during staff meetings; he's notorious for stealing ideas and submitting them as his own." Or, "When I introduce you to Fred Waters, don't take it personally if he acts like he doesn't like you. He applied for your position through job posting, but was rejected. He thinks you cheated him out of a promotion."

Positive statements should be avoided as well. For example, "Janet, I'd like you to meet Rod Perret. Rod can always be counted on to help you meet impossible deadlines."

New employees should be permitted to form their own opinions about their co-workers. Therefore, any statement that is subjective or judgmental should be avoided. Instead, focus on being descriptive. As you approach the desk or office of each worker, briefly describe his or her overall function. Limit yourself to one or two sentences per person so that the new employee will later be able to remember what you said. Think in terms of action words, as described in Chapter 2. For instance, you might want to say, "The next person you will be meeting is Terry Carson. Terry is our office manager. She receives all the work to be typed from the department's assistant vice-presidents, distributes it among the secretaries, reviews the final product, and then returns it to the appropriate A.V.P." Therefore, if the new hire were making notes, he or she could quickly write, "Terry Carson: office manager: Receives, distributes, and returns typing to A.V.P.s."

Familiarization With the Office

Once the introductions have been completed, it is time to show the employee exactly where he or she will be working, and to explain where everything is located. Generally, a sponsor will be assigned to the new person for this purpose. Be certain that the person selected is thoroughly familiar with the office layout and can devote the amount of time necessary to explain everything.

Preparation for this stage of the new employee's first day of work should include a checklist of items to make certain that no details are omitted. This list might include the following points:

1. *Show the employee his or her office or desk.* It is likely that this is the first time the individual will be seeing exactly where he or she will be working. If the employee is to be situated at a desk in close proximity to other workers, explain what the others do in relation to his or her responsibilities. If the employee has a private office, describe any company policies pertaining to pictures on the walls, plants, or other personal touches. Some organizations are rather inflexible about such matters, and employees should be so informed at the outset.

The desks of all new employees should be filled with the necessary supplies (e.g., pencils, pens, pads, staplers, rulers, letter openers, paper clips, rubber bands, tape, and scissors). Additional equipment, such as calculators, computers, typewriters, word processors, or Dictaphone machines, should also be provided, as appropriate. Relevant reference materials, such as a dictionary and a thesaurus, should also be available.

2. *Show the employee where supplies are located and/or explain how to order supplies.* Describe departmental procedures regarding additional supplies. It may be that there is a central supply room and employees merely go there and take whatever they need. If this is the case, take the employee to the room and briefly explain where everything is located. If your organization requires employees to fill out requisition forms for additional supplies, explain where to get the forms, who to give them to when completed, and approximately

how long it takes to receive the requested items. Also explain any exceptions to the regular policies. For example, ordering a new chair or desk will undoubtedly require more paperwork, and probably more signatures, than will requesting a pair of scissors.

3. *Provide the employee with a telephone directory.* All employees should know how they can reach others within the organization. A directory of departments, key employees with corresponding titles, and telephone exchanges should be provided.

4. *Explain how the phone system works.* Many organizations now have rather complex phone systems. It is rare that one can simply pick up a telephone and dial the desired number. Therefore, be certain to thoroughly explain the use of such factors as prefixes, special codes, intercom systems, outside lines, transferring calls, holding calls, and conference calls.

5. *Show the employee the location of rest rooms and water fountains.* It is amazing how many employees hesitate to ask about the location of these two items. It only takes a moment to tell the new employee where the rest rooms and water fountains are located. If there are several throughout the department, point them out.

6. *Explain the time and location of the coffee wagon.* Everyone wants to know how and when they can get coffee, Danish, and the like. If your organization has a food wagon that comes around each department, tell the new hire approximately what time he or she can expect it each day, and exactly where it stops. You might also include any information you have as to what is offered and a sample of prices.

7. *Show the employee the location of photocopy and facsimile (fax) machines and explain how they are used.* Explain any required procedures for their use. In some companies all the duplicating and fax transmissions are done by a clerk. If this is the case, indicate who is in charge of these tasks and where he or she is located. In other organizations, everyone does his or her own photocopying and fax work. In this event, demonstrate how the machines are operated. Also say whom to contact if the machines malfunction.

8. *Show the employee the location of files.* Show the new person where the department's files are located and explain how they are set up. Also describe any procedure for signing out a file.

9. *Show the employee the cafeteria and/or executive dining room.* Take the new employee on a brief tour of the cafeteria. Describe what kind of food is generally offered and the price range. Also provide the hours it is open. If by virtue of his or her title, the employee is

entitled to eat in the executive dining room, include this in your tour as well. Be sure to provide information regarding its hours, reservations if required, method of payment, and policy pertaining to guests.

10. *Show the employee the location of the employee lounge.* If your organization has an employee lounge, take the employee on a brief tour of it. Describe which activities are permitted there, and which are prohibited (e.g., eating, smoking, watching television, playing the radio, or playing games).

11. *Explain the use of company cars.* An employee whose work requires traveling from one organizational location to another is often provided with a company car. If this is the case, explain who the employee should contact for details regarding this matter.

12. *Show the employee any exercise facilities.* More and more companies are reflecting the times by providing their employees with an exercise facility. This may include a running track, gymnastic equipment, and even group exercise classes scheduled before and after working hours. If your organization has such a program, be certain to describe eligibility for and frequency of use, required gear (e.g., sneakers), and hours.

13. *Explain procedures for medical care.* Explain the procedure that is to be followed in the event that an employee requires non-emergency medical care, including any forms to be filled out, and where to go.

14. *Show the employee any child care facilities.* If your organization has a child care program, take the new employee on a brief tour and explain how it operates. Be sure to include eligibility requirements, a description of who watches the children, how many children are assigned to each caretaker, and the cost. Provide the employee with the name of who to contact for additional information.

It is a good idea to give a list highlighting the fourteen categories just described to the new employee so that he or she can jot down notes as you talk. A sample of a checklist for new employees appears in Appendix L. If possible, also provide the employee with a floor plan.

It is important to note that some of the points already mentioned (e.g., seeing the cafeteria, employee lounge, exercise facility, and child care facility) may also be included in a tour conducted as part of the organizational orientation. At this stage, repetition can only serve to reinforce what the employee is being told and shown.

Taking the New Employee to Lunch

By the time the lunch hour rolls around on a new employee's first day of work, he or she is probably feeling somewhat overwhelmed. Therefore, arrangements should be made for someone to take the person to lunch. This is usually done by either the employee's immediate boss or the sponsor who has been in charge of showing the person around. Sometimes, a new employee's co-workers assume this responsibility. In any event, it should be someone who, in all likelihood, will be eating with this person again in the near future.

If your company has a cafeteria, it is a good idea to go there, so that the individual can begin to become familiar with its offerings. In addition, informal introductions to other employees who are in the cafeteria at that time can be made while eating. If the person is an exempt employee, then plan on eating in the executive dining room.

Remember that your purpose in taking a new employee to lunch is to make the person feel welcome and comfortable. Be careful that you do not get carried away, as did the executive who insisted on taking a new clerk in his department to the executive dining room for lunch. His intentions were good, but the gesture was inappropriate. The clerk, quite understandably, enjoyed the experience immensely and fully expected it to be repeated. It was his very first job and he did not realize that the meal he had just had in the executive dining room was an exception to normal procedure. He waited for the vice-president to invite him again, and when the invitation was not forthcoming he began to assume that there was a problem with his job performance. Eventually his work was affected, and his six-month performance review reflected less than satisfactory work.

The End of the Day

It is strongly recommended that new employees attend orientation for at least part of the first day. If this cannot be arranged, then the balance of the day should be devoted to introducing the employee to departmental policies and procedures in some other fashion. A full discussion of departmental orientation appears later in this chapter.

Regardless of how the day is spent, it should conclude the way it began: with a meeting between the new employee and his or her supervisor or manager. A period of approximately thirty minutes should be set aside to discuss what took place during the day and to answer any questions the employee may have. In addition, the following day's agenda should be reviewed.

Organizational Orientation

Virtually all organizations have some sort of orientation program for new employees. Unfortunately, many employers hesitate to invest more than a minimal amount of energy, money, or staff time in this critical stage of a new employee's career. Indeed, some consider it a waste of valuable time—time that could be better spent working. This kind of thinking can have a detrimental effect on both employee performance and attitude and, in turn, result in disciplinary problems and increased turnover. Taking the time to acclimate the new worker to his or her company can have the opposite effect. The employee is more likely to form positive impressions and consequently care more about the quality of his or her work.

The Purpose of Orientation

A well-planned organizational orientation program is designed to help new employees feel welcome and knowledgeable about their new organization. More specifically, it will:

- Give new employees an overview of the organization's history and present status
- Describe the company's overall functions
- Explain the organizational structure
- Describe the organization's philosophy, goals, and objectives
- Explain how vital each employee is in helping to achieve company goals
- Describe the benefits and employee services offered
- Outline the company's standards of performance, rules, regulations, policies, and procedures
- Outline safety and security practices

Naturally, the exact information provided and the amount of time required for an orientation program will vary with each organization. In a small company, for example, a one-day session will probably be adequate. In very large corporations, a full week devoted to orientation may be appropriate. Follow-up sessions several weeks or months later are also recommended. Regardless of the duration of your program, it is critical that the ingredients already outlined be included, and that representatives from human resources and other key departments partake in the presentation of information. Detailed information regarding the content of an organizational orientation program will follow later in this chapter.

Participants

As already stated, all new employees should be required to attend the organizational orientation program. In some companies, new employees in all job classifications participate in the same program. In other companies, one presentation is offered to exempt employees and another is provided for nonexempt employees. This is frequently done for two reasons: First, there are too many new employees for a single program; and second, there is a substantial difference in the specific information offered (e.g., managerial benefits and policies pertaining to executives may differ). In smaller companies everyone generally attends the same session, regardless of job title.

While orientation programs are designed with the new employee in mind, inviting existing employees to attend should also be considered. A refresher on such matters as corporate goals and standards of performance can be very helpful to *all* employees. It can also help motivate existing employees by making them feel that they are still important to the company. Having these individuals attend the same session as do new employees may also be effective, since it allows for an exchange between the newcomers and the existing workers. Usually, however, a separate session is scheduled in order to avoid unnecessary repetition of certain points.

Because discussion is an important element of an effective orientation program, the number of participants should be limited to a maximum of twenty. The ideal group size is from twelve to fifteen. This encourages an exchange between the new employees and still allows for questions to be asked and responded to. Having less than six employees can make the participants feel conspicuous and self-conscious.

Location and Setting

The site selected for your organizational orientation program should be centrally located and convenient for most employees to reach. It should easily accommodate the number of people scheduled to attend, but should not be too large. Tables should be provided, since literature is likely to be distributed and employees will probably want to jot down notes during the course of the presentation. Tables and chairs should be arranged in a casual manner; round tables are preferred over tables and chairs arranged classroom style. For these reasons, auditoriums should be avoided.

Content

As noted at the beginning of this section, there are eight main areas to be covered in an organizational orientation program. These may be expanded to encompass several additional components. Depending on the size and complexity of your organization, the following topics may be considered for inclusion in your orientation program:

History	Training and development
Present status	Growth opportunities
Philosophy, goals, and objectives	Job posting
	Promotions
Structure	Transfers
General expectations of all employees	Other job changes
	Insurance
Overall function	Vacation
General industry information and special terminology	Holidays
	Personal days
Unique organizational features	Sick days
EEO and affirmative action policies	Leaves of absence
	Tuition reimbursement
Rules and regulations	Employees' club
Standards of performance	Pension plan
Grading system	Savings incentive plan
Performance review process	Safety and security practices
Salary increase guidelines	Employment and termination-at-will
Payday	

Generally speaking, an orientation program should emphasize what employees can expect to receive from the organization and what the organization expects to receive from them. In addition, orientation should expose employees to the larger picture of the overall function, status, structure, philosophy, and goals of the organization. It is believed that this holistic view can benefit individuals in their present jobs, help them develop a sense of commitment to the organization, and help them plan a future with the company.

Employee Handbooks

Orientation is an ideal time to distribute and explain the one document that can encompass all of these categories: a well-prepared employee handbook. Like a personnel policies and procedures manual, an employee handbook serves several objectives, among them:

1. It provides a written declaration of a company's commitment to fair employment practices and equal employment opportunity with regard to all employees in all work-related instances.
2. It expresses the basic philosophies of senior management, through both content and tone.
3. It serves as a basic communication tool pertaining to various areas of work.
4. It outlines company rules and requirements as well as clarifying an organization's expectations of its employees.
5. It provides a brief history of the organization, including a description of its primary products and/or services.
6. It outlines the benefits and privileges of working for an organization.
7. It may boost employee morale.
8. It states the employer's commitment or lack thereof to employees with regard to continued employment.

While employee handbooks should be self-explanatory, users of the handbook should be afforded an opportunity to ask questions and seek clarification. In addition, because of possible legal ramifications, companies must ensure that recipients understand its contents. While there is no guarantee that an employee will comprehend the contents of any document, despite all reasonable efforts, employees can be asked to sign a statement that they have received a copy of the company handbook, have read its contents, and understand them. Consider the sample shown in Figure 10-1.

Departmental Representation

The next area to consider in orientation planning is departmental representation, that is, who should conduct and/or be actively

Figure 10-1. Handbook acknowledgment.

This is to acknowledge that I have received and read the company employee handbook in its entirety. Any statements, rules, policies, or procedures I did not understand were explained to me.

I understand that I am to, and will, observe and abide by all amended rules and regulations that may be given to me in writing and made a part of this handbook.

I acknowledge receipt and retention of a copy of this signed statement and the company's employee handbook. A copy of this signed statement will be placed in my personnel file.

Name _____

Signature _____

Department _____

Date _____

involved with the program. Three different groups should be considered: (1) representatives from human resources, (2) experts in each topic, and (3) officers from major departments.

It is generally agreed that someone from human resources should be in charge of the overall program. This entails:

- Planning the content
- Scheduling the speakers
- Preparing the presentation media and supplemental material
- Reserving space
- Scheduling employees
- Making opening and closing remarks
- Introducing each speaker
- Conducting tours

Because of this wide range of responsibilities, the human resources representatives selected should be knowledgeable about the organization and should have presentation skills. The latter is important if enthusiasm and interest are to be generated among the participants. Also, to keep orientation leaders from going stale, a rotational system is recommended, so that no one person conducts orientation every time it is offered.

Experts in various topics should also be involved. For example:

- A benefits expert might discuss insurance, the pension plan, and the savings incentive plan.
- A salary administrator might discuss the grading system, the performance review process, and salary increase guidelines.
- A member of the Training and Development Department might discuss growth opportunities and tuition reimbursement.

As with the human resources representative, these topical experts should be knowledgeable and should possess group dynamic skills. Particularly with dry subjects, such as insurance, it is critical that the presenters are able to facilitate interest and retention.

Finally, all employees, regardless of classification, should be familiar with key organizational officers. Having representatives from senior management participate in the orientation program will accomplish this end. In addition to welcoming new people into the organization, officers might briefly describe the primary functions of their respective departments and discuss how their units relate to the organization as a whole. This will add to the employee's holistic view of the company. Furthermore, minority and women representatives from senior management may serve to promote an organization's EEO and affirmative action policy and inspire future growth.

Format

Orientation information can be imparted in a variety of different ways. In fact, variety is considered essential to the success of a program where a great deal of new information is going to be presented.

There are several formats from which to choose, including lecture by one or more speakers; transparencies or charts; handout materials; films, slides, or videotapes; question-and-answer periods; and tours.

As previously stated, having representatives from various departments participate in orientation is highly desirable. However, regardless of how interesting departmental presentations may be, a straight lecture format is discouraged. Supplemental transparencies and/or charts highlighting key points will further employee understanding and retention of what is being presented. Providing hand-out materials illustrating what has been said is also recommended. Use of professionally prepared films and/or slides can be very effective as well. The primary objection to using a film, as opposed to slides, is that updating a film is far more difficult and expensive than replacing slides. In addition, questions raised during the course of a film must be delayed until the conclusion. Of course the film can be stopped, but this can be disconcerting for viewers.

Growing in popularity is the use of videotape in a modular format. This offers the advantage of an entire orientation program that is portable, allowing for a range of viewing possibilities. For example, before a new hire's first day of work, he or she might be sent a videotape providing a broad overview of the company, its history, philosophies, goals, and products. Having this information when reporting to work on the first day can render the environment less intimidating and, consequently, put an employee more at ease. It is also a good public relations technique, since the new hire may invite other family members or friends to view the tape. Of course, this presumes that all new hires own or have access to a videotape machine. It also presumes that the new employee will actually view and understand the presentation. To ensure this, some organizations show these segments again at orientation; others offer a special session to address any questions home viewers may have. Videotapes also allow employers greater flexibility as to where segments of the orientation may take place. For instance, if a large number of employees are hired for a new satellite location, the videotape portion of the orientation may be conducted there, rather than at headquarters.

Answering questions as soon as they occur is far more preferable than having a formal question-and-answer period. Encouraging a free exchange between speakers and participants promotes a more relaxed, less intimidating atmosphere.

A tour of major company departments is also recommended. This will enable employees to more fully understand how their work relates to the work performed in other units of the organization.

Timing

As was mentioned earlier, employees should be encouraged to attend orientation as soon after beginning work as possible. Indeed, some organizations require new employees to attend before their first day on the job. This is not recommended, since most people continue to work for another employer until beginning a new position. Taking time off to attend an orientation program is usually quite impractical.

The first day of work is usually the best time to begin orientation. Employees are not yet caught up in the details of their jobs, and there is little chance of receiving inaccurate information from other sources. More specifically, the afternoon of the first day is considered ideal. As described earlier in this chapter, the first morning should be devoted to departmental introductions and office familiarization. Once new employees have had the opportunity to become somewhat acclimated to their new environment, they are ready for more detailed information about the organization.

Duration

As previously stated, the exact duration of an orientation program will largely depend on the size and complexity of your organization. In relatively small companies, a minimum of one day is recommended; in very large corporations, a full week or more is usually needed to cover all of the key points.

One alternative that is growing in popularity is the flexible mode orientation program, whereby a general session during the first few days of employment is followed by detailed modules of varying duration in subsequent weeks and months. This method provides employees with basic information at the very beginning of their employment and then provides them with more specific information after they have had an opportunity to become more familiar with their work and surroundings. This progression from general to detailed information also ensures greater retention. The only real drawback to this kind of scheduling is the potential for conflict with departmental deadlines. However, advance notification of session scheduling and cooperation on the part of department heads should preclude any problems of this nature.

Sample Organizational Orientation Program

Following is an example of an organizational orientation program, which may be modified to meet the needs of your particular environment. It has been designed for a fictitious medium-sized bank, Future Savings, and is patterned after the flexible mode concept. It consists of four separate segments: (1) general session, (2) tour, (3) detailed benefits session, and (4) detailed policies and procedures session.

Segment 1: General Session

This segment will provide new employees with a comprehensive view of employment at Future Savings Bank. In general, it will encompass three principal areas: (1) an overview of the banking industry in general, and Future Savings in particular; (2) a synopsis of what Future Savings offers its employees; and (3) a summary of what the bank expects from its employees.

More specifically, the first area—an overview of banking and Future Savings—should cover:

1. A brief description of the banking industry: what it entails, how it compares with other financial businesses, and what makes one bank more successful than another. It is suggested that reference be made to the fact that a bank's long-term, overall success depends on how effectively it utilizes its human resources and on the extent of customer satisfaction.

2. A short summary of the history of Future Savings, citing its origins, tracing its growth, noting its major accomplishments, and describing its present status in the banking community.

3. A description of the bank's philosophy, present status, and objectives.

4. General, frequently used banking terminology. The sooner employees adapt to their new work environment, the sooner they will be able to concentrate on their specific job responsibilities. Familiarity with the unique language of banking will facilitate this adjustment.

5. An overview of the bank's structure and hierarchy. A broad picture of Future Savings and a look at the composition of its major departments (e.g., banking operations, fiduciary, and metropolitan banking) should provide the new employee with an idea of the size and organization of the bank.

6. General information regarding the interrelationship between various departments and functions.

7. Statements regarding the bank's EEO and affirmative action policies. It should be clearly explained that the bank's policy pertains to every aspect of an individual's relationship with Future Savings, including recruitment, interviewing, selection, compensation, benefits, training and development, educational tuition, social and recreational programs, promotions, transfers, relocation, discipline, termination, and all other privileges, terms, and conditions of employment.

The next area to be covered in the first orientation session should be a summary of all the benefits that employees may expect. Because the bank offers so much in the way of benefits, and since there are so many other topics that should also be discussed during this first session, it is recommended that the following benefits merely be mentioned and described very briefly at this point in the program:

- Vacation
- Holidays
- Personal days
- Sick days
- Payday
- Training and development opportunities
- Tuition reimbursement
- Leaves of absence
- Employees' club
- Special bank services

All of these benefits should be described in greater detail in a subsequent orientation session. The purpose at this time is to merely make the employee aware of all the programs available to those working at Future Savings.

Because employees are eligible for insurance coverage immediately upon hire, an in-depth discussion of the following is recommended:

- Life insurance
- Medical and disability insurance
- Travel accident insurance
- Pension plan
- Savings incentive plan
- Other related plans or coverage

The third main area to be mentioned at this first overview session concerns what Future Savings expects of its employees. Once again, the intent here is to familiarize; a more intense session pertaining to rules and policies will follow shortly.

In this regard the following Future Savings policies and procedures should be mentioned:

- Employment and termination-at-will
- Overall expectations of Future Savings employees

- Grading system
- Importance of customer service
- Job posting
- Performance review process
- Promotions
- Rules regarding such matters as attendance and punctuality
- Salary increase guidelines
- Standards of performance
- Transfers
- Safety and security practices

If effectively presented, this general session will accomplish a number of objectives. To begin with, new employees should leave an introductory orientation session with a positive overview of their work environment. At Future Savings this means pointing out all the advantages of working for a bank in general, and the advantages of working at Future Savings in particular. There may be a number of reasons why someone accepts a job at Future Savings, ranging from needing a job, to wanting to work for a financial institution, to specifically wanting to work for Future Savings because of its reputation. Being able to assume the latter would be wonderful but rather unrealistic. It is far safer to assume that most new employees know very little about banking and even less about Future Savings. Therefore, orientation is the bank's opportunity to explain all the attributes of banking and particularly the advantages of working at Future Savings. The reason for doing this is, quite simply, a matter of improving motivation and, thus, productivity. (According to the classical and widely accepted motivational theories of Maslow, McGregor, Herzberg, Ouchi, and others, there is a direct correlation between employee motivation and productivity.) If the bank accepts this relationship as one that is not only valid, but quite effective, then this general orientation program provides the ideal arena for initially creating a highly motivating environment.

To reiterate, one of the goals of this general session is to have new employees leave feeling motivated and inspired about working at Future Savings. This should lead employees to become actively involved with their specific job duties and responsibilities, become an integral part of Future Savings, and plan a long-term future with Future Savings.

Part of the process of making the bank attractive to new employees involves describing all of the benefits that Future Savings offers its staff. The time to boast of all these extras is immediately, reiterating the general benefits outlined during the interviewing process and talking about some others at length.

Inspiring new employees to plan a future at Future Savings, based on a highly motivating environment and available benefits, is a critical aspect of the general orientation session. Equally important, however, is a clearly outlined description of expected employee performance. Employees need to understand at the outset that Future Savings operates on a system of exchange: The advantages of working for the bank are given in exchange for abiding by its policies and rules.

Therefore, another purpose of this first session is to provide new employees with an accurate picture of what working at Future Savings entails, vis-à-vis its overall expectations. It is absolutely critical that all new employees be told immediately upon hire just what the bank requires of them. If these data are clearly and consistently disseminated at the outset, numerous negative performance-related incidents may be avoided. For example, managers and supervisors may assume that employees realize that they should call in when they are not coming to work. However, an employee may previously have worked for someone who did not require this or may have no previous work experience and, therefore, not be aware of this requirement.

It is unfair to assume that any employee—regardless of where he or she may have worked in the past—knows anything regarding the specific policies of a new employer. If the rules are not spelled out in the very beginning, it is conceivable that there may be incidents in subsequent months that could adversely affect that person's chances for growth within the bank. These occurrences can easily be avoided by telling new employees what is expected of them at the very beginning.

The key to successfully disseminating new information lies in creating an environment that is conducive to learning, and presenting the data in a manner that is both interesting and varied. Based on this, the following eleven guidelines are recommended:

1. Create a casual, relatively unstructured environment (e.g., a round table, as opposed to tables and chairs arranged in classroom style).

2. Allow orientation participants to gather over refreshments before the actual session begins. This should help people relax and briefly get to know one another. By the time the session begins, names will have been exchanged and there will not be any unfamiliar faces.

3. Introduce the banking industry and general information about Future Savings, using a short film, slides, or videotape. Using the visual media to accompany anything historical or statistical should not only make the subject more interesting but also help to reinforce the accompanying verbal messages.

4. Distribute a glossary of frequently used banking terminology.

5. Utilize transparencies and charts to highlight the bank's structure and hierarchy.

6. Utilize slides to illustrate the interrelationships between various departments and functions.

7. Incorporate the verbal statements of a human resources representative concerning the bank's EEO and affirmative action policies.

8. Have a presentation by a Future Savings benefits expert about the various insurance plans available. Slides, charts, and transparencies may also be used for this segment. This presentation should be followed by small group discussions relating to the information provided by the benefits expert, so that employees will fully understand their options before completing any of the required insurance cards. The benefits representative could spend a few minutes sitting with each group to clarify any points about which employees have questions.

9. Briefly describe all other Future Savings benefits.

10. Distribute a booklet highlighting the main topics covered and a directory of names, titles, and telephone numbers of people to call with questions relating to the topics described or discussed.

11. Distribute and discuss the employee handbook.

This general orientation session should run for a total of one whole day. It may begin after lunch on an employee's first day of work and then be continued on the following morning. The overnight break will allow employees to digest what has been said thus far, thereby preventing the feeling of being overwhelmed by new material.

Segment 2: Tour

Following the general session, employees should be taken on a tour of the bank's major departments and one typical branch. Seeing a department in action will serve to supplement the information provided in the general session. Arrangements should be made in advance for representatives of each department to guide the employees through the department, explaining how it operates. If specific departmental literature is available, it may be distributed at this time.

In addition to a tour of key bank departments, employees should be shown such places as the following:

- Employee cafeteria and/or executive dining room
- Employee lounge
- Exercise facilities
- Medical unit
- Child care facilities

The hours, functions, and any eligibility requirements of each unit should be described.

It may be that new employees have already been taken on a tour of these places by their department heads. If this is the case, a second trip will contribute to an employee's feelings of familiarization with his or her new environment.

The tour segment should begin on the afternoon of an employee's second day of work and be continued on the morning of the third day.

Segment 3: Detailed Benefits Session

This session will provide detailed information regarding all of the bank's employee benefits. Since an overview of all employee benefits will have been given briefly during the general orientation session and all areas of insurance will have been covered in detail, this session will elaborate on other, noninsurance benefits. It will include:

1. *Vacation.* Details might include eligibility, formula for calculation, and unique stipulations pertaining to holiday add-ons or leaves of absence.
2. *Holidays.* Details might include eligibility, specific dates, any unique stipulations pertaining to absences the day before or after a holiday, and adding holidays onto vacations or leaves of absence.
3. *Personal days.* Details might include eligibility, number of days allowed, purpose, and required procedure.

4. *Sick days.* Details might include eligibility, number of days permitted, uses, and required procedure.
5. *Payday.* Details might include frequency, method, check cashing, advances, and payday occurring during vacations or leaves of absence.
6. *Training and development opportunities.* Details might include programs available, enrollment procedure, eligibility, frequency, and correlation with career planning.
7. *Tuition reimbursement.* Details might include eligibility, types of courses, grade requirements, registration fees, books, maximum number of courses or credits, and procedure.
8. *Leaves of absence.* Details might include types of leaves, maximum duration, eligibility, and effect on employment status, seniority, salary, and benefits. Note that specific federal legislation and, in some instances, state laws govern military leave. Information regarding the employment rights of reservists may be obtained by contacting any one of several area offices of the Office of Veterans' Reemployment Rights (OVRR). In addition, employers may call the National Committee for Employer Support of the Guard and Reserve at 1-800-336-4590.
9. *Employees' club.* Details might include its purpose, what it offers, how events are publicized, and who to contact for detailed information.
10. *Special bank services.* Details might include eligibility and required approval for free checking, travelers checks, safe deposit boxes, installment loans, and advanced checking.

A detailed benefits session will serve two primary purposes: It will show employees that the bank is concerned about their immediate needs and future development, and it will ensure a consistent application of all available benefits to new employees.

Using a variety of training media is recommended in order to ensure a clear understanding of the information presented in this segment. This might include lectures by human resources representatives, followed by discussion; slide or videotape presentations; transparencies and charts; and handout materials.

To foster a comfortable learning session that encourages open communication and questions, an informal seating arrangement and possibly refreshments are recommended.

It is recommended that this benefits orientation session run for one half-day. This amount of time should be sufficient, since some benefits will be reviewed in the general session. In addition, if literature is distributed to new employees when they first report to work, they will be better able to prepare for this in-depth session.

This benefits session will be most effective if conducted approximately one week after the general session. At that time, an elaboration of the specific benefits should reinforce and clarify the information presented during the first couple of days.

Segment 4: Detailed Policies and Procedures Session

This session will provide detailed information regarding the bank's policies and procedures. Because an overview will be presented in the first general session, this more detailed session will elaborate and more specifically explain the bank's policies relevant to all employees. It will include the following topics:

1. *Grading system.* Details might include purpose, and correlation with salary.
2. *Customer service.* Details might include why it is important, whom it affects, and possible ramifications of poor customer service.
3. *Job posting.* Details might include purpose, eligibility, types of jobs posted, how long jobs are posted, requirements, and procedure.
4. *Performance review process.* Details might include purpose, frequency, measurement factors, correlation with standards of performance, and salary increases.
5. *Promotions.* Details might include eligibility requirements, procedures, correlation with grading system, and salary increase guidelines.
6. *Rules regarding such matters as attendance and punctuality.* Details might include importance, possible ramifications of poor attendance and/or punctuality, requirements, and procedure.
7. *Salary increase guidelines.* Details might include procedure, eligibility, frequency, correlation with performance review process, and standards of performance.
8. *Standards of performance.* Details might include purpose, measurement factors, correlation with performance review process, and salary increases.
9. *Transfers and other changes in job classifications.* Details might include eligibility, voluntary and involuntary changes, procedures, correlation with grading system, and salary increase guidelines.

10. *Safety and security practices.* Details might include procedures and guidelines.

A session on policies and procedures that supplements literature describing the bank's requirements and explains the reasons behind some of the rules will set the tone for greater compliance. If an institution expects its employees to obey certain rules and regulations, it has an obligation to provide full and detailed information about these rules and an open exchange to assure clear understanding. Therefore, every opportunity should be provided for employees to ask questions.

To create an environment conducive to learning, a relaxed format is recommended. As already mentioned, an informal seating arrangement and the offer of refreshments might be considered. Varied media will contribute to heightened attention levels and retention of information disseminated. Media might include slide presentations; lectures by human resources representatives, followed by discussion; transparencies and charts; and handout materials.

This policies and procedures session should run for one half-day. This should allow sufficient time to cover the important policies that apply to everyone. As with employee benefits, an overview of policies and procedures will have been presented in the general session and literature will have been presented in advance.

This policies and procedures session should take place no later than two weeks after hiring (one week following the benefits session). By this time, employees will have adjusted somewhat to the new work environment and will therefore be in a better position to understand why certain policies and rules exist, as well as how they apply.

Organizational Orientation Evaluation

Following the last segment of the organizational orientation, each participant should be given a questionnaire for completion. The primary purpose of the questionnaire is to evaluate the content of the orientation program and determine which portions were deemed most informative; how useful the various presentations were; how helpful the visual aids were; how beneficial the printed materials were; how useful the tour was; and what, if anything, should be changed to make the program more effective. In addition, questions regarding such factors as format, timing, location, setting, and duration may be posed.

Questionnaires should be distributed not only to the new hires attending these orientation sessions, but also to managers and department heads responsible for their work. This will provide some additional insight as to the effectiveness of the program overall and the applicability of specific information imparted.

Once a sufficient sample of responses to these questionnaires has been gathered, the results should be culled and analyzed. If a pattern of suggested changes develops, serious consideration should be given to amending the existing program. A sample organizational orientation evaluation form for attendees appears in Appendix M. A slightly modified version may be distributed to managers.

Departmental Orientation

In addition to the topics covered on the employee's first day and during the organizational orientation, there are other areas with which a new employee should be familiar. These topics are most effectively covered during an orientation session conducted within the employee's own department. The person conducting this orientation should be the same person who helped the new employee become acclimated on the first day of work. A rapport with this person will have already been established, thereby making the employee feel more comfortable.

Content

Departmental orientation should focus on specific job-related areas. Following are some topics considered relevant for inclusion:

1. *Departmental responsibilities.* Details might include origins, overall function, and both long-term and short-term goals.
2. *Department structure.* Details might include the identification of specific functions and the incumbents in specific positions.
3. *Disciplinary procedure.* Details might include an outline of the general disciplinary procedure, sample infractions, and ramifications of same.
4. *Grievance procedure.* Details might include steps to follow, people to contact, time frames, and examples of legitimate grievances.
5. *Hours of work.* Details might include starting and quitting times and alternative work arrangements.

6. *Interrelationship between own department and other departments.* Details might include a description of the flow of work between departments and the key individuals to contact in other departments.

7. *Job duties and responsibilities.* Details might include a description of exact tasks to be performed, expected frequency of performance, areas of responsibility, and interrelationship with other jobs, both within the department and with other departments.

8. *Meal and break periods.* Details might include how meal and break periods are scheduled and frequency and duration of breaks.

9. *Meal money.* Details might include eligibility for meal money, maximum amount, and procedure.

10. *Overtime.* Details might include requirements, eligibility, frequency, and scheduling.

11. *Personal telephone calls.* Details might include under what circumstances personal telephone calls are permitted.

12. *Personal visitors.* Details might include where personal visitors may be met, and I.D. requirements.

13. *Reporting relationships.* Details might include direct and indirect reporting relationships and who is in charge during absences of the people normally in charge.

14. *Smoking regulations.* Details might include both restrictions and areas where smoking is permitted.

15. *Time records.* Details might include sign-in sheets, and records of sick days, vacation days, and personal days.

16. *Vacation scheduling.* Details might include how vacations are scheduled, who approves vacation requests, and how far in advance requests should be made.

It is advisable to have a topical checklist for these categories, similar to the one used on the employee's first day of work, in order to make certain that nothing is omitted. Giving a copy to the new employee so that he or she can take notes as you talk is also advised.

Materials Used

If the new employee will be working in a supervisory or managerial capacity, be certain to provide him or her with a copy of the organization's personnel policies and procedures manual. Take time to familiarize the individual with the overall content, explaining how and when the manual is to be used. Also be certain to mention the person who should be contacted if clarification is needed. Additional group training in the proper use of this important company tool should be provided at some point in the near future, and the new supervisor or manager should be so advised.

If deemed appropriate, also provide the new employee with a departmental table of organization. Go over it with the employee, describing the primary functions of each position and individual as you do so.

In addition, provide the employee with work manuals, instructions, or other printed materials relative to his or her specific job.

Timing

It is recommended that this departmental orientation take place on the afternoon of the employee's third day on the job, if at all possible. Having by this time received a general introduction to his or her environment, he or she should now receive full departmental information before actually beginning to work.

Summary

This chapter has provided information relative to three different aspects of orientation for new employees: the first day of work, organizational orientation, and departmental orientation. Important components of each aspect of orientation were described and recommendations were made regarding such matters as timing, duration, and format. Recommendations for orientation evaluation were also made. In addition, a sample organizational orientation program was provided, consisting of four distinct segments: a general session, a tour, a detailed benefits session, and a detailed policies and procedures session.

The following orientation schedule has been recommended:

Day 1:   A.M.—Familiarization with the office
            P.M.—Organizational Orientation, Segment 1: General Session

Day 2:   A.M.—Organizational Orientation, Segment 1: General Session (Conclusion)
            P.M.—Organizational Orientation, Segment 2: Tour

Day 3:   A.M.—Organizational Orientation, Segment 2: Tour (Conclusion)
            P.M.—Departmental Orientation

Week 2:   One half-day—Organizational Orientation, Segment 3: Detailed Benefits Session
Week 3:   One half-day—Organizational Orientation, Segment 4: Detailed Policies and Procedures Session

Readers are urged to modify the model program and schedules to suit the needs of their particular environment.

Appendix A
Work Environment Checklist

Working Conditions

- Extensive standing
- Ventilation
- Exposure to chemicals or fumes
- Space
- Noise level
- Types of machinery or equipment

Location

- Permanent
- Temporary
- Rotational
- Options available

Travel

- Purpose
- Locations
- Frequency
- Duration
- Means of transportation

Schedule

- Work arrangement
- Hours
- Days of the week
- Meal breaks and other scheduled breaks
- Required overtime

Other Factors

Appendix B
Job Description Form

Job Description

Job title:

Division/Department:

Reporting relationship:

Location of job: Work schedule:

Exemption status: Grade/Salary range:

Summary of duties and responsibilities

Primary duties and responsibilities

1.

2.

3.

4.

5.

6.

7.

8.

9.

Performs other related duties and assignments as required.

Job title:

Division/Department:

*Education, prior work experience,
and specialized skill and knowledge*

Physical environment/working conditions

Equipment/machinery used

Other (e.g., customer contact or access to confidential information)

Job analyst:
Date:

Appendix C
Job Posting Notice Form

Job Posting Notice

Job title:
Division/Department:
Location: Job no.:
Summary of primary duties
   and responsibilities:
Exemption status: Grade/Salary range:
Work schedule/Working
   conditions:
Qualifications/Requirements:

Closing date:

Job Posting Eligibility Requirements

1. You must be employed by Valdart, Ltd. for at least twelve consecutive months.
2. You must be in your present position for a minimum of six months.
3. You must meet the qualifications/requirements listed above.
4. Your most recent evaluation must reflect your job performance as satisfactory or better.
5. You must notify your immediate supervisor/manager of your intent to submit a job posting application.

Job Posting Application Procedure

1. Complete a job posting application form, available in the Human Resources Department.
2. Return the completed form to the Human Resources Department and give a copy to your immediate supervisor/manager by the closing date noted above.
3. You will be contacted within three working days of receipt of your application.

Appendix D
Job Posting Application Form

Job Posting Application

(Please print or type)

Name: Date:
                                        Telephone ext.:

Present job title: Present div./dept.:

Present grade: Present salary:

Name of present
  supervisor/manager:

Position applied for: Job no.:

Job Posting Eligibility Requirements

1. You must be employed by Valdart, Ltd. for at least twelve consecutive months.
2. You must be in your present position for a minimum of six months.
3. You must meet the qualifications/requirements listed on the job posting notice for this position.
4. Your most recent evaluation must reflect your job performance as satisfactory or better.
5. You must notify your immediate supervisor/manager of your intent to submit a job posting application.

Job Posting Application Procedure

1. Submit the original copy of this form to the Human Resources Department; submit the yellow copy to your immediate supervisor/manager; keep the white copy for yourself.
2. You will be contacted within three working days of receipt of your application.

Appendix E
Sampling of Job Ads

Although job ads vary in terms of content, approach, layout, and specific design, all ads should contain certain key elements. This includes information about the company (even "blind" ads should describe the organization), job requirements, and responsibilities. In addition, a statement regarding benefits and compensation should be offered, as well as contact information. Reference to being an equal opportunity employer should be made as well. Of course, the overall appearance should be eye-catching and easy to read.

Following is a sampling of five ads illustrating varying degrees of effectiveness.

Job Ad Number 1: Account Executive/Vendor Liaison

Account Executive/Vendor Liaison

AT NATWEST, SUCCESS IS IN THE CARDS.

In this case it means handling Visa and Mastercard, along with FDR, Envoy, and many other NatWest vendors.

We're one of the Northeast's thriving financial institutions with a tremendous growth record and opportunities for career advancement. This particular opportunity is for an individual who can act as a liaison with all areas of the merchant business and coordinate activities by supplying support and assistance in problem solving, monitor ACH and vendor transmissions, provide service to major accounts, develop and implement new services, and more.

A knowledge of Visa/Mastercard regulations and FDR processing systems, authorization, data capture systems and terminals is required, plus strong communication and analytical skills. Some experience with independent systems work would be a definite asset.

If you're the professional we're looking for, ready for the rewards and benefits of joining a leader like NatWest, please send your resume, in confidence, to: *Human Resources Department, Dept. AE, National Westminster Bank USA, 3 Huntington Quadrangle, Melville, NY 11747.* We are an equal opportunity employer M/F.

National Westminster Bank

Source: Newsday, March 18, 1990. Courtesy of Human Resources, National Westminster Bank, USA.

Overall Appearance: Very neat, orderly, and professionally presented. Logo identifies company. Variation in size and boldness of print effective. Eye-catching, clever statement following job title.

Job Specifications: Sufficient information about job duties and requirements to alert readers as to level of skill and knowledge sought. Specific reference to monitoring "ACH" and a knowledge of "FDR" processing is an effective screening device, since individuals without knowledge of these terms are not likely to apply. Absence of reference to specific number of years' experience or educational achievements is appropriate.

Information About the Organization: Simply and directly stated. Lack of detail assumes knowledge on the part of the readers.

Benefits and Compensation: Fails to mention benefits or compensation.

Contact Information: Department title provided in lieu of name of person to contact to preclude numerous calls anticipated from unqualified candidates.

EEO Information: Minimally stated.

Job Ad Number 2: Director of Human Resources

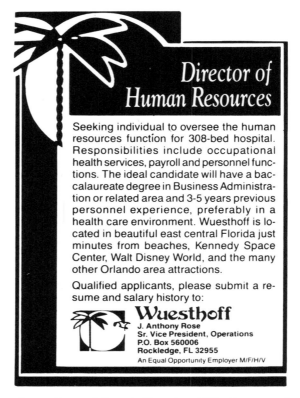

Source: Personnel Journal, November 1989. Courtesy of Wuesthoff Memorial Hospital, Rockledge, Florida.

Overall Appearance: Eye-catching use of graphics; alternating use of black and white is striking. Variation in use of print effective.

Job Specifications: Considering the scope of duties usually associated with jobs of this title, minimal description of responsibilities. Reference to "ideal candidate" makes degree requirement and three to five years previous personnel experience acceptable, although it does not stipulate what level of experience. Preference for experience in health care environment appropriately stated.

Information About the Organization: Description as a 308-bed hospital is insufficient. Reference to location and surrounding attractions effective.

Benefits and Compensation: Fails to mention benefits or compensation.

Contact Information: Name and title of person to contact clearly stated. Use of post office box number eliminates possibility of telephone inquiries.

EEO Information: Addition of "H/V" is effective.

Job Ad Number 3: Healthcare Recruiter

Overall Appearance: Very neat and orderly; lack of highlights or variation in boldness and size of print does not permit rapid scanning of contents by reader.

Job Specifications: Stipulation of degree requirement and specific number of years' prior experience questionable, particularly for the level of this job. Relevance of background in advertising and marketing techniques unclear. Reference to possible frequent travel is significant in that it may serve as either a "screening" statement or an added attraction.

Information About the Organization: Describing Fairbanks Memorial as an acute care facility and the sole provider in the area is sufficient. Reference to attractions in the community is well presented.

Benefits and Compensation: Vague language.

Contact Information: Offering interested candidates a choice of writing, calling, or using a fax machine is helpful.

EEO Information: No reference is made to being an equal employment opportunity employer.

HEALTHCARE RECRUITER
Fairbanks Memorial Hospital, a 177 bed acute care facility serving the northern region of Alaska has a challenging opportunity for a qualified individual to recruit applicants for health care positions. May require frequent travel. Must have two years experience in Human Resources plus two additional years in the health care field. A degree is required, preferably in human resources management, health care, or marketing. Must have good background in advertising and marketing techniques. The hospital is the sole provider located in Fairbanks in the beautiful Tanana Valley on the Chena River. The community is the home of the University of Alaska, offers downhill and cross-country skiing, excellent hunting, fishing, hiking, and other outdoor opportunities. Excellent compensation and benefits. **Contact Sandra Haselberger, 1650 Cowles, Fairbanks, AK 99701, 907-451-3499; FAX 907-452-5776.**

Source: Personnel Journal, June 1990. Courtesy of Fairbanks Memorial Hospital.

Job Ad Number 4: Associate Marketing Brand Manager

Source: The New York Times, March 18, 1990. Courtesy of
Schieffelin & Somerset Co.

Overall Appearance: Graphics are a real eye-catcher; placement of information off to one side reads well. Logo identifies company. Variation in size and alternating use of black and white print effective.

Job Specifications: Maximum number of years' experience identifies level of job. Description of specific knowledge and skills well done (assuming excellent oral presentation skills are an integral part of the job). College degree requirement is questionable.

Information About the Organization: Minimally stated.

Benefits and Compensation: Specific salary information clearly informs potential applicants of what they may expect. Minimal statement regarding benefits; reference to career opportunities implies career planning, job posting, or the like.

Contact Information: Clearly stated.

EEO Information: Minimally stated.

Job Ad Number 5: Chief Executive Officer

Overall Appearance: Professional in design, but information is too cramped. Greater variation in size and boldness of print would make content easier to read.

Job Specifications: Detailed description of required skills and knowledge. Use of phrases such as "Progressively responsible experience and demonstrated success . . ." and "Proven effectiveness . . ." clearly identifies nature and level of qualifications sought. Advanced degree requirement is questionable, since scope of responsibilities is unclear. Further requirement that this degree be "in an area related to the mission of the AACD" is vague.

Information About the Organization: Comprehensive description about the organization clearly identifies its status, size, scope, budget, and membership.

Benefits and Compensation: Vague language.

Contact Information: Clearly stated, except that reference to request for additional information is unclear.

EEO Information: Addition of "Women and minorities are encouraged to apply" is effective.

CHIEF EXECUTIVE OFFICER—*(Executive Director)* The American Association for Counseling and Development (AACD), with Headquarters in Alexandria, Virginia, is a professional and scientific, not-for-profit, organization, with an annual budget of $5.5 million, representing 56,000 counselors, human development specialists and administrators, and related mental health professionals. The Executive Director has a unique opportunity to work with a staff of 84 volunteer leaders from diverse backgrounds. The successful candidate should possess the following qualifications:
• Progressively responsible experience and demonstrated success in supervision and management of complex organizations, including supervision and development of professional and support staffs.
• Competence and executive experience in oversight of the preparation, implementation, and evaluation of budget and fiscal plans.
• Proven record of professional development.
• Proven effectiveness in government, public, and community relations.
• Demonstrated effectiveness in working with individuals from diverse backgrounds.
• Ability to organize and allocate human and financial resources.
• Proven organizational development and strategic planning skills.
• Knowledge of public policy development and the legislative process.
• Clear understanding of the needs of a diverse membership and ability to provide leadership for programs and services to meet such needs.
• An advanced degree in an area related to the mission of the AACD. Earned Doctorate and appropriate professional credential preferred.
Salary and fringe benefits will be commensurate with training and background.
Interested persons should send a letter of interest and vita to: **Executive Director Search, P.O. Box 1403, Ann Arbor, MI 48106.** Additional materials will be requested. The deadline for application is January 5, 1990.
AACD is an equal opportunity/affirmative action employer. Women and minorities are encouraged to apply.

Source: Training & Development Journal, December 1989. Courtesy of ERIC/CAPS, University of Michigan.

Appendix F
Application for Employment Form

APPLICATION FOR EMPLOYMENT

(Please Print)

Valdart, Ltd. considers applicants for all positions without regard to race, religion, sex, national origin, age, veteran status, disability, or any other legally protected status.

Date: _____

Name:_____
          last   first   middle

Address: _____
         number   street   city   state   zip code

Phone No.: (___)_____ Social Security No.: _____
         area code

Position(s) Applied For: _____

Hours and Days Available to Work: _____

Have you ever filed an application at Valdart, Ltd. before?
   ( ) Yes ( ) No   Date: _____ Position(s): _____

Have you ever been employed by Valdart, Ltd. before?
   ( ) Yes ( ) No Dates: _____ Position(s): _____

Do you have any relatives already employed by Valdart, Ltd.?
              ( ) Yes ( ) No

   If yes, please list names and departments: _____

Are you above the minimum legal working age?
             ( ) Yes ( ) No

Are you legally permitted to work in this country?
( ) Yes ( ) No

If yes, will you be prepared to produce proof at the time of hire, in accordance with the Immigration Reform and Control Act of 1986?
( ) Yes ( ) No

*Have you ever been convicted of a felony? ( ) Yes ( ) No
If yes, please explain: _____

_____

_____

_____

_____

*A positive response will not necessarily affect your eligibility to be hired.

Do you have any physical, mental, or medical impairments that would interfere with your ability to perform the job for which you are applying?
( ) Yes ( ) No

If yes, please explain: _____

_____

_____

_____

_____

As related to the position applied for, what languages do you speak, read, and/or write?

_____( ) Speak ( ) Read ( ) Write Degree of
Fluency
_____

_____( ) Speak ( ) Read ( ) Write Degree of
Fluency
_____

_____( ) Speak ( ) Read ( ) Write Degree of
Fluency
_____

What professional organizations or business activities are you involved with, relative to your ability to perform the job for which you are applying? _____

_____

_____

_____

Employment Experience

Please list present or most recent employer first. If additional space is needed, continue on a separate sheet of paper. Include part-time employment and military service, if any.

Employer:_____ Phone No.:_( )_____
                                                      area code

Address: _____
                  number   street   city   state   zip code

Position(s): _____

Super./Mgr.: _____

Dates Employed: From: _____ To: _____
                                      mo.   yr.   mo.   yr.

Reason for Leaving: _____

_____

_____

Description of Primary Responsibilities: _____

_____

_____

_____

- -

Employer:_____ Phone No.:_( )_____
                                                      area code

Address: _____
                  number   street   city   state   zip code

Position(s): _____

Super./Mgr.: _____

Dates Employed: From: _____   To: _____
                        mo.   yr.   mo.   yr.

Reason for Leaving: _____

_____

_____

Description of Primary Responsibilities: _____

_____

_____

_____

_____

— —

Employer: _____ Phone No.: ( ) _____
                                             area code

Address: _____
          number   street   city   state   zip code

Position(s): _____

Super./Mgr.: _____

Dates Employed: From: _____   To: _____
                        mo.   yr.   mo.   yr.

Reason for Leaving: _____

_____

_____

Description of Primary Responsibilities: _____

_____

_____

_____

_____

— —

Employer:_____ Phone No.:_( )_____
                                                    area code

Address: _____
              number   street   city   state   zip code

Position(s): _____

Super./Mgr.: _____

Dates Employed: From: _____ To: _____
                                    mo.   yr.   mo.   yr.

Reason for Leaving: _____

_____

_____

Description of Primary Responsibilities: _____

_____

_____

_____

Education and Training

Type of School	Name and Location	No. Years Completed	Honors Received; Diploma/Degree	Course of Study
Elemen. School				
Jr. High/ High School				
Trade, Business, or Technical				
College/ Univ.				
Graduate/ Profess.				
Other (explain)				

Please describe any additional academic achievements or extracurricular activities relative to the position for which you are applying:

_____

_____

_____

Additional Qualifications

Please identify any additional knowledge, skills, qualifications, publications, or awards that will be helpful to us in considering your application for employment: _____

_____

_____

_____

References

Please provide the name, address, and phone number of three additional references, other than present/former employers:

name	address	phone no.

1. _____
2. _____
3. _____

Special Notice to Disabled Veterans, Vietnam Era Veterans, and Individuals With Disabilities

Government contractors are subject to Section 402 of the Vietnam Era Veterans Readjustment Act of 1974, which requires that they take Affirmative Action to employ and advance in employment qualified disabled veterans and veterans of the Vietnam Era; and Section 503 of the Rehabilitation Act of 1973, as amended, which requires that they take Affirmative Action to employ and advance in employment qualified disabled individuals.

(Definitions)

1. Veteran of the Vietnam era means a person who served more than 180 days of active service, any part of which was during the period August 5, 1964, through May 7, 1975, and who was discharged or released with an other than dishonorable discharge or discharged or released because of a service-connected disability.

2. Special Disabled Veteran means a veteran entitled to compensation for a disability rated at 30% or more, or rated at 10% or 20% if determined to be a serious employment handicap, or a person discharged or released from active duty because of a service-connected disability.

    If you consider yourself to be covered by one or both of these Acts, and wish to be identified for the purposes of proper placement and appropriate accommodation, please sign below. Submission of this information is voluntary and failure to provide it will not jeopardize employment opportunities at Valdart, Ltd. This information will be kept confidential.

    ( ) Disabled   ( ) Disabled Veteran   ( ) Vietnam Era
                                                        Veteran

                    Signed_____

Agreement

I certify that the statements made in this application are correct and complete to the best of my knowledge.

I understand that false or misleading information may result in termination of employment.

I authorize Valdart, Ltd. to conduct a reference check so that a hiring decision may be made. In the event that Valdart, Ltd. is unable to verify any reference stated on this application, it is my responsibility to furnish the necessary documentation.

( ) You May   ( ) You May Not contact my present employer.

( ) You May   ( ) You May Not contact the schools I have attended for the release of my educational records.

Disclaimer

If accepted for employment with Valdart, Ltd., I agree to abide by all of its policies and procedures. If employed, I understand that I may terminate my employment at any time without notice or cause, and that the Employer may terminate or modify the employment relationship at any time without prior notice or cause. In consideration of my employment, I agree to conform to the rules and regulations of the Employer and I understand that no representative of the Employer, other than the President or Human Resources Officer, has any authority to enter into any agreement, oral or written, for employment for any specified period of time or to make any agreement or assurances contrary to this policy. If employed, I understand that my employment is for no definite period of time, and if terminated, the Employer is liable only for wages and benefits earned as of the date of termination.

I also agree to have my photograph taken for identification purposes if hired.

Signed _____

Date _____

Do Not Write Below This Line

Interviews

Human Resources Interviewer: _____ Date: _____

Comments: _____

_____

_____

Results: _____

Dept./Div. Interviewer: _____ Date: _____

Comments: _____

_____

_____

Results: _____

Dept./Div. Interviewer: _____ Date: _____

Comments: _____

_____

_____

Results: _____

Employed: ( ) Yes ( ) No

If Yes: Title _____

Dept. _____

Date of Hire _____

Starting Salary _____

AN EQUAL OPPORTUNITY EMPLOYER M/F/V/D

Appendix G
Completed Application for Employment Form

APPLICATION FOR EMPLOYMENT

(Please Print)

Valdart, Ltd. considers applicants for all positions without regard to race, religion, sex, national origin, age, veteran status, disability, or any other legally protected status.

Overall appearance neat; legible; easy to read

Date: __Nov. 21, 1991__

Name: __Perkins__ __Valerie__ __Danielle__
　　　　　last　　　　　　first　　　　　　middle

Address: __23 Turner Ave., Tyrone　NY　65010__
　　　　　number　street　　　　city　　state　　zip code

Phone No.: __(123)555-2085__ Social Security No.: __515-48-6234__
　　　　　area code

Position(s) Applied For: __Ass't. to Dir. of Human Resources__

Hours and Days Available to Work: __M-F; 8:30-6__

Have you ever filed an application at Valdart, Ltd. before?
　　( ) Yes　(X) No　Date: _____　Position(s): _____

Have you ever been employed by Valdart, Ltd. before?
　　( ) Yes　(X) No　Dates: _____　Position(s): _____

Do you have any relatives already employed by Valdart, Ltd.?
　　　　　　　　(X) Yes　( ) No

omission

　　If yes, please list names and departments: _____

Are you above the minimum legal working age?
　　　　　　　　(X) Yes　( ) No

Are you legally permitted to work in this country?

(**X**) Yes   (   ) No

If yes, will you be prepared to produce proof at the time of hire, in accordance with the Immigration Reform and Control Act of 1986?

(**X**) Yes   (   ) No

*Have you ever been convicted of a felony?   (   ) Yes   (**X**) No

If yes, please explain: _____

_____

_____

_____

_____

*A positive response will not necessarily affect your eligibility to be hired.

Do you have any physical, mental, or medical impairments that would interfere with your ability to perform the job for which you are applying?

(   ) Yes   (**X**) No

If yes, please explain: _____

_____

_____

_____

_____

As related to the position applied for, what languages do you speak, read, and/or write?

Spanish____(**X**) Speak   (**X**) Read   (**X**) Write   Degree of Fluency **good**_____

French____(**X**) Speak   (**X**) Read   (**X**) Write   Degree of Fluency **fair**_____

_____(   ) Speak   (   ) Read   (   ) Write   Degree of Fluency _____

Job does not require additional language skills

What professional organizations or business activities are you involved with, relative to your ability to perform the job for which you are applying? **Member of Human Resource Develop-** **ment Specialists; and Personnel Specialists of** **America**

Employment Experience

Please list present or most recent employer first. If additional space is needed, continue on a separate sheet of paper. Include part-time employment and military service, if any.

Employer: **Q & R, Ltd.**   Phone No.: **(123) 555-4044**
                                                                area code

Address: **23-85 E. 36th St. Tyrone, NY 65010**
                number   street   city   state   zip code

Position(s): **Personnel Assistant**

Super./Mgr.: **Thomas Richards**

Dates Employed: From: **5/89**   To: **Present**
                                      mo.   yr.   mo.   yr.

Reason for Leaving: **No room for advancement**

gap of 1 mos. between jobs needs clarificat.

Description of Primary Responsibilities: **Recruiting and** **interviewing nonexempt employees; reference checks;** **processing new hires; Assist with policies & procedures;** **salary admin.; performance appraisals; EEO forms.**

Employer: **Roxbury Med. Ctr.** Phone No.: **(712) 555-1900**
                                                                area code

Address: **2500 Oxford Blvd. Roxbury, Conn. 36401**
                number   street   city   state   zip code

Position(s): **Personnel Assistant**

Super./Mgr.: **Eileen Cannali**

Dates Employed: From: **9 / 87** To: **9 / 88**
  mo. yr.   mo. yr.

"Red Flag"

Reason for Leaving: **Personal**

Description of Primary Responsibilities: **Recruiting and Interviewing nonexempt employees; references; processing new hires; benefits; orientation.**

Employer: **Global Imports, Inc.** Phone No.: **(712) 555-2200**
  area code

Address: **1725 Union Ave., Roxbury, Conn 36401**
  number street city state zip code

Position(s): **Administrative Ass't.**

Super./Mgr.: **Jessica McDonald**

Dates Employed: From: **10 / 86** To: **8 / 87**
  mo. yr.   mo. yr.

Reason for Leaving: **No room for advancement**

Description of Primary Responsibilities: **Responsible for running the Personnel Dept.**

job title needs explanation

needs clarification

"Red Flag"

pattern of reasons for leaving to starting to emerge

Employer: **Vanderbilt Movers**   Phone No.: _(123)_____

area code

Address: __1948 Tunney Blvd. Tyrone, NY 65010__

number   street   city   state   zip code

Position(s): **Office Manager** _____

Super./Mgr.: __Robert LaBlanca_____

Dates Employed: From: __1 / 86__ To: __12 / 86__

mo.   yr.   mo.   yr.

Reason for Leaving: __Conflicted with schedule at__
__school.__ _____

_____

Description of Primary Responsibilities: __Distributed work__
__of 6 AVP's and VP's to secretaries.__ _____

_____

_____

omission

Overlap in dates with Global

Frequency of job changes
1/86-12/86
10/86-3/87
9/87-9/88
5/89-Pres

Education and Training

Type of School	Name and Location	No. Years Completed	Honors Received; Diploma/Degree	Course of Study
Elemen. School	Wilson— Roxbury, Conn.	6		general
Jr. High/ High School	Roxbury Jr. H.S + Roxbury H.S., Conn.	6	HS Diploma	general
Trade, Business, or Technical	N/A			
College/ Univ.	Roxbury Univ, Conn.	4	BA degree	English
Graduate/ Profess.	Tyrone Law School	1 ½		Law
Other (explain)				

Inconsistency between courses of study and employment

Please describe any additional academic achievements or extracurricular activities relative to the position for which you are applying:

graduated college with honors – 3.6 cum index

Additional Qualifications

Please identify any additional knowledge, skills, qualifications, publications, or awards that will be helpful to us in considering your application for employment: **excellent communication skills**

References

Please provide the name, address, and phone number of three additional references, other than present/former employers:

	name	address	phone no.
1.	Jeff Brixton		712-555-5591
2.	Joel Meyers	19 Lodge Ave. San Carlo, CA 02070	213-555-0082
3.	Rob LaBlanca	24 Apple Dr. Tyrone, NY 65010	123-555-3319

omission

Former employer

Special Notice to Disabled Veterans, Vietnam Era Veterans, and Individuals With Disabilities

Government contractors are subject to Section 402 of the Vietnam Era Veterans Readjustment Act of 1974, which requires that they take Affirmative Action to employ and advance in employment qualified disabled veterans and veterans of the Vietnam Era; and Section 503 of the Rehabilitation Act of 1973, as amended, which requires that they take Affirmative Action to employ and advance in employment qualified disabled individuals.

(Definitions)

1. Veteran of the Vietnam era means a person who served more than 180 days of active service, any part of which was during the period August 5, 1964, through May 7, 1975, and who was discharged or released with an other than dishonorable discharge or discharged or released because of a service-connected disability.

2. Special Disabled Veteran means a veteran entitled to compensation for a disability rated at 30% or more, or rated at 10% or 20% if determined to be a serious employment handicap, or a person discharged or released from active duty because of a service-connected disability.

If you consider yourself to be covered by one or both of these Acts, and wish to be identified for the purposes of proper placement and appropriate accommodation, please sign below. Submission of this information is voluntary and failure to provide it will not jeopardize employment opportunities at Valdart, Ltd. This information will be kept confidential.

(   ) Disabled   (   ) Disabled Veteran   (   ) Vietnam Era
                                                          Veteran

Signed_____

Agreement

I certify that the statements made in this application are correct and complete to the best of my knowledge.

I understand that false or misleading information may result in termination of employment.

I authorize Valdart, Ltd. to conduct a reference check so that a hiring decision may be made. In the event that Valdart, Ltd. is unable to verify any reference stated on this application, it is my responsibility to furnish the necessary documentation.

(   ) You May   (✗) You May Not contact my present employer.

(   ) You May   (   ) You May Not contact the schools I have attended for the release of my educational records.

omission

Disclaimer

If accepted for employment with Valdart, Ltd., I agree to abide by all of its policies and procedures. If employed, I understand that I may terminate my employment at any time without notice or cause, and that the Employer may terminate or modify the employment relationship at any time without prior notice or cause. In consideration of my employment, I agree to conform to the rules and regulations of the Employer and I understand that no representative of the Employer, other than the President or Human Resources Officer, has any authority to enter into any agreement, oral or written, for employment for any specified period of time or to make any agreement or assurances contrary to this policy. If employed, I understand that my employment is for no definite period of time, and if terminated, the Employer is liable only for wages and benefits earned as of the date of termination.

I also agree to have my photograph taken for identification purposes if hired.

Signed *Valerie D. Perkins*

Date **11/21/91**

Do Not Write Below This Line

Interviews

Human Resources Interviewer: _____ Date: _____
Comments: _____
_____
_____

Results: _____

Dept./Div. Interviewer: _____ Date: _____
Comments: _____
_____
_____

Results: _____

Dept./Div. Interviewer: _____ Date: _____
Comments: _____
_____
_____

Results: _____

Employed: ( ) Yes ( ) No
If Yes: Title _____
Dept. _____
Date of Hire _____
Starting Salary _____

AN EQUAL OPPORTUNITY EMPLOYER M/F/V/D

Appendix H
Interview Evaluation Form

Applicant: _____

Position: _____

Additional factors, as relevant:

Clerical skills: _____
_____
_____

Verbal communication skills: _____
_____
_____

Writing skills: _____
_____
_____

Technical skills: _____
_____
_____

Numerical skills: _____
_____
_____

Language skills: _____
_____
_____

Other job-related information: _____
_____
_____
_____

Overall evaluation:
    (   ) Meets job requirements
    (   ) Fails to meet job requirements

Additional comments: _____
_____
_____
_____

Interviewer: _____

Appendix I
Employment Reference Form for Exempt Positions

Exempt Employment Reference Check

Date: _____

Applicant's name: _____   Position: _____

Person contacted: _____   Title: _____

Company: _____   Telephone no.: (_____) _____

Address: _____

The above named individual has applied to Valdart, Ltd. for employment. He/She has listed you as a former employer, and has authorized us to conduct a reference check. We need your assistance in verifying and providing certain information regarding his/her work performance:

1. _____ worked in the _____
   department as a(n) _____
   from _____ to _____.
   (   ) correct (   ) incorrect
   If incorrect, please explain.

2. His/Her primary responsibilities included: _____
   _____
   _____
   _____
   (   ) correct (   ) incorrect
   If incorrect, please explain.

Applicant's name: _____   Position: _____

Person contacted: _____   Company: _____

----

3. He/She stated that his/her reason for terminating employment
    with your company was: _____

    _____

    (   ) correct (   ) incorrect
    If incorrect, please explain.

    How would you evaluate his/her overall work performance?

5. What were his/her greatest strengths?

6. What were the areas in which he/she required improvement
    and/or additional training?

7. What made him/her an effective supervisor/manager?

Applicant's name: _____   Position: _____

Person contacted: _____   Company: _____
----

8. How did he/she handle job-related situations involving pressure? Involving difficult tasks?

9. How would you describe his/her management style? Decision-making style?

10. Please provide an example of the type of decision he/she would commonly have to make on the job, and the ramifications of this decision.

11. How effectively did he/she handle meeting deadlines?

12. How did he/she generally respond to repetitious tasks? To new assignments?

Applicant's name: _____   Position: _____

Person contacted: _____   Company: _____
----
13. Please describe any work-related travel required, in terms of location, duration, and frequency.

14. This job calls for the ability to: _____
    What experience did he/she have in doing this?
    (Note: This question can be expanded to encompass several different factors. Use your job description as a guide.)

15. How effectively did he/she interact with peers? Senior management? Employees?

16. Would you rehire him/her?
    (   ) yes (   ) no
    If no, why not?

17. Is there anything else we should know about his/her work performance?

                    Reference conducted by: _____

Appendix J

Employment Reference Form for Nonexempt Positions

Nonexempt Employment Reference Check

Date: _____

Applicant's name: _____ Position: _____

Person contacted: _____ Title: _____

Company: _____ Telephone no.: (   ) _____

Address: _____

The above named individual has applied to Valdart, Ltd. for employment. He/she has listed you as a former employer, and has authorized us to conduct a reference check. We need your assistance in verifying and providing certain information regarding his/her work performance:

1. _____ worked in the _____
   department as a(n) _____
   from _____ to _____.
   (   ) correct (   ) incorrect
   If incorrect, please explain.

2. His/her primary responsibilities included: _____
   _____
   _____
   _____
   (   ) correct (   ) incorrect
   If incorrect, please explain.

Applicant's name: ＿＿＿＿＿＿＿ Position: ＿＿＿＿＿＿＿＿＿

Person contacted: ＿＿＿＿＿＿＿ Company: ＿＿＿＿＿＿＿＿＿

----

3. He/She stated that his/her reason for terminating employment
   with your company was: ＿＿＿＿＿＿＿＿＿＿＿＿＿＿＿＿
   ＿＿＿＿＿＿＿＿＿＿＿＿＿＿＿＿＿＿＿＿＿＿＿＿＿＿＿＿＿

   (   ) correct (   ) incorrect
   If incorrect, please explain.

4. How would you describe his/her attendance record? Punctuality
   record?

5. How would you evaluate his/her overall work performance?

6. What tasks did he/she perform particularly well?

7. What were the areas in which he/she required improvement
   and/or additional training?

Applicant's name: ———————   Position: ————————

Person contacted: ——————   Company: ———————
- -

8. How closely did you need to supervise his/her work?

9. How did he/she respond to requests to work overtime? To be on call?

10. How did he/she respond to repetitious tasks? To new assignments?

11. How effectively did he/she interact with co-workers? With management?

12. This job calls for the ability to: ———————————.
    What experience did he/she have in doing this?
    (Note: This question can be expanded to encompass several different factors. Use your job description as a guide.)

Applicant's name: _____ Position: _____

Person contacted: _____ Company: _____
----

13. Would you rehire him/her?
    (   ) yes (   ) no
    If no, why not?

14. Is there anything else we should know about his/her work
    performance?

Reference conducted by: _____

Appendix K
Selection Checklist

Instructions for Use

The Selection Checklist on the following page can be a valuable tool in the selection of the best possible candidate for any given job. The form is most effectively utilized when the qualifications or qualities of each promising applicant are evaluated according to the ten categories listed. This may best be accomplished by applying the following rating scale:

1 Exceeds the requirement or trait sought
2 Satisfactorily meets the requirement or trait sought
3 Minimally meets the requirement or trait sought
4 Fails to meet the requirement or trait sought
5 Offers an alternative trait that may satisfactorily substitute for the requirement or trait sought
6 Offers an alternative trait that does not satisfactorily substitute for the requirement or trait sought

Each rating should also be accompanied by supportive job-related information and examples, as ascertained during the interview.

Sample
Selection Checklist

Position:	B. Way	J. Dix	J. Sam	R. Hon
Work History:				
Education:				
Intangibles:				
Reactions to Key Questions:				
Nonverbal Communication:				
Salary Require.:				
Reasons for Leaving Previous Employers:				
Potential:				
Appropriate Job Match:				
Other:				

Appendix L
Checklist for New Employees

1. Office/desk
   a. Functions of other workers situated nearby
   b. Policies regarding pictures, plants, and other personal items
   c. Desk supplies:
      1. Pencils and pens
      2. Pads and other paper
      3. Stapler
      4. Ruler
      5. Letter opener
      6. Paper clips
      7. Rubber bands
      8. Tape
      9. Scissors
   d. Equipment:
      1. Calculator
      2. Computer
      3. Typewriter
      4. Word processor
      5. Dictaphone machine
   e. Reference materials:
      1. Dictionary
      2. Thesaurus
2. Supplies
   a. Location
   b. Procedure
   c. Exceptions

3. Telephone directory
4. Phone system
   a. Prefixes
   b. Special codes
   c. Intercom
   d. Outside numbers
   e. Hold
   f. Conference calls
5. Rest rooms; water fountains
6. Coffee wagon
   a. Time
   b. Location
   c. Offerings
   d. Cost
7. Photocopy and facsimile (fax) machines
   a. Location
   b. Procedure for operation
   c. Changing paper
   d. Malfunction procedure
8. Files
   a. Location
   b. Procedure for signing out files
9. Cafeteria/executive dining room
   a. Location
   b. Food offered
   c. Cost
   d. Hours
   e. Reservations required (dining room)
   f. Method of payment (dining room)
   g. Guests (dining room)
10. Employee lounge
    a. Rules regarding its use
11. Company car
    a. Who to contact for additional information

12. Exercise facilities
    a. Location
    b. Facilities offered
    c. Eligibility
    d. Hours
    e. Requirements for use
13. Nonemergency medical care
    a. Location
    b. Procedure
14. Child care facilities
    a. Location
    b. Eligibility
    c. Caretakers
    d. Cost
    e. Who to contact for additional information
15. Other

Notes

_____
_____
_____
_____
_____
_____
_____
_____
_____
_____
_____
_____
_____
_____
_____
_____
_____
_____
_____

Appendix M
Organizational Orientation Evaluation

The purpose of this questionnaire is to evaluate the effectiveness of Valdart's organizational orientation program. Please answer the following questions as frankly and specifically as possible. Your identification is not required.

1. How would you evaluate the overall content of the program?

2. What segments did you find to be the most interesting and/or informative?

3. What segments did you find to be the least interesting and/or informative?

4. What segments have proved to be most beneficial in your position?

5. What segments have proved to be least beneficial in your position?

6. How interesting/informative were the visual aids?

7. How useful have the printed materials been in your position?

8. How would you describe the tour?

9. Please evaluate each of the speakers in terms of their ability to convey the subject matter, sustain your interest, and respond to questions.

10. How would you rate the location and setting of the orientation?

11. How would you rate the duration of the program?

12. How would you rate the format of the program?

13. When do you feel would be the most appropriate time for a new hire to attend orientation?

14. What other areas would you like to see covered during orientation?

15. Are there any topics you feel should be deleted from the existing program?

16. Please feel free to make any additional comments with regard to the program.

17. Please provide a summarizing statement reflecting your overall evaluation of the orientation program.

Index

AARP (American Association of Retired Persons), 8–9, 10, 113
achievement tests, 212
acquired immune deficiency syndrome (AIDS), 114, 118–119
   hot line for, 225
   testing for, 224–225
action words, in job descriptions, 44–45
active listening, in interview, 151–153
address, proper form of, 248
adverse impact, 204
advertising
   billboard, 68, 80
   newspaper and magazine, 52–54, 77
   radio or television, 63–64, 79
   samples of, 280–285
Aetna Life and Casualty Co., 5
affirmative action, 4, 105, 108–110
   and applicant record keeping, 91–92
   goals of, 49, 53, 109
   impact of, 128–129
affirmative action plans, 56
   factors in establishing, 110
Age Discrimination in Employment Act of 1967, 112–113

aggressive applicants, interviewing, 171
AIDS (acquired immune deficiency syndrome), 114, 118–119
   hot line for, 225
   testing for, 224–225
Albemarle Paper Co. v. Moody, 207
alcoholics, 114
Alexander & Alexander Consulting Group, 224
alternative work arrangements, 13, 19–26
American Association of Hispanic CPAs, 16
American Association of Retired Persons (AARP), 113
   "How to Recruit Older Workers," 10
   Worker Equity Initiative, 8–9
American Bar Association, Subcommittee on Drug and Alcohol Abuse in the Workplace, 223
American Indian Science and Engineering Society, 16
American National Standard Specifications for Making Buildings and Facilities Accessible to, and Usable by, the Physically Handicapped, 115

American Psychological Association, 206
  Committee on Ethical Standards, 217
American Society for Training and Development, *Buyer's Guide & Consultant Directory,* 73
Americans with Disabilities Act of 1990, 11, 116–118
American Telephone & Telegraph, 5, 12
  Work and Family program, 17
angry applicants, interviewing, 171
appearance, of applicant, 101
Apple Computer Co., 17
applicant record keeping, affirmative action and, 91–92
application forms, at-will statement on, 141
aptitude tests, 212
Asians, in labor force, 3
Association of Personnel Test Publishers, 228
associations, as recruitment source, 71, 81
at-home work, 19, 23–24
Atlantic Richfield, 24
at-will doctrine, 128, 138–143, 242
audience, for recruitment, 48

bad faith in employment, 142
Bakke, Allan, 126
balance and reflex performance checks, 222
Bank of America, 17
basic skills, 2
  training by corporations, 5
B. Dalton Bookseller, 5
benefits, 39–40
  in orientation, 263, 267–269
  for part-time employment, 20
Bennett Mechanical Comprehension Test, 215
BFOQ (bona fide occupational qualification), 113, 129–130
bias, from referrals, 101

billboard advertising, 68, 80
biological clock, 21, 93
bisexuals, 116
blind ads, 54
blood tests, for drugs, 222
body language, 102–103, 149, 151, 154–157, 240
  of interviewer, 156, 159
bona fide occupational qualification (BFOQ), 113, 129–130
bonus, for hiring, 39
Bristol-Myers Squibb Co., 59
brochures, for school recruitment, 58–59
Buckley Amendment, 237
budget, and recruitment, 48
Burger King, Crew Education Assistance Program, 14–15
Bush, George, 126
Business & Legal Reports, 220
business services, 2
Buyer's Guide & Consultant Directory (American Society for Training and Development), 73

cable television, 63
cafeteria, 251–252
call-ins, as recruitment source, 57
Camara, Wayne, on handwriting analysis, 218
Career Counseling Network, 65
CareerLine, 63
Catalyst, "Flexible Work Arrangements: Establishing Options for Managers & Professions," 19
Center for Public Resources, 5
child care, 17–18, 252
chronemics, 103
citizenship requirements, and discrimination, 124
Civil Rights Act of 1866, 106
Civil Rights Act of 1964, 54, 56, 107–108, 206
Civil Rights Act of 1990, 126–127
Civil Service Commission, 204

close-ended questions, 158, 161–162
COBRA (Comprehensive Omnibus Benefits and Retirement Act), 118
college degree, requiring, 136
color psychology, 218
common-law doctrine of qualified privilege, 232
company cars, 252
company expectations, 265
company information, 159
    place for, in interview, 147–148
company objectives, and employee selection, 239
company policies, in orientation, 269–270
comparable worth, 111
Comprehensive Omnibus Benefits and Retirement Act (COBRA), 118
compressed workweek, 22–23
computer-administered tests, 209–210
computer diskettes, for recruitment, 59
computer industry, 2
computerized systems for recruitment, 64–65, 79
Computer Programmer Aptitude Battery, 215
Connecticut v. Teal, 207–208
construct validity, 205
Consultants News, 56
consulting firms, 72–73, 81
Consulting Psychologists Press, *CPP Catalog of Tests and Materials for Business,* 217
content validity, 205
contractors, independent, 25–26
control of interview, 172
core hours, 21
Corning Glass, 24
Council for Aid to Education, 15
cover letters, 88
CPP Catalog of Tests and Materials for Business (Consulting Psychologists Press), 217

Crawford Small Parts Dexterity Test, 215
Creating a Flexible Workplace (Olmsted and Smith), 19
credit reporting, 2
criterion-related validity, 205
critical tracking test, 222–229

data processing industry, 2
Days Inn of America, Inc., 9, 11–12, 13–14
defamation of character, reference checks and, 231–232
departmental orientation, 271–273
    timing of, 273
departmental representation, in orientation planning, 257–259
department heads, interviews by, 30
DiCosala v. Kay, 144
Direct Mail List Rates and Data (Standard Rate and Data Service), 62
direct mail recruitment, 62–63, 79
Directory of Executive Recruiters, 56
disabled persons, 11–13
    for at-home work, 24
    legal protection of, 114–115
    physical exams for, 219
    recruitment of, 12
    testing of, 210
disciplinary procedures, 141, 271
discrimination, 106–128
    affirmative action, 108–110
    Age Discrimination in Employment Act of 1967, 112–113
    AIDS, 118–119
    Americans with Disabilities Act of 1990, 116–118
    Civil Rights Act of 1866, 106
    Civil Rights Act of 1964, 107–108
    Employee Polygraph Protection Act, 126
    Equal Pay Act of 1963, 111–112
    national origin, 124
    preemployment inquiries and, 130–131, 132–135

discrimination (*continued*)
  Rehabilitation Act of 1973, 114–
    115
  religious, 122–124
  reverse, 126
  systemic, 49
  systemic, employee referral
    programs and, 52
  testing and, 206–208
  Vietnam Era Veterans Readjust-
    ment Act of 1974, 119
dislocated workers, 2
displaced workers, 2
documentation of interview, 181–
  200
  descriptions in, 188–189
  job-related facts in, 184–188
  opinions in, 183–184
  recording direct quotes of appli-
    cant in, 185–187
  subjective language in, 182–183
  summarization in, 198, 199
dominant applicants, interviewing,
  172
Drug-free Workplace Act of 1988,
  221
drug tests, 220–224
  guidelines for, 224
drug users, 114, 116
duties of job, familiarization with,
  29–30
Dychtwald, Ken, 25
  on older workers, 7–8

Eastman Kodak Co., 15
education, 4
  EEO guidelines and, 131, 136–
    137
  in job familiarization, 30–32
  questions on, 164–166
educational assistance programs, 58
educational references, 237–238
educational requirements, problems in changing, 137
Educational Testing Service, 214
800 numbers, *see* toll-free phone
  numbers

80 percent rule of thumb, 204
Ekman, Paul, 156
elder-care programs, 18–19
emotional applicants, interviewing,
  172
employee handbooks
  as contracts, 138–139
  job security in, 140
  and orientation, 257
employee leasing, 26, 75–76, 81
employee lounge, 252
employee medical records, retention of, 220
Employee Polygraph Protection
  Act, 126, 226
employee referral programs, 51, 77
Employee Retirement Income
  Security Act of 1974 (ERISA),
  118
employees' club, 268
employee selection
  responsibility for, 29
  uniform guidelines on, 204–206
employers, liability for employee
  behavior, 144
Employers' Tests and Services
  Associates, 213
employment agencies, 54–56, 77
employment and termination-
  at-will doctrine, 138–143, 242
employment application, form for,
  286–301
employment contract, job offer
  letter as, 242
employment services, government
  regulation of, 56
engineering jobs, 3
English as second language, 6
environment
  for interviews, 94–96
  multicultural, 15–16
  work, 34–37, 275
Enzyme-Linked Immunosorbent
  Assay test, 225
equal employment opportunity, 4,
  31, 49, 87, 105, 234
  impact of, 128–129
  open questions and, 163

Equal Employment Opportunity Commission, 107, 204
and age discrimination, 112
on sex-referent language in employment advertising, 54
equal opportunity employer, 56
Equal Pay Act of 1963, 90, 111–112
ERISA (Employee Retirement Income Security Act of 1974), 118
ethnocentrism, 103–104, 153
evaluation, of organizational orientation, 270–271
Executive Order 11246, 56, 108–109
Executive Order 12564, 221
Executive Orders, on affirmative action, 108–109
executive search firms, 65
exemption status, 37–38
and recruitment, 49
exempt positions
reference form for, 304–307
telephone screening for, 85
exit interviews, 141, 233
expectations of company, 265
experience
EEO guidelines and, 131, 136–137
job relatedness of, 137
questions on, 166–170
eye contact, 154

Facial Affect Scoring Technique, 156
facsimile machines, 23, 251
Fair Credit Reporting Act of 1971, 56
Fair Employment Practices: Summary of Latest Developments, 113
Fair Labor Standards Act of 1938, 37, 56
Family Education Rights and Privacy Act, 237
family issues, work and, 16–19
federal government, doing business with, 109

fetal protection, 121
files, showing new employee location of, 251
films, for orientation, 260
Financial News Network, 63
first day of work, 247–254
familiarization with office on, 250–252
introductions on, 249–250
lunch for new employees on, 253
meeting with manager at end of, 253–254
first impressions, 100–101
Flanagan Aptitude Classification Test, 216
"Flexible Work Arrangements: Establishing Options for Managers & Professions" (Catalyst), 19
flextime, 21–22
Foley v. Interactive Data Corporation, 142
Ford Motor Company, 5
Foreign Service, 225
format for interviews, 147–148
forty-hour workweek, 16
Forty Plus, 10
four-fifths rule of thumb, 204
functional illiterates, 4

Gaines v. Monsanto, 144
Gallup survey, on older workers, 8
gamblers, 116
General Accounting Office, 125
General Aptitude Test Battery, 216
General Motors, 5
generic job descriptions, 42
genetic testing, 219
geographic location, 35–36
Globe Research Corporation, 68
government agencies, as recruitment source, 61–62, 79
government regulation, and job application forms, 87
graphology, 217–218
Great American Savings Bank (San Diego), 9

grievance procedures, 141, 271
Griggs v. Duke Power Co., 207
group size, for orientation, 255
growth opportunities, familiariza-
    tion with, 40

hair analysis, for drug use, 223
handicapped persons, *see* disabled
    persons
hand-out materials, for orientation,
    260
Hand-Tool Dexterity Test, 215
handwriting analysis, 217–218
health care workers, AIDS testing
    of, 225
health services, 2
hearing-impaired applicants, test-
    ing of, 210
Hewlett-Packard Company, 21
high school diploma, requiring,
    136
hiring
    bonus for, 39
    negligent, 143–145
Hispanics, 3
holidays, 267
homeless, 13–14
homosexuals, 116
honesty tests, 227–228
Honick, Joseph, on employee leas-
    ing, 75
hours of work, 271
HR News, 11
Hudson Institute, "Workforce
    2000: Work and Workers for
    the 21st Century," 13
human resources specialists
    interviews by, 29–30
    networking by, 71–72
hypothetical questions, 162
Hyundai, 69

icebreakers, 247–248
I.D. card national, 125
Illiterate America (Kozol), 4
immigrants, 16

Immigration Reform and Control
    Act of 1986, 16, 124
implied contract rights, 138
in-basket tests, 213
independent contractors, 25–26
industrial psychologists, 206, 217
industries, fast-growing, 2
Industry-Labor Council on Em-
    ployment and Disability, 118
information, providing to appli-
    cant, 159–161
in-house temporary agencies, 75
in-house training programs, 5
I-9 form, 124–125
intangible job requirements, 240
integrity tests, 227
intelligence tests, 215–216
intergenerational center, 18
internal promotions, 49
International Business Machines
    Corporation, 5, 18, 21, 69
*International Union v. Johnson Con-
    trols,* 121
interruptions, of interviews, 94
interview preparation, 28, 83–104
    application and résumé review,
        86–91
    and interviewer's review of his or
        her own perceptions, 100–104
    telephone screening in, 83–86
    see also job familiarization
interviews, 7, 146–180
    active listening in, 151–153
    closing, 179–180
    considering applicant's feelings
        during, 100
    developing rapport in, 149–150
    of disabled applicants, 12–13
    encouraging applicant to talk
        during, 157–159
    environment for, 94–96
    evaluation form for, 302–303
    first question in, 150–151
    format for, 147–148
    guidelines and pitfalls for, 177–
        179

for job with no requirements, 191–192
note taking during, 153–154
objectives of, 96
one-on-one vs. team, 172–174
planning questions for, 96–99
of problem applicants, 170–172
providing applicant information during, 159–161
scheduling of, 92–94
stress, 174–177
tape-recording of, 189–190
types of questions for, 161–164
see also documentation of interview
introductions, on first day of work, 249–250
introductory remarks, on first day of work, 247–249
Inwald, Robin, 227

J. C. Penney Co., 23
Job Accommodation Network, 11, 118
job analysis, 42
job applicants
appearance of, 101
considering feelings of in interview, 100
problem, 170–172
recording direct quotes of, 185–187
job application
appearance of, 88
completion of form for, 6
form for, 87
review of, 86–91
job changes, frequency of, 89
job clearinghouse, for older workers, 10
Job Corps, 225
job description, 6, 29, 41–46, 160, 192–193, 239–240
categories of information in, 46
form for, 276–277
guidelines for, 42–44
for job posting, 50

job fairs, 60, 78
job familiarization, 28–47
benefits, 39–40
education and prior work experience in, 30–32
exemption status, 37–38
growth opportunities, 40
intangible requirements in, 32–33
job description in, 41–46
job duties and responsibilities, 29–30
reporting relationships in, 33–34
salary ranges, 38–39
union status, 40
work environment, 34–37
job information, 159
place for, in interview, 147–148
job knowledge tests, 212–213
job offer
letters making, 241–242, 243
to temporary workers, 74
job opportunities, 2
job posting, 49–51, 77
form for, 278–279
job-related facts, in interview documentation, 184–188
job relatedness, of work experience, 137
job requirements, and discrimination, 108
job restructuring, for disabled persons, 114–115
job rotation, 36
jobs
fast-growing, 3
number lost, 1981–1986, 1
job security, in employee handbook, 140
job sharing, 20–21
jobs with no requirements, interviewing for, 191–192
job titles, and duties, 90–91
John Hancock, 17
Johnson, Lyndon, 108
Johnson & Johnson, 17

Johnson Controls, Inc., 121
just cause, for termination, 138

Kennedy, John F., 108
Kids-to-Go, 17
kleptomaniacs, 116
Kozol, Jonathan, *Illiterate America*, 4

labor force, *see* work force
labor shortage, 2
laws on employment, 105–145
lawsuits, from drug testing, 222
leading questions, 163
lead poisoning, 121
leasing, employee, 26
leaves of absence, 40, 268
　mandatory for pregnancy, 120
legal advice, xii
letter of job offer, 241–242, 243
letters of rejection, 241, 242, 244–
　245
Leven, Michael, 14
Levi Strauss & Co., 20
Liberty Mutual Insurance Group, 5
lie detector tests, 226
life insurance, 39
listening, active, in interview, 151–
　153
literacy, in workplace, 4–7
loaded questions, 162
location, for organizational orienta-
　tion, 255–256
Los Angeles County/U.S.C. Medical
　Center, 61
lunch, for new employees, 253
Lüscher personality test, 218

magazine advertising, 52–54, 77
Mailer's Guide (Post Office), 62
mailing lists, recruiting from, 62
Mainstream, Inc., 118
Management Review, 75
mandatory pregnancy leaves, 120
McDonald's Corporation, and older
　workers, 9
meal breaks, 272

mealtime stress interviews, 176–
　177
medical and disability insurance, 39
medical assistants, 2
medical care, company procedures
　for, 252
Mental Measurements Yearbook, 216
Miike, Lawrence, 222
military, as recruitment source, 69–
　70, 80
minimum standards, setting, 31
Minnesota Clerical Test, 215
Minnesota Multiphasic Personality
　Inventory, 216
minorities, 2, 3, 15–16
morale, and unsatisfactory working
　conditions, 35
motivation, and productivity, 264
motor disabilities, and testing, 211
motor work samples, 213
multicultural environment, 15–16
multiple choice questions, 161
Myart v. Motorola, 206–207

Nabisco Brands, 5
National Academy of Science, 2
National Association of Personnel
　Consultants, *National Directory
　of Personnel Consultants by Spe-
　cialization,* 73
National Association of Rehabilita-
　tion Facilities, 12
National Black MBA Association,
　16
National Business Education Asso-
　ciation, 213
National Computer Systems Profes-
　sional Assessment Services, 214
National Conference of Commis-
　sioners on Uniform State Laws,
　127
National Council on the Aging, 18
*National Directory of Personnel Con-
　sultants by Specialization* (Na-
　tional Association of Personnel
　Consultants), 73

national I.D. card, 125
National Labor Relations Act, 40
national origin discrimination, 124
National Staff Leasing Association, 76
National Support Center for Persons with Disabilities, 11
National Westminster Bank USA, 18
Native Americans, in labor force, 3
Naugles, 9
negligent hiring, 143–145
 reference checks and, 232–233
nervous applicants, interviewing, 170–171
networking, 60
new employees
 checklist for, 314–316
 selection of, 3
newspaper advertising, 52–54, 77
newspaper inserts, 71, 80
New York Business Group for Health, 19
New York Telephone, 5
nonexempt positions, 37
 interviews for, 92–93
 recruitment of, 48
 reference form for, 308–311
 telephone screening of, 84–85
nonverbal communication, 102–103, 149, 151, 154–157, 240
note taking, 153–154, 192–199
 point system for, 190–191
notification of chosen candidate, 241–242

objective language, in interview documentation, 182
objectives
 of interviews, 96
 of orientation, 264
observation, in job analysis, 42
Occupational Safety and Health Act (OSHA), 118, 220
O'Connor Finger Dexterity Test, 215

office familiarization, on first day of work, 250–252
Office of Federal Contract Compliance Programs, 109
Office of Personnel Management, 204
Office of Technology Assessment, 227
Older Women's League, 18
older workers, 2, 7–10
 for at-home work, 24
 reasons for working, 9–10
Olmsted, Barney, *Creating a Flexible Workplace*, 19
Olsten Corporation, 5
on-campus recruiting, 58, 78
one-on-one interview, vs. team, 172–174
on-site recruitment, 76, 81
on-the-job accidents, 8
open-ended questions, 93, 151, 158, 163–164
open house, 61, 78
opinions, in introductions, 249
organizational orientation, 254–261
 content of, 256–257
 duration of, 261
 evaluation form for, 317–318
 evaluation of, 270–271
 location and setting for, 255–256
 participants in, 255
 sample program for, 261–270
 timing of, 260–261
orientation, xii, 246–274
 benefits of, 264
 company policies in, 269–270
 departmental, 271–273
 departmental representation in, 257–259
 employee handbooks and, 257
 first day of work, 247–254
 format for, 259–260
 organizational, 254–261
 purpose of, 254–255
 tour in, 266–267
OSHA (Occupational Safety and Health Act), 118, 220

outplacement firms, 67–68, 80
overhead costs, flextime and, 21
over-the-counter drugs, and drug
    testing, 222
overtime, 272

Pacific Bell, 23
Pacific Islanders, in labor force, 3
paralegals, 2
participative management, 26
part-time employment, 19, 20
    for full-time workers, 25
Pathfinders/Eldercare, 18
payday, 268
payroll, annual temporary, 74
perceptions, in interview prepara-
    tion, 100–104
performance appraisals, 40, 228
permanent employment, offer to
    temps, 74
personal computers, 23
personal days, 40, 267
pesonality tests, 216–219
personal references, 230, 238–239
Personnel Administrator, 11
*Personnel and Career Assessment
    Catalog 1990* (Psychological
    Corporation), 216
personnel files, 56–57, 78
Personnel Journal, 68
Personnel Manager's Legal Reporter,
    220
personnel policies manuals, as
    contracts, 138–139
personnel psychologists, 206
personnel services, 2
Personnel Tests for Industry, 215
pharmaceutical work, polygraph
    testing for, 226
Philadelphia Newspapers, Inc., 6
photocopy machines, 251
physical exams, preemployment,
    115, 117, 219–220
physical tests, 214–215, 218–219
physical working conditions, 34–35
Pitney Bowes, Inc., 21

Pizza Hut, 12
Polaroid Corporation, 5
policies, for testing, 208–211
polygraph tests, 226–227
preemployment inquiries, and
    discrimination, 130–131, 132–
    135
preemployment physical exams,
    117, 219–220
preemployment screening, and
    remedial training, 6–7
preemployment training, 66–67, 80
Pregnancy Discrimination Act of
    1978, 120–121
President's Committee on Employ-
    ment of People with Disabili-
    ties, 11, 118
privacy
    drug testing and, 221
    for interview, 94
    national I.D. card and, 125
    reference checks and, 231–232
    rejection letters and, 245
private businesses, with public
    accommodations, 117
private office, company policies on,
    250
probationary period, 140
probing questions, 162
problem applicants, interviews of,
    170–172
productivity
    motivation and, 264
    worker age and, 8
professional associations, as recruit-
    ment source, 71
professional journals, advertising
    in, 53
professional positions
    search firms to fill, 54–56
    time allotment for interviewing,
    92
professionals, for testing, 216–217
professor programs, as recruitment
    source, 58
profit-sharing programs, 40

promotions, 40, 49
testing and, 208, 213
Psychological Corporation, 213
1990 Personnel and Career Assessment Catalog, 216
psychologists, 206
industrial, 217
psychomotor tests, 214–215
public accommodations, private businesses with, 117
pupillary-reaction test, 223–224
Purdue Pegboard, 215
Purdue University, 213
pyromaniacs, 116

Quaker Oats Co., 20
qualified privilege, common law doctrine of, 232
questionnaires, in job analysis, 42
questions
answering, in orientation, 260
close-ended, 158, 161–162
first, in interview, 150–151
hypothetical, 162
for interviews, 161–164
leading, 163
loaded, 162–163
multiple choice, 161
negative reactions to answers, 102
open-ended, 93, 151, 158, 163–164
planning, for interviews, 96–99
probing, 162
specific examples of, 164–170
QUIZ, Inc., 214

radio advertising, 63–64, 79
random drug testing, 220–221
rapport, in interview, 149–150
Reagan, Ronald, 221
record retention
of employee medical records, 220
of testing, 211
recruitment
of disabled, 12

employment trends and, 3
factors affecting, 48–49
innovations in, 2
of older workers, 10
on-site, 76, 81
and work at home, 23
recruitment sources, 48–82
billboard advertising, 68, 80
computerized systems for, 64–65, 79
consulting firms, 72–73, 81
direct mail, 62–63, 79
employee leasing, 75–76, 81
employee referral programs, 51–52, 77
employment agencies and search firms, 54–56, 77
government agencies, 61–62, 79
job posting, 49–51, 77
military, 69–70, 80
newspaper inserts, 71, 80
open house, 61, 78
outplacement firms, 67–68, 80
personnel files, 56–57, 78
preemployment training, 66–67, 80
professional associations as, 71–72, 81
radio and television advertising, 63–64, 79
research firms, 65–66, 79
response cards, 68–69, 80
schools, 58–60, 78
temporary help agencies, 73–75, 81
voice ads, 76, 81
walk-ins, call-ins, and write-ins, 57, 78
Recruitment Today, 69
reference checks, 7, 230–239
educational, 237–238
evaluating, 239
form for exempt positions, 304–307
form for nonexempt positions, 308–311

reference checks (*continued*)
  and guidelines for obtaining
    information, 233–235
  and guidelines for releasing
    information, 233
  and invasion of privacy and
    defamation of character, 231–
    232
  and negligent hiring, 232–233
  personal, 238–239
  by telephone, 235–236
  written, 236–237
referrals, bias from, 101
*Regents of the University of California
  v. Bakke,* 126
Rehabilitation Act of 1973, 114–
  115, 118
rejection letters, 241, 242, 244–245
religious discrimination, 122–124
Remington Products, Inc., 18
repetition, to encourage applicant
  to talk, 157
reporting relationships, 33–34, 272
reports, *see* documentation of
  interview
research firms, for recruitment,
  65–66, 79
response cards, 62, 68–69, 80
responsibilities of job, familiarization with, 29–30
rest rooms, 251
résumé
  appearance of, 88
  review of, 86–91
reverse discrimination, 126
Rocco, Inc., 6
Rockefeller College, Professional
  Development Program, 119
Rockwell International, 63
rotation of job location, 36

sabbaticals, 25
salary, description of, 140
salary ranges, 38–39
  of men vs. women, 111

salary requirements, 240
  discussions of, at interview, 160
  reviewing, 89–90
salary reviews, 40
San Francisco AIDS Foundation,
  119
Saturdays, requirement to work on,
  122
schedule, 36–37
scholarships, 14
school recruiting, 58–60, 78
screening
  overreliance on tests for, 203
  by telephone, 83–86
search firms, 54–56, 77
seating arrangement, for interviews, 95–96
security-related tests, 218–219
  polygraph testing, 226
selection
  in employment process, xi
  of new employees, 3
selection of applicant, 230–245
  checklist for, 312–313
  decision maker for, 241
  notifying candidate, 241–242
  see also reference checks
self-employed workers, 25
Senior Employment Service, 10
service industries, 2
severance pay, 127
sex discrimination, in salary, 90
sexual harassment, 107
shy applicants, interviewing, 170–
  171
sick days, 268
sign-on bonus, 39
silence, to encourage applicant to
  talk, 159
skills, test of, 213–214
slides, for orientation, 260
Smith, Suzanne, *Creating a Flexible
  Workplace,* 19
smoking regulations, 272
Social Security recipients, 10
Society for Human Resource Management, 224

specific job descriptions, 42
Spring Industries, 5
standard hours of work, 37
Standard Metropolitan Statistical Area, 109
Standard Oil Co. (Indiana), 5
Standard Rate and Data Service, *Direct Mail List Rates and Data*, 62
stereotypical thinking, 103
strength and endurance tests, 214–215
stress interviews, 174–177
Stride Rite Corp., 18
subjective language, in interview documentation, 182–183
summarization, 158
  in active listening, 152
  in interview documentation, 198, 199
Sundays, requirement to work on, 122
supplemental work force, 25
supplies, 250–251
Surgeon General's report on AIDS, 225
systemic discrimination, 49
  employee referral programs and, 52

tailored testing, 210
talkative applicants, interviewing, 171
tape-recording of interviews, 189–190
tax incentives, for hiring disabled workers, 12
Tax Reform Act of 1986, 12
team interview, vs. one-on-one, 172–174
telecommuting, 23
telephone directory, 251
telephone references, 233, 235–236
telephones, personal calls on, 272
telephone screening, 83–86

telephone system, 251
telephone voice ads, 76
television advertising, 63–64, 79
  of open house, 61
Television Employment Network, 63
temporary help, 24–25
  older workers as, 9
temporary help agencies, 2, 73–75, 81
termination, employers' rights on, 127
testing, 201–229
  for AIDS, 224–225
  alternatives to, 228
  characteristics of, 202–203
  computer-administered, 209–210
  of disabled applicants, 210
  and discrimination, 206–208
  policies for, 208–211
  and promotion, 208
  pros and cons of, 203
  validation of, 204, 205
tests, 211–228
  achievement, 212
  aptitude, 212
  development of, 206
  for drugs, 220–224
  intelligence, 215–216
  job knowledge, 212–213
  personality, 216–219
  physical ability and psychomotor, 214–215
  physical and security-related, 218–219
  polygraph, 226–227
  in prescreening, 7
  work samples as, 213–214
  written honesty, 227–228
Texas Instruments, 5
Thomas, Franklin A., on affirmative action, 109
thought speed, 153, 236
Thurstone Test of Mental Alertness, 215
time overlaps, in applicant's work history, 88

time records, 272
timing
  of departmental orientation, 273
  of organizational orientation,
    260–261
toll-free phone numbers
  for advice on accommodating
    disabled workers, 11
  for AIDS hot line, 225
  for literacy groups, 5
tort damages, 142
tour, in orientation, 266–267
trade tests, 212
training, 2, 4
  opportunities for, 268
  preemployment, 66–67, 80
Training & Development Journal, 7
  on sabbaticals, 25
transvestites, 116
travel, 36
Travelers Insurance Company, 5–6,
    18
  and older workers, 9
Truth-in-Lending Act, 56
tuition reimbursement, 268
  forms for, 140
turnover
  older workers and, 9
  and unsatisfactory working
    conditions, 35
typing tests, 213

UAW-Ford Eastern Michigan Uni-
    versity Academy, 6
Uniform Employment Termination
    Act, 127–128
*Uniform Guidelines on Employee
    Selection Procedures*, 210, 228
unions, 40
  and religious beliefs, 123–124
Union Special, 69
United States Architectural and
    Transportation Barriers Com-
    pliance Board, 118
U.S. Bureau of Labor Statistics, 1
U.S. Census Bureau, 2

U.S. Chamber of Commerce, 227
U.S. Department of Commerce, 74
U.S. Department of Defense, 221,
    225
U.S. Department of Education, 4
U.S. Department of Health and
    Human Services, 221
U.S. Department of Justice, 204
U.S. Department of Labor
  on exemption classification, 38
  Office of Federal Contract Com-
    pliance Programs, 204
U.S. Department of Labor Statis-
    tics, on literacy, 4
U.S. Department of the Treasury,
    204
U.S. Department of Transporta-
    tion, 221
U.S. Employment Service, 216
U.S. Justice Department, Special
    Counsel for Immigration
    Related Unfair Employment,
    125
U.S. Public Health Service, 225
United Technologies, 5
Urban League, 5–6
urine testing, for drugs, 221–222

vacations, 40, 267, 272
validation of tests, 204, 205
verbal work samples, 213
videotapes, for orientation, 260
Vietnam Era Veterans Readjust-
    ment Act of 1974, 119
Vietnam War veterans, testing for
    drug use, 221
visually impaired applicants, testing
    of, 210
voice ads, 76, 81
voluntary reduced work-time pro-
    grams, 25

Wagner Act, 40
walk-ins, as recruitment source, 57,
    78
Walt Disney World, 61

water fountains, 251
Watson, Clara, 208
Watson v. Fort Worth Bank & Trust, 208
Wells Fargo, 25
whistle-blowing, 138
women, 2, 3, 13
  wage discrimination and, 111
word-of-mouth recruitment, 51
  and discrimination, 108
work environment, 34–37
  checklist for, 275
work ethic, new, 1
work experience, in job familiarization, 30–32
work force
  changing, 1–4
  components of, 7–16
  profile of, for year 2000, 3
  supplemental, 25

"Workforce 2000: Work and Workers for the 21st Century"
  (Hudson Institute), 13
work history, of applicant, 88
work logs, 42
workplace literacy, 4–7
work samples, 213–214
workweek, compressed, 22–23
write-ins, as recruitment source, 57,
  78
write-up of interview, *see* documentation of interview
written honesty tests, 227–228
written references, 236–237
Wygant v. Jackson, 126

years of experience, specifying
  number of, 137
youth, 14–15

zero tolerance policy, 221